C000257410

Best of Breed

Best of Breed

The Hawker Hunter FR10

By Nigel Walpole

First published in
Great Britain in 2006
By Pen and Sword Aviation
An imprint of
Pen and Sword Books Ltd
47 Church Street
Barnsley
South Yorkshire
S70 2AS

Copyright © Nigel Walpole 2006

ISBN 1 84415 412 2

The right of Nigel Walpole to be identified as the author of this work has been
asserted by him in accordance with the Copyright, Designs and Patents Act 1988.

A CIP record for this book is available from the British Library

All rights reserved. No part of this book may be reproduced or transmitted in any form or by any
means, electronic or mechanical including photocopying, recording or by any information storage
and retrieval system, without permission from the Publisher in writing.

Typeset by Mac Style, Nafferton, E. Yorkshire
Printed and bound in the UK by Biddles Ltd

Pen and Sword Books Ltd incorporates the imprints of Pen and Sword Aviation, Pen and Sword
Maritime, Pen and Sword Military, Wharncliffe Local History, Pen and Sword Select, Pen and Sword
Military Classics and Leo Cooper.

For a complete list of Pen and Sword titles please contact
Pen and Sword Books Limited
47 Church Street, Barnsley, South Yorkshire, S70 2AS, England
E-mail: enquiries@pen-and-sword.co.uk
Website: www.pen-and-sword.co.uk

Dedication

I dedicate *Best of Breed* most appropriately to my Dutch wife, Margreet, who plunged unwittingly but wholeheartedly into the Hunter fraternity in 1965, and whose expertise in the English language has been invaluable in all my writings.

The author's profits from *Best of Breed* will be donated to Combat Stress, the Ex-Services Mental Welfare Society.

The author

Group Captain Nigel Walpole OBE BA RAF (Ret'd) passed out from the Royal Air Force College, Cranwell, in 1954 and joined 26 (Hunter) Day Fighter Squadron in Germany a year later. He then served on 79 (Swift FR5) Squadron in Germany and USAF RF-101 Voodoo units in South Carolina on an exchange posting. On promotion to squadron leader he carried out staff duties in support of the Hunters in Aden before taking command of 234 Hunter DF/GA Squadron at 229 OCU in 1964 and subsequently II (AC) Hunter FR10 Squadron in Germany. He gained a soldier's perspective of air power as the Wing Commander Brigade Air Support Officer with 16 Parachute Brigade before commanding 12 (Buccaneer) Squadron briefly in 1972 and going on to fly Jaguars as Officer Commanding Strike Wing at RAF Bruggen. Appointed Group Captain Operations, RAF Germany, in 1982, he ended his service career as Assistant Chief of Staff Offensive Operations, Second Allied Tactical Air Force, and retired to become Weapons Advisor to British Aerospace, Stevenage. This is his fourth book of its type and he has written a number of articles for international aviation magazines. He and his wife Margreet now live in Suffolk.

Contents

Acknowledgements

Best of Breed has found the light of day as a result of encouragement and assistance from Sir Sandy Wilson and Lady Thomson, material assistance with the photographs from Alan and Collette Curry and the stalwart work of David Baron in coupling his fast-jet expertise with the power of the pen to labour through my drafts. I am also indebted to the Ministry of Defence for allowing the use of photographs which might have originated from Crown sources, staff of the Public Records Office for their help and to the Officers Commanding Nos II (AC) and IV (AC) Squadrons, squadrons which remain fully operational to this day, for allowing access to their archives.

Of course, there could have been no book of this sort without many textual contributions and photographs from the players of the time and for these I thank: Peter Atkins, David Bagshaw, 'Dickie' Barraclough, Sandy Burns, Ray Bannard, Tim Barrett, Mike Barringer, Ben Bennett, Roy Bowie, Ralph Chambers, Hugh Cracroft, Bryan Carter, Al Cleaver, 'Moose' David, Ray Deacon, Jim Dymond, Dickie Dickinson, 'Duckie' Drake, George Eccleston, AVM Ron Elder, ACM Sir David Evans, Keith Garrett, Mike French, AVM Sam Goddard, Chris Golds, Air Cdre Peter Gover, 'Hoppy' Granville-White, Bob Hillman, Geoff Hall, Peter Highton, Air Cdre John Houghton, David Jenkins, ACM Sir Richard Johns, Air Cdre Pat King, George Lee, Roger Lindsey, Peter Lewis, David Lockspeiser, Al Mathie, Peter Marshall, Mike McEvoy, Brian Meadley, Air Cdre Frank Mitchell, Jock McVie, Bill Norton, Mike Nuttall, Stan Peachy, Stu Penny, Ken Petrie, Mike Plimmer, Alan Pollock, Roger Pyrah, Peter Rayner, Peter Riley, Colin Richardson, Jerry Saye, Eric Smith, AVM Sir John Severne, Ian Sharples, Eric Sharp, Ken Simpson, Air Cdre David Thornton, Air Cdre Peter Taylor, Air Cdre Tim Thorn, Sam Toyne, Fred Trowern, Air Cdre Owen Truelove, Ian Worby, AM Sir John Walker, Taff Wallis, Alan Walpole, Alex Weiss, Derek Whitman, Roger Wilkins, ACM Sir Keith Williamson and 'Oscar' Wild.

Finally, if I have omitted any contributors I do apologise, as I do to those whose inputs I have not been able to use. I am grateful to you all.

Glossary

AAA	Anti-aircraft Artillery	FGA	Fighter Ground Attack
AAC	Army Air Corps	Flt Cdr Ops	Flight Commander Operations
AC	Army Co-operation	Flt Cdr Trg	Flight Commander Training
ACE	Allied Command Europe	FOD	Foreign Object Damage
ADDF	Abu Dhabi Defence Force	FR	Fighter Reconnaissance
ADF	Automatic Direction Finder	FRA	Federal Regular Army
ADIZ	Air Defence Identification Zone	GAF	German Air Force
		GCA	Ground Control Approach
AFCENT	Air Forces Central Europe	GCI	Ground Control Interception
AFNORTH	Air Forces Northern Europe	GDA	Gun Defended Area
AOC	Air Officer Commanding	GGS	Gyro Gunsight
AOG	Aircraft On Ground (awaiting spares)	GLO	Ground Liaison Officer
		GLS	Ground Liaison Section
APC	Armament Practice Camp	HBL	Hadramaut Bedouin Legion
APRF	Arabian Peninsular Reconnaissance Force	HE	High Explosive
		IFF	Identification Friend or Foe
ARR	Airborne Radio Relay	IFR	Instrument Flight Rules
ASP	Aircraft Servicing Platform	IFREP	In-Flight Report
ASOC	Air Support Operations Centre	IP	Initial Point
ASSU	Air Support Signals Unit	IRE	Instrument Rating Examiner
ATAF	Allied Tactical Air Force	JARIC	Joint Air Reconnaissance Intelligence Centre
BAF	Belgian Air Force		
BASO	Brigade Air Support Officer	JHQ	Joint Headquarters
BASOC	Brigade Air Support Operations Centre	JSPI	Joint School Photographic Interpretation
BDA	Battle Damage Assessment	LAA	Light Anti-aircraft Artillery
C3I	Command, Control, Communications and Intelligence	LFA	Low Flying Area
		MFPU	Mobile Field Processing Unit
		MISREP	Mission Report
CAP	Combat Air Patrol	MU	Maintenance Unit
CAS	Chief of the Air Staff	NAVWASS	Navigation and Weapons Aiming Sub-System
CFS	Central Flying School		
CO	Commanding Officer	NBC	Nuclear, Biological and Chemical
COC	Combat Operations Centre		
CR	Central Region	NLF	National Liberation Front
CRE	Central Reconnaissance Establishment	NORTHAG	Northern Army Group
		OCU	Operational Conversion Unit
DFCS	Day Fighter Combat School	ORB	Operations Record Book
DFGA	Day Fighter Ground Attack	PAI	Pilot Attack Instructor
DME	Distance Measuring Equipment	PI	Photographic Interpreter
		PIU	Photographic Intelligence Unit
DZ	Drop Zone	PR	Photographic Reconnaissance
EAP	Eastern Aden Protectorate	QFI	Qualified Flying Instructor
ECM	Electronic Counter measures	QGH	Controlled Approach Through Cloud
EEI	Essential Elements of Information		
		RDAF	Royal Danish Air Force
FAC	Forward Air Controller	RNLAF	Royal Netherlands Air Force
FAF	French Air Force	RNoAF	Royal Norwegian Air Force
FASOC	Forward Air Support Operations Centre	RSAF	Republic of Singapore Air Force

RP	Rocket Projectile	Tac Recce/Recon	Tactical Reconnaissance
RSO	Range Safety Officer	TAR	Tactical Air Reserve
SAC	Senior Aircraftsman	TOC	Tactical Operations Centre
SACEUR	Supreme Allied Commander Europe	TOS	Trucial Oman Scouts
		TOT	Time on Target
SAM	Surface-to-Air Missile	TRS	Tactical Reconnaissance Squadron
SAS	Special Air Service		
SASO	Senior Air Staff Officer	UHF	Ultra High Frequency
SEA	South East Asia	USAFE	United States Air Force Europe
SOAF	Sultan of Oman's Air Force	VFR	Visual Flight Rules
SOC	Sector Operations Centre	VHF	Very High Frequency
SOR	Special Occurrence Report	VISREP	Visual Report
Taceval	Tactical Evaluation	WAP	Western Aden Protectorate

Foreword
Air Chief Marshal Sir 'Sandy' Wilson KCB AFC

When asked from time to time during my career what aeroplane I have enjoyed flying the most I have never had any hesitation in naming the Hunter, and I am sure I am not alone in this feeling. To me the Hunter is the Spitfire of the jet age. But, of course, there were Hunters and Hunters and the author sets out his views on why he believes the fighter reconnaissance version was the 'best of breed'.

In this book the author, Nigel Walpole, a former expert fighter reconnaissance pilot captures the aircraft, the role and, most importantly, the ethos and personalities of the band of Cold War pilots who flew the aircraft in Germany or in the Middle East during the 1960s. There can be few better qualified to tell this story as he flew the RF-101 Voodoo and the Swift before commanding No. II (AC) Squadron at Gutersloh, flying the Hunter FR10 at the height of the Cold War.

His comments on the pros and cons of peacetime competition flying are instructive, as are his views on the imperatives of realistic operational training, remembering that Tactical Evaluations were in their infancy in the Hunter era. He rightly highlights the over-emphasis on 'photographic evidence' and the failure of the tasking agencies to exploit the value of timely 'in-flight reports'. He also questions the contention that existed in those days that fighter reconnaissance was a role which could only be performed by very experienced pilots.

In operational terms, the FR10 acquitted itself extremely well in the Radfan Campaign and, looking back with the benefit of hindsight, I am in no doubt that the FR Hunter would have been equally successful if it had ever been put to the ultimate test in the Central Region of NATO. Indeed, one can only imagine what could have been made of this great aircraft had it been treated to progressive capability upgrades as happened to the later Jaguar. Sadly, this magnificent Hunter served for less than a decade in this role.

What bring this story truly to life are the amusing anecdotes and photographs from the FR10 era. Whilst some of the stories may seem a little out of place when viewed through today's spectacles they do underline the special atmosphere that existed in the 1960s, both in Germany and the Middle East. I think it is true to say that the Hunter FR force played and worked hard and the author has painted a canvass which reflects this balance. I was privileged to fly this aircraft both as a junior pilot and later as a flight commander at Gutersloh and look back on those times with great affection.

Whether you have flown this aircraft or not, I am sure you will enjoy the way in which Nigel Walpole tells the story of the Hunter FR10. As he did in his previous book 'Swift Justice', he uses a light touch and the book is amply illustrated with some wonderful photographs. For those who have flown the aircraft, the book will bring back evocative memories of an aircraft and its people, not just the pilots but those all important support personnel – engineers, photographic specialists, ground liaison officers and photographic interpreters – who made up the FR world.

It is for you the reader to judge if the Hunter FR10 was indeed the 'best of breed'. For me it certainly was, not in the sense that it was technically better than any other mark of Hunter, but simply that with its especially adapted cockpit, its cameras and guns, it was a perfect platform for the low level reconnaissance role.

Sandy Wilson

Preface

The fighter reconnaissance (FR) version of the Hunter, the FR10, entered service with the RAF in 1961 to replace the Swift FR5. *Best of Breed* describes work and play within the FR fraternity of the 1960s, with many of the personalities involved adding their memories to the factual framework drawn from official sources. The text recalls the aircraft's strengths in the role, the training of 'chosen men' and their commitments in NATO, Aden and Bahrain.

Feeling strongly then and now about the employment (and sometimes misemployment) of our FR assets, I make no apology for indulging my views on how armed reconnaissance could and should have contributed to the land/air battle, and to what extent this was reflected in practice, in our training, exercises and operations with the FR10 – and in the diverse support which was so essential to its effectiveness. Inevitably, this touches on matters of policy, management and the ever-contentious academic competitions which occupied NATO's tactical reconnaissance (tac recce) forces for much of their time in the 1960s. My views did not always chime with those of my peers or the hierarchy at that time, and my central beliefs have remained unchanged with hindsight. It is, of course, important to bear in mind that what is written here relates solely to the equipment available in the 1960s and the modus operandi of that period, and not to the navigation equipment, reconnaissance fits and concepts of today.

To this end, I have relied not only on my first-hand experience on Swift, Hunter, USAF RF-101 (Voodoo), Buccaneer and Jaguar strike/attack/recce squadrons, but also on that of many others similarly involved. I was also able to see FR from a soldier's perspective, and how it might contribute best to operations on the ground, while serving with 16 Parachute Brigade. Finally, I discovered the realities of reconnaissance planning, coordination and management when responsible for targeting and tasking the NATO offensive and recce resources of the Second Allied Tactical Air Force (2ATAF).

I would like *Best of Breed* to be more than a reminder to those who had the privilege of serving with the Hunter FR force of our life and times in days of sometimes high tension but relative peace, which had the potential to contribute much in any land/air war and could provide a great deal of personal satisfaction in a wonderful lifestyle. In bringing work and play together, *inter alia*, within a simple but serious didactic text, I seek to dismiss some of the misconceptions about the role which existed then and may have endured to this day. In sum, I have tried to do justice to the aircraft itself and the Hunter FR force as a whole, in an honest portrayal of our life at the time and proper tribute to one part of the professional, well-rounded RAF of the 1960s.

Best of Breed may generate heartfelt debate within the wider Hunter community but, in the context of front line service, I hope to lead the reader into accepting that the FR10 justified the claim in the title.

Chapter 1
Hawker's Best

A fighter reconnaissance (FR) variant of the Hunter had been under consideration at Hawker Aircraft throughout the gestation of the Hunter and the Swift but, given the aircraft's success in other fighter roles, Hawker's order book was soon full so the option was late in development. The firm took the lead itself in the mid-1950s by modifying and evaluating WT780, a Hunter F4, with an array of five cameras in the nose compartment. With perfect timing the configuration was pronounced successful by all involved and, with the RAF having monitored progress with covert interest, the Ministry of Supply issued Air Staff Specification FR164D in 1957. Hawker was well-prepared and XF429, a Hunter F6 modified to carry the three oblique cameras (no vertical stations), was taken on its maiden flight by Hawker test pilot Hugh Merewether on 7 November 1958. This aircraft was jokingly referred to as the 'Hunter Mk. 9^1/$_2$'; it was, of course, the embryo FR10.

Hawker test pilot David Lockspeiser became involved in the trials and on one of his camera test runs in late 1959 he photographed a 'target of opportunity' (the first of many for the FR Hunters), on the Goodwood racetrack near Chichester – a new Formula 1 racing car being tested by Aston Martin, supposedly under great secrecy. There was no avoiding the eye from the sky.

The RAF was entirely satisfied with the outcome of this initial evaluation and, after successful service trials, ordered thirty-three of these 'new' aircraft (converted from Hunter F6s). The FR10 was very similar to the FGA9 but incorporated port, starboard and nose-facing Vinten F95 oblique cameras; the gunpack was retained with its four 30-mm Aden cannon but the radar ranging was discarded to make room for the cameras and there was no provision for bombs or rockets. Armour plating gave some protection to the pilot and increased the weight

Trial Run. Hunter F6 WT780 was initially trialled with five F95 cameras, but the two cameras in a vertical station were removed in the FR10. *Brooklands Museum via David Lockspeiser*

Steady Ahead. The all-important G4F compass took pride of place on the FR10's instrument panel, unobscured by the control column. *Ken Simpson*

Target of Opportunity. Hawker test pilot David Lockspeiser found this new Aston Martin racing car on test at Goodwood Circuit while he was evaluating the camera system in Hunter XF426. *David Lockspeiser*

in the nose to keep the centre of gravity within bounds. The external tank capacities mirrored those of the FGA9, but fuel in the 230 gall tanks inboard was gauged. Distance Measuring

Clear Ahead. The standard Gyro Gunsight was fixed and offset to one side in the FR10 – to allow a better view ahead for map reading at very low levels, early target acquisition and visual reconnaissance. *Ken Simpson*

Equipment (DME) gave way to a miniature radio compass, as did the very high frequency (VHF) radio to ultra high frequency (UHF) equipment. A brake parachute was added and a gearing system was introduced to dampen aileron sensitivity at high indicated airspeed when flying at low level. The role equipment included a voice recorder.

There were significant differences between the FR10 and the FGA9 in their cockpit layouts, the ergonomics of the FR10 being particularly beneficial to low-level operations. The upper port centre panel of the FGA9, which contained the weapons and stores jettison switches, was removed, the latter easily accessible in the FR10 on the port wall, while a fixed gunsight was offset to starboard, both modifications greatly improving forward vision. The radio controls were moved from the port shelf into the space vacated by the panel and gunsight, enabling the pilot to change frequencies without the distraction of looking down into the cockpit. An independent stopwatch holder, fuel warning 'bingo' lights, F95 camera operating and footage indicators were also positioned to be seen at a glance, again obviating the need to look into the cockpit. The all-important G4F compass was moved up and to the left from behind the control column, for quicker reference (also helping instrument flying). All this made low flying easier and safer, allowing the pilot to concentrate on his lookout, map reading and reconnaissance.

Oblique Excellence. Vinten's F95 cameras, set obliquely in port, nose and starboard stations, were the best to be had at the time for the FR10's modus operandi. *School of Photography*

The cockpit layout of all the RAF FR10s was the same, a boon to flight safety while minimising the risk of selecting the wrong switch ('switchery pigs'), an all too common problem in other marks of the aircraft. Hunter fighter/ground attack (FGA) pilot Alan Pollock, who negotiated

Eyes and Teeth. This IV Squadron FR10 gives a proper impression of the massive power of its four 30 mm Aden cannon. (available for use offensively or defensively), the closed nose camera eyelid and the starboard camera port. *Sam Goddard*

additional flying in FR10s, noted this admirable uniformity, contrasting it with some eighteen possible permutations in the FGA9. Combining all these attributes with the performance of the aircraft made the FR10 a perfect platform for the dual roles of recce and attack, and justifies the claim that this aircraft was the best of the Hunter breed.

The only obvious visible differences between the FR10 and the FGA9 were the three camera ports and perhaps the external tankage. The FR10 invariably carried 230 gall drop tanks inboard and 100 gall tanks outboard, whereas the FGA9s were normally fitted with four tanks for ferry flights only and were seen more usually without the outboard 100 gall tanks, enabling them to carry rockets or bombs and allowing better manoeuvrability.

Both aircraft were equipped with either the Avon Mk 203 or 207 axial-flow gas turbine engine, developing 10,000 lb or 10,150 lb static thrust respectively at sea level, by which they easily achieved their maximum permitted speed of 620 kts. The FR10's special gearing, provided in anticipation that powered aileron control would be undesirably light for the role, was rarely used – pilots soon getting used to the sensitivity. The 'follow-up' tailplane, most relevant to manoeuvring in the upper airspace, was retained but not used in high-speed low level FR operations. The author, having flown many hours in both the Hunter and the Swift, claims that the Swift gave a steadier ride at very low level, with the pilot able to fly almost 'hands off' at speeds up to 600 kts in an aircraft which could generally sustain greater damage from bird strikes and other incidental problems inherent in operational low flying. The Swift could also out-accelerate the FR10, but only by using its very thirsty reheat, and decelerate faster with its airbrake-cum-flap, but the Hunter FR10, with its brake parachute, could land on shorter runways.

The early marks of Hunters had their problems. With only 2,200 lb of fuel, the air defence F1 was very limited in range and endurance and trips of 35-45 minutes at high level were typical, but the aircraft was so light that it was possible to reach heights in excess of 50,000 ft. They had no on-board navigation aids, other than DME, could not initially fire their guns (their very *raison d'etre*!) and the early Avon engine was very prone to surging. The FR10 had improved engines and additional fuel, the gun firing problems had been solved, 'Sabrinas' were fitted below the fuselage to capture the cartridge links and the aircraft had a radio compass.

In the late 1950s and early 1960s, several official and unofficial initiatives were taken in attempts to enhance the Hunter's operational effectiveness, but few were adopted. David Lockspeiser remembers a very low cost modification to the gunpack which would replace two of the Aden cannon with two Sidewinder heat-seeking missiles, leaving the two remaining guns with an additional 20 rounds of ammunition. This would have been welcomed by many Hunter pilots on the front line and, incidentally, by the Central Fighter Establishment during the author's time there in 1962, but the option was rejected, allegedly on the grounds that the Sidewinder was obsolescent (variants are still in use some forty-five years later!) and that the Hunter "had only a few years of service left".

The Ministry and Hawker had timed the whole FR10 project perfectly to coincide with the withdrawal of the Swift FR5 in the early 1960s, the airframes of which were becoming very weary, and its replacement offered greater flexibility and adaptability within the commonality of a large family of Hunter aircraft. Moreover, despite residual nostalgia for the Swift, it could not be denied that the Hunter FR10 was generally very much more effective in the FR role: it had a better operational range, greater manoeuvrability, double the firepower and a far more credible self-defence capability.

Once the decision had been made, Hawker lost no time in modifying the F6s earmarked for conversion to the FR10. Five of these aircraft were completed by November 1960, with delivery to Nos II (AC) and IV (AC) Squadrons continuing apace throughout 1961. Another success story in British military aviation had begun.

What Might Have Been. A private venture, to replace two of the Hunter's Aden cannon with two Sidewinder missiles, failed to secure official support. *David Lochspeiser*

The Ultimate Product. Operationally configured with 2 x 230 gallon and 2 x 100 gallon external tanks from the start, the FR10 went through its service with the RAF without any significant visual modifications or additions. *Ray Deacon*

Chapter 2
On the Role

Bringing to a close NATO's major reconnaissance competition Royal Flush in 1963, General Lyman Lemnitzer, Supreme Allied Commander Europe (SACEUR), said: "Without the capacity for timely and effective reconnaissance, the commander's ability to influence the course of the battle is seriously, even disastrously, handicapped".

To many, air reconnaissance in the Cold War meant photography, and in the case of high level, strategic, photographic reconnaissance (PR) this was reasonable. In the context of tactical reconnaissance (tac recce), and in particular FR, it should have meant much more, but here too many believed that photography was all that mattered and this was reflected in many tac recce competitions, conveniently judged on photographic excellence. The author, who learned the need for reliable, up-to-date intelligence in the successful prosecution of a fast-moving air/land battle from his flying days, three years with the British Army and in NATO's battle management, saw it differently. Given sensible targeting and tasking, confidence

among 'customers' in visual sightings of essential elements of information (EEI) only, and the necessary communications to pass the bare details to an appropriate agency without delay in an In Flight Report (IFREP), visual reconnaissance can provide invaluable real time intelligence. Also with this transmitted data, all is not lost if the cameras fail, photo cover of the target is found to be inadequate, an aircraft fails to return or is forced to divert to a base without photographic facilities. In any event the time taken to interpret information from photographs, or in getting the photographs themselves to those in need of them, may be too long to be of use to those already engaged in battle.

The FR10 pilot could also deal directly with certain lucrative, fleeting targets caught unawares (a nuclear missile convoy is usually quoted here) with the Hunter's four highly effective 30-mm Aden cannons, or he could call up a strike force, lead it to the target and mark it with the guns. In a European war there were many possible situations in which such

Central Europe. The 2ATAF area of responsibility.

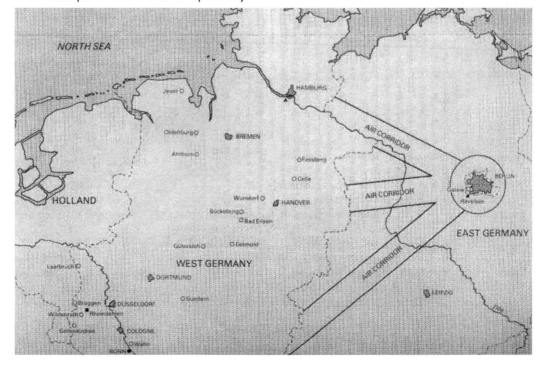

Fast and Low – The Way to Go.

In the UK and Germany 250 ft was the minimum permitted height in training, transiting and overflying the targets at speeds up to 600 kts. *II Sqn*

FR10 pilots in Aden and Bahrain could be authorised progressively down to 50 ft, where all FR pilots would seek to be in war. *Ralph Chambers via Ray Deacon*

In war, FR10 pilots would make good use of terrain masking in the Sauerland, Harz and Solling. *II & IV Sqn Archives*

immediate action could have been crucial and would have been justified; any delays, such as waiting for photo confirmation, almost certainly would have rendered subsequent follow-up action superfluous – a fact proven so often in the Vietnam War. Having said that, the cardinal principle on which such action should have been based was that an FR10 mission should not ordinarily have been disrupted, or this valuable asset be put at any unnecessary risk, and guidelines were there to ensure this. Also, despite being very capable with the FR10's guns in the air-to-air mode, the pilot should have engaged hostile aircraft only to survive, or when

essential to obtain the information required and return home with it.

Operational training in the Hunter FR10 should have reflected every aspect of this potential, to enable the pilots to reach and acquire their targets, assimilate target information visually, operate their F95 cameras to best effect and take offensive or defensive measures if justified. This chapter takes a look at each of the component parts of a total FR10 armed recce package – beginning with certain imperatives in the generation of a task.

Right away the planners might have been faced with a dilemma that called for a compromise. There was unlikely to be any merit in prioritising safety at the expense of completing the task satisfactorily. On the other hand there was no point in exceeding sensible requirements and losing the aircraft in the process. The onus in the first place was, therefore, on those responsible for targeting and tasking, often hidden underground well away from the realities outside and sometimes lacking the necessary expertise in the art of the possible. There are too many stories from the recce fraternity who engaged in live and paper exercises during the Cold War, and coincidentally the very hot war in Vietnam, of tasks sent down to the front line which, in one way or another, did not seem essential or were unnecessarily risky, although to be fair, those at the 'sharp end' did not always have the 'big picture' which should always drive the tasking. In NATO's Central Region (CR) Hunters were sometimes tasked in war contingency plans and exercise training beyond their tactical range or into unacceptable weather, or to repeat missions

covered satisfactorily only shortly before (this certainly led to the loss of US aircraft in Vietnam). The FR10s were frequently required to obtain full photo cover of major airfields, about which many static features would already be known from other means of surveillance in peacetime, or to look for unspecified activity over large areas, both tasks requiring passes at very vulnerable heights or multiple runs over defences that were quickly alerted. Those setting the reconnaisance task should of course have been aware that the FR10 had no vertical cameras or night recce capability, the pilot neither able to see to fly at operational low level at night nor recce his targets with the naked eye without illumination (no night vision goggles in those days). Also they should have been aware the FR10 cameras had limitations at dawn and dusk. But all these facts were sometimes overlooked. Examples of poor targeting and tasking recur as this history of the FR10 unfolds.

All this is not to minimise the potential of the Hunter recce force; it had a significant contribution to make over a wide variety of targets, was very responsive and could survive. Its visual and photographic tasks would have included pre and post-strike recces, route recces, recce/attack interface – the pilot always remaining vigilant for 'opportunity' targets.

Much of Germany was often covered by fog or very low stratus but FR pilots pressed on above or between layers, holding their heading and planned speed, using whatever helped them en route (typically church spires, radio aerials, chimneys and train smoke) and hoping that their targets would be in the clear. *Roger Wilkins*

Targets could be static (bridges, airfields, infrastructure, missile and gun sites, harbour facilities, communications and radar) or mobile (troops/equipment encamped or on the move, helicopter operations, ship movements etc.). Each environment (European, arctic, desert, maritime, tropical et al) had its own problems, calling for different approaches and some specialised training.

When pilots, for whatever reason, considered their assigned tasks imprudent they could of course point out the implications and risk factors and have their concerns passed up the line, but this would often lead to acrimonious, time-consuming debate thus negating the value of the rapid response inherent in tac recce. Far better to have the task originators (army and air force) well educated in the capabilities and limitations

Camera Excellence. Three exceptionally effective Vinten F95 cameras, set obliquely in port, starboard and forward nose stations, gave the FR10 force a low level photographic capability unique in NATO at the time.

Low-level Surveillance. The F95 camera could reveal useful detail from very low level. *Peter Lewis*

I've Got Your Number! F95 photo at high speed and very low over RAF Scharfoldendorf, Germany. *Sandy Burns*

Spotter Spotted. F95 sees ACC Auster under poor camouflage. *John Turner*

Hello Sailor! Sandy Burns gets up close and friendly for this F95 shot of HMS *Bulwark* off Aden. *Sandy Burns*

No 468 GLS. In 1966, with Major Peter Heath and Captain John Clark at the helm, 468 GLS provided II (AC) Squadron with invaluable support. *John Clark*

of the recce assets available to them during peacetime – rather than wait for them to learn on the job in war. Equally essential was the appointment of high quality, up-to-date specialists in their respective roles on the battle management staffs and to have them well-rehearsed in day-to-day and exercise training. Filtering recce requests at that stage minimises poor tasking at the outset.

With such education and essentially joint operational training involving all the elements of the recce force in peacetime, the recce aircrews could hope for tasking on EEIs only, this

No 261 GLS. Major Brian Cobb and Captain Mike Nuttall headed No 261 GLS in support of IV (AC) Squadron. *IV Sqn*

allowing them to plan viable and survivable tactics. In the case of that favourite target, the major airfield, for instance, the single-seat FR10 pilot could then overfly or stand-off at very low level, with all cameras operating, concentrating on such specifics as damage to the main runway, general activity on the airfield and types of aircraft. These factors would be at the core of his immediate, short in-flight report, the single pass having sufficed and the mission given every chance of survival. The successful recce mission starts with the customer and the battle management cells – but then the recce pilot must reach his target.

In Europe's Cold War of the 1960s there was no alternative but for the FR10s to transit from their main base at RAF Gutersloh to their targets at very low level, thus limiting them to operations in East Germany. The proliferation of ever more effective radar assisted anti-aircraft artillery (AAA), surface-to-air missile (SAM) systems, and Warsaw Pact fighters, together with the lack of electronic countermeasures (ECM), would have denied them the use of upper airspace. Moreover, the Hunters were not equipped with the sophisticated navigation systems in common use today, to enable them to remain on track in or above the perennial low cloud which covered much of Germany for the greater part of the year, and then to descend safely to low level to resume the accurate map reading which would keep them clear of known defences and take them to their targets with the precision needed.

Theoretically, the range of an FR10 could be increased by flying an initial leg at high level, followed by a descent to low level in friendly airspace (with some Allied radar assistance, if necessary, available and free of jamming). However, taking into account the geography of the area, the war tasks assigned and a rule of thumb which precluded such a profile unless the high level leg was circa 100 nm long, this was rarely an option from Gutersloh. High speed pilot navigation at the lowest levels permitted was therefore the order of the day.

Similar arguments applied to the approaches to, overflight and egress from targets where local defences were likely to have been most formidable. Ideally, the FR10 would be flown at the highest possible speed (circa. 600 kts) and the lowest possible level (less than 50 ft over flat terrain), but neither the excellent F95 camera nor the human eye was likely to be able to satisfy

Bridge Recce.

So essential to movement on the ground, bridges would be obvious targets for FR in war and competition. This three-span, twin track, through-type steel girder truss rail bridge, with masonry piers and abutments could be a target. *Alex Weiss*

This bridge, believed to be in a deep ravine in the Italian mountains, might have been acquired only in the final seconds of the target run at operational low level, thus limiting time for ideal photograph and a comprehensive visual report. *II Sqn*

With construction of most significant bridge targets for the FR10s in Germany already known, the requirement in war should have been limited to essentials (eg. Is the bridge serviceable?) *IV Sqn*

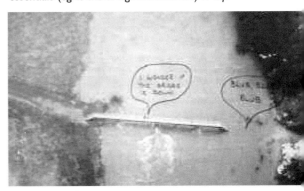

'over the target requirements' on these parameters, so one or both would have to be compromised for the minimum time required to obtain the necessary information. On anything but a pin-point target (say a bridge) all three cameras might be selected and triggered throughout the pass, bearing in mind that the more film exposed the longer it would take to process and interpret. Camera selection and operation was therefore crucial but, despite the simplicity of the Hunter system, there have been cases in training where, in the tension of the moment, the pilot has got it wrong, even forgetting to press the camera button. From his visual sightings, and using a form of shorthand, the pilot would jot down key target information on his kneepad as soon as it was relatively safe to do so after leaving the target, and prepare his IFREP. Egress on the homeward leg would again be as low and as fast as possible, skirting known defences both on the hostile and friendly side of the border. Part of the homeward leg could be flown at high level, perhaps to divert to an alternative base or for fuel or weather considerations, but climbing out only when clear of hostile defences. In particular, safe recovery procedures through 'friendly' SAM belts and Gun Defended Areas (GDA) called for high-level

flight because few FR pilots had any confidence in those defences.

The inherent value of this real time information was recognised at that seat of learning, the RAF Staff College, in briefing notes which stated that 'Commanders can obtain information from visual reconnaissance far more quickly than by any other present day means by in-flight reporting'. There could have been nowhere better to put this to the test than on the front line in Germany, or in the real combat conditions in Aden, but the author believes that in the Hunter FR10's nine-year history this simple expedient was given too little attention.

Bridge Building. NATO and Warsaw Pact armies had mobile bridging equipments of all sorts, well rehearsed to supplement or take the place of static facilities destroyed in battle. These made excellent peacetime training targets.

Pontoons found during route recce. *Sandy Wilson*

Getting into position (non-tactically!). *Peter Riley*

PI's annotation of multi-bridge building. *Sandy Wilson*

German self-propelled ferry. *Al Mathie*

True, attitudes did become more positive in the 1960s, Northern Army Group (NORTHAG) and 2ATAF leading the way in Northern Germany by sending small groups of soldiers equipped with standard radios into the field during exercises to receive and relay IFREPS. Pilots were then required to route close to these pre-planned reporting points (often an unwelcome diversion for them) but, using equipment which was then notoriously unreliable, they often failed to make two-way contact with the ground. In this event they would transmit 'blind', hoping that their reports were being received and that they could complete them before they were 'jammed'. When they were successful, the ground nodes would then pass on these messages to battle staffs, hopefully without error or delay. Perhaps all participants had to take some blame for failings in a system which had been made to work most effectively by the *Luftwaffe* in Spain in the 1930s and by the Germans again in WW2 between the Panzers and Junkers 87 aircraft. Cold War army and air commanders seemed slow to appreciate its value; too many were loath to believe visual reports derived from overflights at the speeds and heights which were to some officers equally unbelievable. Had they had more faith in the pilots, better equipment might have been provided and the whole system rehearsed more regularly. Pictures were almost always demanded, not only as convincing evidence of what was or was not there, but because they were invaluable for the well-rehearsed and perfectly orchestrated debriefings which had the highest priority throughout and in the aftermath of most peacetime exercises.

Presentations of such perfection were unlikely to have taken place in war. The stark reality was that, despite the rapidity with which they were returned to the airfield, processed and printed, photographs would rarely get from there to units in the field in time to influence the battle. Had commanders correlated visual reports with photographs in peacetime they might have given more priority to visual reports and benefited greatly from them.

Fortunately, owing much to the determination of energetic protagonists of in-flight reporting, a better understanding of its value filtered up the line during the 1960s, leading to more regular training. IFREPS even became an integral part of Royal Flush competitions until some participating nations demanded that, for flight safety reasons, the competitors should climb to and maintain 1,000 ft in clear weather (which was not always possible) to transmit their findings in three thirty-second reports. However, these safety conscious demands hardly reflected the realities of war in a heavily defended ECM environment.

One of the author's long term friends in the post-WW2 German Air Force (GAF), *Oberst* Gert Overhoff, a leading advocate of in-flight reporting who would go on to command the Tripartite Tornado Training Establishment, believed that, even at the time of the FR10s, Warsaw Pact ECM made it necessary for these reports to be completed within 10 seconds and helped evolve procedures by which this was possible. A 'line thrust' system was developed for pre-planned route searches in which aircrew and battle staffs placed identical, gridded overlays between common start and finish points on their target maps, so that coded positions could be passed simply, briefly and accurately in the air. Similar measures were

evaluated but most were rejected outright as too complicated, too lengthy or simply unusable in single-seat recce aircraft. In fact, where reports could be passed at very low level direct to troops in contact, say to a Forward Air Controller (FAC) or Brigade Air Support Officer (BASO), or to an airborne attack package following close behind, some messages might be passed in the clear without undue risk to security.

Airborne messages can of course be intercepted and used against the sender. During Exercise Marshmallow, in November 1969, the author parachuted into the Solling region of the then West Germany (on the border with East Germany) as the forward air commander for 15 (Scottish) Parachute Battalion, carrying an A43 ground-to-air radio. By chance he overheard a message from the leader of four Belgian F-104s flying as 'enemy', awaiting instructions from the FAC of the Canadian Vingt Doux infantry battalion (also 'enemy') to attack the paras. Unheard by the FAC he was able to instruct the fighter bombers to change frequency, on which he then instructed them to abort their mission and they returned to base. The paras would live to fight another day and would have been even more impressed had the pilot tasked to deliver prints to them of a local sighting a mere one hour before not jettisoned them from the airbrake of his Hunter while taxying out.

The campaign against dissident factions in South Arabia offered proof of another valuable contribution which could be made by the FR10s, that of visual sightings leading to a recce/attack interface. Flight Lieutenant Roger Pyrah, commanding 1417 Flight at RAF Khormaksar in Aden in 1964-65, did much to perfect this joint effort in the region, using the recce pilot's special ability to find targets and pass their exact positions, if necessary marking them with the FR10's guns for an attack package to acquire more easily (in this case the FGA9 Hunters from Khormaksar). In this scenario, there was little chance of the target escaping in the short time between recce and attack, rendering secure communications unnecessary (Chapter Nine). In the European theatre there was too little of this interface in the Hunter years, but subsequently Jaguar FR aircraft were used to relay up-to-the-minute information to assist Tornado bombers locate mobile targets. Moreover, the GAF made arrangements for its Southern (navigation) Fixer Service to take on a war role, with an appropriate

Airfield Recce. With the flexible and mobile Warsaw Pact air power (including massive fleets of attack helicopters) greatly exceeding that of NATO, airfields and airstrips of all sorts were primary targets for FR.

Main Operating Base (MOB). FR10s were unlikely to find such an easy target as this MOB in war – RAF Laarbruch later 'toned-down'. *Sandy Wilson*

Simulated Forward Operating Base (FOB). Siegerland, with its interesting mix of ancient and modern aircraft, was a popular peacetime target. *Sandy Wilson*

Vertical Photography. The FR10 had no credible high-level vertical photo capability in a hostile environment. *Roger Wilkins*

RAF Salalah. Full cover of large airfields was hard to achieve with oblique cameras only – and survive against strong ground defences. *Derek Whitman*

frequency switching plan, to receive IFREPs and relay them to specified customers.

Recce aircraft could also pass their sightings to customers via an Airborne Radio Relay (ARR)

aircraft flying with relative safety in friendly airspace at high level. Use of this 'air bridge' was simplicity itself, with short messages passed in simple code, again on pre-planned frequencies. This 'air bridge' concept was promoted 'bottom-up' and trialled successfully using the two-seat fast-jet trainers established in RAF Germany, but it was not adopted officially during the Hunter era.

Visual sightings relayed by any of these means could have a very timely and productive impact on events and would certainly have been possible in many circumstances, even for single-seat FR or FGA pilots. The option was practised regularly by the II (AC) Squadron FR10 pilots during the author's time at Gutersloh (1964-1967), albeit 'in house' using an ARC-52 radio installed with self-help below the operations desk. This facility allowed aircraft to be re-tasked in flight (simulating new and immediate priorities), IFREPS to be received and recce/attack operations triggered. This was the type of training that should have been run by the established battle management teams using the facilities in place for war.

Continuous use of the FR10s in these ways would have increased confidence in such measures, none of which depended on successful photography. That said, photographs can of course play a major part in war and the FR10, with all its organic support, had much to offer here too. The excellent F95 oblique camera, developed to replace the F24 in use up to and including the time of the Meteor FR9s, was originally evaluated in Germany on the Meteor. It was found to be very successful and entered front line service in the Swift FR5, again with great success. For fast, low level work it was unparalleled at that time. Fitted with 4-inch or 12-inch focal length lenses with the 70-mm wide film, it allowed considerable magnification before grain size became a problem. To avoid blurring at very high speeds, exposure times of up to 1/2,000 second were achieved with a strip aperture in a focal-plane endless-shutter blind of Neoprene silk, which admitted light as it passed over a film gate at a cycle rate of four or eight frames/second. The film magazines, loaded in darkness but easily detached from their lens units in less than 10 seconds, each contained enough film for 500 exposures. With all these attributes, while measuring 11 x 9 x 6 inches and weighing only 16 lb (with a four-inch lens and magazine) – this was an ideal camera for the FR10.

The associated switches came easily to hand. Camera heating was activated by the starter bar below the instrument panel, with either G90 or F95 cameras selected by a switch on the port consol. Individual selectors for the three cameras were also positioned on the port consol, in order to determine the cycle rate of four or eight frames/second, and an iris control switch allowed the selection of ambient light values between dull, normal and light (if automatic exposure control was not fitted). Correct camera operation, by a button on the stick top, could be checked by three green lights on the starboard glare shield and three camera-magazine contents indicators mounted on the starboard instrument panel.

Whereas other contemporary recce aircraft had viewfinders to enable their pilots to position targets on the film with competition accuracy, FR10 pilots had no such help and learned to do so with their own cues until it became an almost subconscious action based on a sixth sense. In so doing, they were able to devote more attention to visual sightings of their targets, to keeping clear of obstacles and looking out for hostile aircraft. Having checked the correct operation of the cameras selected, and remembered to trigger them over the target, the pilot would then direct the camera(s) vertically at the ground in a clearing burst to signify the end of that run. He might leave one or more of his cameras selected when over hostile territory in anticipation of a target of opportunity, but peacetime competitions required the minimum sensible use of film to expedite processing and interpretation.

During the return to base an IFREP would be transmitted, if only 'blind', after which the pilot might start preparing his Visual Report (VISREP) while the targets were fresh in his mind. All this time he had to remain vigilant for active defences, both hostile and 'friendly', remember to change his Identification Friend or Foe (IFF) code according to mandatory procedures when penetrating friendly airspace, and to concentrate on flying his aircraft safely, often in difficult conditions. It would always be a busy trip home.

Whether FR missions should be flown by single aircraft or in pairs depended on several factors. Taking a war scenario first, the paucity of assets and economy of effort alone would probably have dictated the use of single aircraft in Europe – unless the targets were considered of such size or importance that a second aircraft was deemed necessary. A wingman not only provided redundancy but a measure of protection for his leader and a back-up should the primary aircraft become unserviceable or destroyed at any stage of the flight; if necessary a second aircraft could also help in any search and rescue operation. The choice between these two

Radar and Missile Sites. Static radar and missile sites were relatively simple targets, whereas mobile equipments could be hard to find. The difference was made clear from peacetime training against static targets (Type 80 radars, Nike and Hawk sites) and mobile (Flycatcher radars, Pershing and Honest John missiles).

Honest John Missiles. *Jack Bowland*

British Type 80/Type 13 Radar Site. *Sandy Wilson*

American Nike Missile Site. *Sandy Wilson*

Military Deployed. Perhaps the most difficult targets for the FR pilots were those military units in the field skilled in camouflage. For good reason there were few photographs of good camouflage and even less accurate visual reports – but there were many mobile targets which failed to conceal themselves adequately.

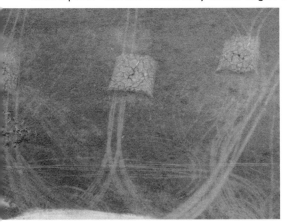

'Dead Ants'. Prostrate soldiers (left) did nothing to conceal their poorly camouflaged guns, with tracks to and from their precise locations. *Sandy Wilson*

Nearly There. Man-made facilities provide excellent concealment but this signals vehicle falls short, while radio aerials silhouetted against the skyline helped the low flying FR10s. *Sandy Wilson*

Attention Getters. Better camouflage for guns, but tracks and nearby support vehicles (whitewall tyres) give the game away. *Sandy Wilson*

Fooled? These dummy missiles (made from drop tanks?) might deceive the eye but not the camera. *IV Sqn*

options also depended on the degree of opposition expected. During the air war in Vietnam the use of single or pairs of Voodoo tactical reconnaissance aircraft was determined by a constant reappraisal of all these fundamental considerations, and others, in ever-changing circumstances. In Europe the FR10 pilot would have wished to fly as fast and low as possible, keeping transmissions to a minimum, using the aircraft's impressive manoeuvrability strenuously to maximise terrain masking, avoid obstacles and unexpected defences should they appear, perhaps welcoming poor visibility and low cloud for greater security. In these conditions a wingman would have his work cut out merely to stay with his leader, let alone provide

Desert Reconnaissance. The very variable desert terrain, with few landmarks on poor maps and often obscure targets, required a particular expertise, different tactics and techniques.

Heading and speed had to be held steady over flat, featureless desert terrain. *Ralph Chambers via Ray Deacon*

Roger Pyrah found these rebel positions in the Jebel Radfan. *Roger Pyrah*

With equally sharp eyes, Tim Thorn spotted the bivouacs of these dismounted troops in the desert scrub. *Tim Thorn*

Movement. Any movement, disturbance in the sand, tracks or dust could attract the eye from the sky. Armour moving in daylight was a rare sight *Alex Weiss*

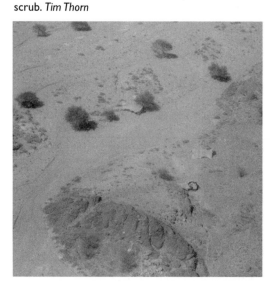

continuous cross-cover while navigating himself so that he could take over should the need arise, thus largely negating his theoretical value. Add this reasoning to the need for economy of effort and it was generally concluded that FR10 operations would normally have involved single aircraft only.

In training, the considerations were very different. Defensive cross-cover was of course no longer a primary factor (even if practical) but when flights were to be made over very difficult, unpopulated or inhospitable terrain (such as the deserts of the Middle East) a second man could be desirable or necessary for flight safety or

On Track? Bedouin villages, ill-defined, absent from or mis-plotted on maps, were often all there was to aid map reading. *Ralph Chambers via Ray Deacon*

search and rescue reasons. In fact, most executives in the FR business generally rejected pairs flying, other than for checks or other special purposes, as wasted effort.

In 1965, however, II Squadron in Germany adopted pairs flying as a general but not inviolate rule, in an attempt to make sortie results more transparent and raise operational standards. This was coupled with a 'trip of the day' programme in which all available pilots covered the same targets in the same time window and therefore in more or less the same weather. This was no academic competition, with all the temptations and non-operational practices which characterised Royal Flush, Sassoon and Big Click exercises (Chapter Seven). Planning and flying pairs, with all operational pilots, regardless of experience taking equal turns in the lead and as wingman, on strictly operational profiles and practices, generated greater demands than were likely when individuals did their own thing from start to finish. Over time, any repetitive errors were revealed and hopefully remedied, with a regular and mutually beneficial cross-fertilisation of ideas. Some pilots complained that they found it rather daunting to have their performance monitored continuously, but any extra pressure should have been welcomed in going some small way to simulate war conditions, rather than the alternative of a generally pressure-free individual sortie. The argument that a set daily programme of pairs missions wasted some precious training hours is refuted. Wingmen were programmed

with a full workload; not only did they have to keep formation (position depending on weather etc.) and navigate precisely themselves, always aware that at any point in the sortie they might be ordered (on the squadron 'natter' frequency or by their leader) to take the lead. They were also required to render visual reports and photographs on all the targets, the pressure on them increased further with in-flight re-tasking, diversions or interceptions by 'bounce' aircraft. During this time II Squadron always exceeded its annual flying task.

Using these tactics and training, would the FR10s have been able to succeed in their war missions (survival being implicit in this success)? To help answer this question the author took views from ex-Soviet and East German air defence radar specialists, AAA gunners and MiG fighter pilots in the wake of the Cold War. *Oberst* Alfred Lehmann, who manned East German early warning and aircraft control radars in the late 1950s and early 1960s and went on to command a comprehensive network of sites, was confident in their ability to detect intruders, either single aircraft or mass raids, and to provide some form of fighter control – provided they were not at very low level. He admitted, however, that these early systems would not have been able to detect or trace aircraft flying at the heights and speeds that the FR10 pilots intended to fly. It is believed that the Warsaw Pact did have visual observers at strategic points and in depth along the Inner German Border, equipped with radios to report the headings and estimated airspeeds of Allied aircraft entering their airspace. It seems unlikely, however, that at the outset of a general war in the 1960s, this system would have been sufficiently well rehearsed, or the defences responsive enough, to make best use of such warnings.

Later, an enhanced network was made to work to good effect in Vietnam but the circumstances there were very different to those at this stage in Europe. It is not known how effective their electronic counter counter measures (ECCM) would have been against the almost negligible ECM available to NATO at that time. Likewise, ex-MiG pilots Klaus Jurgen Baarz, who became

Self-Defence. Only in extremis, when in imminent danger from hostile aircraft, and without detriment to their primary recce task, FR10 pilots might take the offensive – and they were trained for this contingency.

Chris Golds, in a 14 Squadron Hunter F6, holds an outgoing Swift FR5 in his gunsight. The FR10 would not be such easy prey. *Chris Golds*

Practice makes perfect – but this is a little too close! *IV Sqn*

Deputy Commander of the East German Air Force/Air Defence, and Klaus Heinig, while again proud of their capabilities, agreed that they would have been very lucky to catch Hunters flying among the trees at the very high speeds, especially without early warning. Similar opinions came from Dr Dusan Schneider, who served in the Czech Air Force from 1952 to 1969 flying the MiG-15bis, MiG-17PF and MiG-21. He does recall that on the day before Stalin's death in 1953, Czech MiG-15bis from Pilsen shot down a USAF F-84 from Bitburg AB in Germany, one of two which had strayed into their airspace, and that in 1959 Czech MiG-19s forced an Italian Air Force F-84 to land at Hradec Kralov AB. The embarrassed pilot left his cockpit muttering: "Mamma mia, Mamma Mia, Madonna mia, Madonna mia", and was returned later to Italy by train. However, these aircraft did not have the performance of the FR10 and they were not flying at operational low level.

Finally, the author obtained a highly reliable account of MiG-15 capabilities and limitations from an exceptionally able ex-RAF fighter pilot, Mark Hanna who, when chief pilot of the 'Old Flying Machine Company', flew the aircraft in mock combat against F-86 and Hunter fighters. Mark found the Russian aircraft to be directionally unstable, the light but rather ineffective ailerons giving a poor rate of roll, and that the MiG had a tendency to 'dutch roll' and 'pitch-up' well within the permitted speed range. He was not comfortable in the MiG at the high speeds required to attempt to intercept the

Hunters at ultra low-level and 600 kts, and it seems unlikely that the MiG-17 would have been much better but, given sufficient warning and effective intercept control, the MiG-21 could have posed a much greater threat to the Hunters.

Whether it was as a result of clandestine intelligence or simply from sensible, professional deduction, the author was able to confirm that MiG satellite bases had been set up close to the most likely penetration points for NATO aircraft, shortening response times and perhaps making the maintenance of Combat Air Patrols (CAP), with the vast numbers of fighters available, wholly viable. A *Diensthabendes*, equivalent to the NATO Quick Reaction Alert (QRA) force, was required to be airborne in 8 minutes by day and 10 minutes by night. Even in the 'quiet' years of the Cold War the East German Air Force, heavily biased to air defence, had to maintain 90 per cent of its fighters combat ready at all times – every twelve-aircraft squadron holding four aircraft at 30 minutes readiness. The numbers of aircraft training and rehearsing war procedures in the airspace close to the IGB were so high that half the force would fly training sorties on alternative days only. Although the actual proficiency of the pilots in the air could not be judged, it is known that they flew approximately half the number of training hours allocated to NATO pilots, but of

Route Reconnaissance. FR10 pilots in all theatres could expect to be tasked with route recces of many different sorts — each with particular problems.

Only in conditions of air superiority (such as here in Aden) could this route be viewed from height — but how to follow it at very low level? *Roger Pyrah*

Easy to follow but easy too for the defences in this desert terrain. *IV Sqn*

course much depended on the content of each flying hour. The fact remained that any Allied aircraft entering their airspace would face overwhelming odds and would have to use every means possible to survive.

The USAF experience in Vietnam, even against less organised AAA defences, suggests that guns would have posed the main threat to low flying Hunters in Eastern Europe, which for the reasons given could not escape them by flying above their range. All the Hunters could do, therefore, was both to avoid known GDAs and anticipate where the guns were most likely to be concentrated – then to fly as low and as fast as possible, using terrain masking to the maximum

Before and After. Pre and post-strike recces were for real only in Aden, as in this 'before and after' cover provided by Roger Pyrah, 1417, Flight in the Wadi Tayme. Any war in Europe would have generated many similar requirements. *Roger Pyrah*

Ship Ahoy! FR10 pilots in Europe were trained to spot and recognise Soviet shipping, particularly in the Baltic and Mediterranean, as were those in Aden and Bahrain in their coastal waters, in the Indian Ocean, Red Sea and Persian Gulf.

Riga Class in the Baltic. *Al Mathie*

Unidentified Fast Patrol Boat in the Baltic. *Pete Riley*

Ancient Mariner in Skaggerak. *Pete Rayner*

to delay detection and make firing solutions difficult. The AAA defences were impressive: Soviet 57-mm S60 guns, with PUAZO-6-60 fire directors and SON-9 fire control radars, were thick on the ground in regiments of 24 guns, accompanied by similar numbers of 85-mm guns. These were supplemented by other regiments of 37-mm guns and by the formidable ZSU-23/2 and 23/4 Shilka mobile, radar-laid AAA. A warm welcome awaited any NATO aircraft.

The Warsaw Pact SAM threat to jets flying in Europe at very low level became significant in the 1960s, with the Soviet-built SA-4 'Ganef' and the portable SA-7 'Grail', with its infra-red detection and guidance system optimised for low-level defence, hard to avoid. All that said, coupled with his own experience in offensive and air defence exercises against contemporary NATO weapons systems in Germany, the author believes that, given the necessary prerequisites in targeting and tasking, and strict adherence to the fully operational training outlined above, the FR10 pilots stood a good chance of completing their missions safely.

Team effort was the name of the game and essential to effective air reconnaissance. The academic competitions provided graphic demonstrations of this and the work of the support agencies, specifically the squadron photographic tradesmen, Ground Liaison Sections (GLSs), Mobile Field Processing Units (MFPUs) and Photographic Interpreters (PIs). A British Army GLS, attached to each recce squadron, would normally comprise two Ground Liaison Officers (GLOs) (majors or captains) and four to six other ranks. They would be involved in the action from the start of a mission, the officers preparing briefing material for the pilots on the targets and the defences likely to be encountered, the soldiers producing target maps (1:100,000 or 1:50,000 scale), while pilots planned their routes (on 1:500,000 maps).

Opportunity Targets. The FR pilots were encouraged to photograph and report back on any additional targets of possible interest seen en route.

FR10 pilots practiced their *en route* photography on any target of interest, such as this ski jump at Winterberg. *Roger Wilkins*

With sharp eyes, Peter Gover of IV Squadron, spotted two human targets besporting themselves among the trees high in the Teuterberger Wald – and called for corroboration from any other FR10 airborne. Classic FR opportunity. *Peter Gover*

The structure, organisation and contribution made to this joint effort by the PIs and the MFPU is outlined more fully in Chapter Eleven 'Film Stars'. Suffice it to say here that their importance cannot be over emphasised.

The whole support team came together as the recce aircraft taxied to a stop as close as possible to the MFPU, the pilot signalling which cameras had been used. Following the necessary safety procedures, the pilot would stop-cock the engine and the camera magazines would be off-loaded within seconds to be speeded to the processing van by the fastest means possible (by foot, bicycle or dispatch rider). Within a very few minutes the wet film would be on the light table for identification of the targets and selection of negatives by the PI, assisted by the pilot and the GLO, for analysis and printing. The pilot would then begin writing his VISREP and the PI his Mission Report (MISREP). The first prints could be available within 15 minutes from 'engine off', with the aim of completing the initial package of information gleaned from a sortie within 30 minutes. Should further analysis reveal additional information a 'Hot Report' would follow. The flight line had done its job – but how would all this material be handled thereafter?

This highly visible and very impressive team effort came at the end of a line which began with those who selected the targets and tasked the missions in the battle management cells, and those who generated and maintained the aircraft on the flight line and were responsible for the essential equipments therein (communications, cameras, weapons etc.) During the recce missions airborne radio relays and communications nodes on the ground had to remain on the alert for what could be all-important IFREPS. Likewise, Allied defences had to be ready to give returning friendly aircraft safe passage in strict accordance with published procedures, while air traffic agencies stood by to render assistance in their recovery. This was indeed a truly collective effort.

Tactical Evaluations (Tacevals), exercises and competitions proved that, with all those involved working in harmony, a typical FR mission had the potential to make a significant contribution to the tactical land/air battle and, depending on the means employed, to do so within a very short timeframe from an air reconnaissance request to completion of the package of information required. The greatest concern of all involved in this frenetic effort at station level was the length of time it might take to get the intelligence gathered from there to the requesting agency – and what use was made of it there. In some three years with the British Army the author can recall only one occasion when, other than via an in-flight report, the results of a recce request generated in the field reached them in time for the information to be of use in the battle. Prints were, however, always welcomed for use in VIP briefings!

Chapter 3
Training the Best

The initial, specialised training of pilots destined for the Meteor FR9 and its successor the Swift FR5 in the 1950s was founded at RAF Stradishall in Suffolk. The Meteor T7 was used for dual checks and the camera equipped FR9 for operational training. This was the route taken to the front line by most first-tour pilots but a stepping stone bypassed by some experienced jet fighter pilots who undertook type conversion and FR familiarisation on front-line squadrons. When the Hunter FR10 replaced the Swift, this training was transferred to No. 229 Operational Conversion Unit (OCU) at RAF Chivenor, on the River Taw Estuary in North Devon. Chivenor was a much loved station despite its WW2 accommodation and single 2,000 yard runway; it had a good weather factor and lay conveniently close to low flying areas and the weapons range at Pembray, with the only significant operating disadvantage being the lack of ideal diversions. This was where those pilots assessed to have the right potential would become acquainted with FR. Among their attributes, these 'chosen men' needed the ability to navigate and fly safely at very low levels and the airmanship to cope with the unexpected. They usually operated alone, often out of radio contact and at extreme ranges. These pilots had to anticipate bad weather and

be able to divert from, and recover to track following distractions caused by weather and (simulated) hostile attention. Meticulous flight planning and comprehensive target study was a *sine qua non*, while visual acuity and a retentive memory were needed for visual reconnaissance. Success in the role depended on an independence of mind, determination and integrity.

In the early 1960s, FR training was conducted by the OCU's No 1 Squadron (234 Squadron in its war role), commanded by Squadron Leader Ron Wood. Conversion to the Hunter F6 and F9, using the Hunter T7 two-seat aircraft, was followed by instruction in basic pilot navigation (predominantly map reading) at low level (progressively down to a minimum of 250 ft) at

Senior flight commander and ex-FR pilot, Flight Lieutenant Peter Highton, led the flypast to mark the boss's farewell. *Author*

In at the Start. Squadron Leader Ron Wood, OC 1/234 (R) Squadron, 229 OCU, RAF Chivenor, the squadron initially responsible for FR training on the Hunter. *Pete Highton*

Sample Only. The faces of all FR course members would adorn the walls of the WW2 Wing Operations at Chivenor until the end; these pilots among many who went to make their mark (in one way or another!) within the FR 10 fraternity. (Rear, L to R): Flt Lts Frank Mitchell and Slash Slaney (II Sqn); (Front, L to R) Flt Lts Iain Weston (IV Squadron) and Ken Simpson (1417 Flt). *RAF Chivenor via Hoppy Granville-White & Tim Webb*

speeds increasing from 360 to 420 kts and higher. Targets for visual reconnaissance, simple at first but gradually more difficult to find, identify and report on, were injected into this programme as the student progressed. Additional sorties ensured continuity in general handling, formation, instrument flying etc and regular checks were carried out in the two-seat Hunter T7 or by 'chase' pilots to ensure that the required standards were being achieved. A comprehensive ground training syllabus, to which the army GLOs and later PIs made important contributions, introduced the student to the EEIs of targets against which he could expect to be tasked in war (military vehicles, airfields, bridges etc).

Low-level training sorties mirrored those practised in Germany, typically over 600 nm to cover three targets with initial point (IP) to target runs at speeds ranging from 360–540 kts, these speeds determined by the tasks, stage of training, range, terrain and weather. Tracks to IPs for each target, with turning circles and time intervals (1 or 2 minutes) appropriate to the speeds flown at each juncture were marked on 1:500,000 scale route maps. For final runs from the IP to target, the pilot transferred to larger scale maps, usually 1:50,000, folded to a convenient size and again marked with tracks and time marks, perhaps at 10 second intervals. Although in the first years the OCU had no aircraft equipped with reconnaissance cameras it was assumed in this training that they were. For instance, tracks would be offset to one side of the target to optimise visual reconnaissance opportunities while allowing for the required photographic cover with the side oblique cameras. Direct overflight of a target would offer excellent photo cover with the nose-facing camera, but limited the visual option when the target became obscured under the aircraft's nose. Egress from each target would take account of tactical imperatives, with the next leg ideally starting over an easily identified feature on map and ground.

As in the CR of Europe, the constantly changing low flying regulations, prohibited areas and general restrictions in the UK added complications to flight planning, as did the mandatory avoidance of all towns and large villages, hospitals, stud farms et al, but these no-go areas were used to advantage to simulate GDAs and SAM-defended areas. With these factors (as would be the case in war), it was rarely possible to plan straight lines between targets and constant changes of heading increased navigational difficulties. Throughout the course students were taught to 'stay ahead of the aircraft', seeking to tie up natural and man-made features on the ground with the map according to the required track and time marks. When airborne they had to be ready to take avoiding action from pockets of unforecast weather, other aircraft and even birds causing deviations from track and timing; while human errors in navigation and aircraft emergencies also intruded to likewise distract the pilot. A student clever or fortunate enough to stay on track could expect an instructor flying chase to introduce synthetic difficulties to increase the tension and test the student's reaction. He might call in a 'bounce' aircraft to evaluate all-round look out and evasive tactics, task a target of opportunity or require an unplanned diversion. FR students could never expect an easy ride, especially towards the end of the course when competition between them became the name of the game – again reflecting peacetime recce practices in NATO.

No. 229 OCU was blessed throughout with a wealth of diverse experience among its instructors; those heading the FR course were no exception and were invariably given a great deal of latitude in their conduct of this training. The author took command of No. 1 Squadron from Ron Wood in early 1965, when the FR course was in the very able hands of Flight Lieutenant Fred Trowern, late of II Squadron in its Meteor FR9 days, and Flight Lieutenant 'Porky' Munro, who had also cut his teeth on the FR9 and progressed to the Swift FR5 on 79 Squadron. Their successors were Flight Lieutenant John 'Johnny' Morris, a veteran of the air war in Korea, and Lieutenant Bob Ponter, an exchange officer who had flown the multi-role Scimitar in the Royal Navy. Fred was noted for his paternal touch while Johnny Morris was undeniably more forceful in his demands on the

ground and in the air. Initial FR training was in good hands.

The introduction of the Swift FR5 and the perceived demands of FR had led to a policy of selecting newcomers to the role who not only showed the right potential but also had previous fast jet experience, preferably in ground attack and this continued up to the time of the author's arrival on 229 OCU – when even diehard FR men were beginning to question the need for such a policy. So it was that the rule was relaxed progressively, firstly in 1965 with candidates taken from other fast jet roles, followed by ex-flying instructors who had demonstrated the right ability and, later, selected 'first tourists'. For example, Flight Lieutenant Dick Johns came from the Javelin all-weather force and after a basic conversion to the Hunter had no great difficulty with the FR course. He was followed by Flight Lieutenants Sandy Wilson, Pete Gover and Geoff Hall, who had been 'creamed off' after their pilot training to become Qualified Flying Instructors (QFIs) and returned directly to the training organisation for their first productive tour. As such, they were all considered to be of above average ability in the air and on the ground but, lacking the benefit of that front line, fast jet experience, there was some scepticism over their prospects.

Flight Line Chivenor. This line up of Hunter F6s, on which FR pilots trained in the early 1960s, represented about one quarter of the aircraft on the apron at Chivenor on a busy day. The aircraft are probably manned for a mass flypast. *Jerry Saye*

Test Cases. In the early days, those selected for FR10 courses had invariably completed at least one fast-jet tour. In 1965, however, it was found that selected ex-QFIs could meet the demands without that prerequisite. (L to R) Flt Lts Sam Toyne (Staff), Sandy Wilson and Geoff Hall (II Sqn), Pete Gover (IV Sqn) and George Cole (Staff). *Sandy Wilson*

The Trail Blazer. Having shown that previous fast jet experience might not be necessary to meet the requirements of FR, Flying Officer Ron Elder then proved that selected men could be taken direct from advanced flying training, pass the course and go on to excel in the role. *Ron Elder*

The arrival of the QFI students at Chivenor was grist to the mill for Johnny Morris, who had now taken over the FR course and given it a new momentum, some would say demanding too much even from those students holding the originally more stringent credentials. His final 'Operational Phase' provided the ultimate challenge, with combination sorties that tested the students' ability to map read (the fundamental art) very precisely at high speed and the lowest authorised level; to acquire, identify and report in detail EEIs which were hard to find and complex to report and with every distraction thrown in. Sandy Wilson remembers: 'During trips in the final phase over unfamiliar terrain in a detachment to Scotland, Sam Toyne in the chase aircraft never stopped talking to me, calling in a 'bounce', tasking targets of opportunity and otherwise diverting my attention'. In 41 hours (in addition to those allocated to convert to the Hunter), Sandy had faced tests which might have qualified him at this time for operational status on

I Know Who You Are. White spines identified the FR10s at Chivenor – this one flown by Jim Dymond. *Jim Dymond*

command. His Log Book records a great deal of (actual) instrument flying, with many a controlled descent through cloud (QGH) and Ground Control Approach (GCA) recoveries – reminders of how the weather in the 'sucker hole' of Chivenor could hamper low flying. He too remembers John Morris calling for nothing but the best and Bob Ponter providing an interesting insight into carrier-style landings during dual sorties in the Hunter T7. In his final three trips he competed against fellow students, Flight Lieutenants John Thomson, Stu Penny, Derek Whitman and Roger Wilkins (all of whom became well-respected FR pilots) covering electronics, airfield, bridge, harbour and line search targets. The fact that each of these sorties was timed and completed in 40 minutes suggested that they were flown at very high speeds. Modesty prevents Hoppy from revealing the winner.

Inevitable horse trading for the finite resources produced by a centralised servicing system at 229 OCU to cater for all the needs of the basic air defence, ground attack courses and other fast jet training, led to the formation in 1967 of a third squadron, No. 79 (Reserve) Squadron (once an FR squadron), for specialist courses including that for FR. The squadron was commanded first by Squadron Leader Sam Toyne, a one-time flight commander on II Squadron. He recalls that the necessary resources were brought together and the squadron firmly established over one weekend with no significant interruption to the OCU's busy programme. The new incumbents begged, borrowed or otherwise acquired their every need – the wartime spirit evident as a coffee bar sprang to life in parallel with the operations desk, while four Hunter F6s and two newly acquired Hunter FR10s were towed to their flight line on the northern perimeter of the airfield. With F95 cameras in their own FR10s the OCU students were now better able to learn the rudiments of airborne oblique photography at Chivenor, albeit adding to their workload. The established aircraft of 79 Squadron would soon sport the famous Salamander insignia of this one time Battle of Britain unit and its FR10s would be

a front-line squadron. Johnny Morris was indeed a hard task master but he had learned well from his days in Korea and wanted his students to be prepared for the harsh realities of war. The QFI 'guinea pigs' proved the sceptics wrong, all three passing the course with flying colours and going on to become very successful in their new role; they had broken the mould and opened the way for others who had not already proved themselves on fast jet squadrons. They were well chosen men.

Flight Lieutenant 'Hoppy' Granville-White, already an experienced Hunter FGA pilot from a tour on No. 208 Squadron in Aden, passed through the course in the winter of 1965–66; Squadron Leader Stanford Howard now in

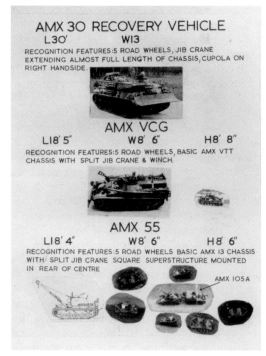

AMX 30 RECOVERY VEHICLE
L30'   W13
RECOGNITION FEATURES:5 ROAD WHEELS, JIB CRANE EXTENDING ALMOST FULL LENGTH OF CHASSIS, CUPOLA ON RIGHT HANDSIDE.

AMX VCG
L18' 5"   W8' 6"   H8' 8"
RECOGNITION FEATURES:5 ROAD WHEELS, BASIC AMX VTT CHASSIS WITH SPLIT JIB CRANE & WINCH.

AMX 55
L18' 4"   W8' 6"   H8' 6"
RECOGNITION FEATURES:5 ROAD WHEELS BASIC AMX 13 CHASSIS WITH SPLIT JIB CRANE SQUARE SUPERSTRUCTURE MOUNTED IN REAR OF CENTRE

AMX 105A

Recognition Training. Much ground training at Chivenor and on the front line provided guidance on recognition of friend and foe; typically, this card illustrates the detail FR pilots were expected to memorise. *Sandy Wilson*

identified further by their white spines and fins. Meanwhile, the boss's 'Shelty' dog took up residence in the crewroom, ready to welcome (or otherwise) the transient hounds belonging to the many army officers who would undergo FAC training on the squadron.

The FR Flight itself was now commanded by Flight Lieutenant Bill Armstrong, assisted by Flight Lieutenants George Cole and Jim Dymond. Flight Lieutenant Eric Lockwood, a PI with great experience and an unrivalled reputation in FR, joined the team to capitalise on the photography produced by the FR10s, together with Major Peter Heath, the GLO who had served with Eric on II Squadron. Eric had been posted in from RAF Brampton, the home of photographic interpretation on the other side of the country where he had recently set up house, but Sam Toyne softened the blow by arranging for him to be flown home in a Meteor T7 at the weekends. Eric accepted this gratefully, if with some trepidation, until his Meteor was pelted with hail stones in a horrendous storm and he decided thereafter to travel by car. Eric provided a most professional contribution to the FR courses; he not only prescribed photographic requirements but took the lead in the all-important ground instruction which preceded and continued throughout the flying phases. The

234(R) Squadron. Captain Bernie Bogoslosky, the USAF Exchange Officer on 234(R) Squadron leads a formation of 16 instructors (including the FR staff) to celebrate the Britain of Britain anniversary in 1964. *Jerry Saye*

'Late Initials' Tim Thorn runs in on Runway 27 over the original hutted camp at Chivenor. *Tim Thorn*

syllabus included instruction in tactics and techniques for the visual recognition of likely target arrays (military equipments, airfields, barracks, bridges, dams, oil installations, missile sites, electronics etc.) and the identification of their key features. This was necessary on the Warsaw Pact side of the border as a war contingency and on the friendly side for the many peacetime competitions. After two weeks

The Scenic Route. Jim Dymond skirting the North Devon Coast. *Jim Dymond*

of uninterrupted groundschool the flying phase began with similar intensity.

The aforementioned regulations and restrictions which governed peacetime low flying imposed additional pressures on all involved in supervising, planning, routeing and flying the sorties, but it was imperative to avoid violations in order to preserve the low flying concessions so essential to effective operational training. Likewise, there was every need to placate the anti-noise lobby; even to jest about any misdemeanour in this context carried a risk, as Sam Toyne found, perhaps to his detriment. While taking time out for coffee in 79 Squadron's crewroom, Sam's station commander enquired how his last trip had gone. He replied: "Splendid sir, one odd thing though, I was chasing a student in Wales, way off track, when we flashed over two or three hundred blokes dressed in white on the banks of Lake Bala, all staring up at us with their mouths wide open". It was at the time of the National Eisteddfod in Wales when the bards were at their most vociferous and Lake Bala had been notified formally as a particularly sensitive area to be avoided at all cost. The station commander was not amused.

In 1969, Squadron Leader Chris Golds took command of 79 Squadron, a unit for which he had acquired a great respect some decade before in its previous incarnation as a Swift FR5 Squadron located with his Hunter FGA squadron at RAF Gutersloh. He had joked that all the FR men needed to know about their cameras was 'F8 at a fortnight', a joke which might now come back to haunt him. He recalled too that, 'if we could catch the portly Swift at low level we could nail it, but catching it was the trick. With its afterburner selected this grandson of the Spitfire could fairly bound across the nap of the earth and we fighter jocks would soon run out of fuel so a victory was hard to come by'. The Swift, like other front line tac recce aircraft of the time (the RF-101 and RF-104) could out-run but not out-turn the fighters, whereas the FR10, with its greater manoeuvrability, was a different proposition and defensive combat was a part of the training syllabus. Chris also brought with him more than 2,000 hours of Hunter air defence and ground attack experience; he had been the Middle East Air Force staff officer responsible for the FR flight in Aden and was no newcomer to Chivenor, having been awarded the AFC for his exemplary work on the OCU during a previous tour there.

Besides these professional qualifications Chris was well known and greatly admired throughout the fast-jet community as a humorist, raconteur and aviation artist. He was, therefore, an ideal choice for training the best on this multi-role squadron.

On arrival in March 1969, Chris set about proving to himself, his highly qualified instructors and his students, that he was up to the job, by joining No. 49 FR Course. On his own admission he was just a little daunted, particularly by the need to satisfy the very high demands set by the new head of the FR team, Bill Armstrong. He was well aware that Bill was 'known for his low level navigation skills but not his patience – even with his boss to be.' Chris's graphic account of this training sortie is instructive: 'My last trip was a 'three targets on each of three legs' bash around the UK and I set off with about a half-ton of maps and my brain in a spin. On the last leg, with my score just enough to gain a pass, I nailed target No. 1 but missed No. 2. With my chances of becoming the squadron commander now diminishing rapidly, I just had to get target No. 3, a railway tunnel set into a steep hillside – and suddenly there it was, at 'three o'clock'. I broke right and fired my starboard F95, pulling some 7 'G', well beyond the limits for my still partially-full 230 gall tanks, then reversed hard to avoid hitting the ground above the tunnel. So to my great relief I passed the course, celebrating that memorable Friday evening in the Chivenor bar with Bill Armstrong and his right hand man, Jim Dymond. Perhaps they were relieved that they had not found it necessary to 'chop' their new boss, but not half as relieved as I was! The fighter recce course was the hardest work I ever had to do in the flying world and I regularly got home to my quarter very late in the day to find my two young children fast asleep and my wife gritting her teeth – but never complaining'.

Not all of Chris's peers who had been on fast jets for some years approached the FR course so seriously. Sam Toyne remembers two highly respected squadron leaders, both destined to command FR10 squadrons, who seemed to think that the course would be a 'doddle' and an opportunity to brush up on their bridge. Seven hours a day of lectures and tests throughout the two week groundschool quickly disabused them of this and to their credit they soon buckled down to pass without difficulty. There was a price to pay for being one of the chosen few.

For Chris there was no respite; he took over 79 Squadron on the Monday following completion of the course. Early in his tour his PI joked that he had to leave the title strip off the bottom of his boss's 9 x 9-inch negatives so that there was more room for the target, but this did not last long; Chris soon got it right having learned quickly that there was a little more to airborne photography than 'F8 at a fortnight'. Then, on 1 April 1970, after one year in command and at the height of his flying career, he was grounded with diabetes. Unable to accept the offer of demotion to flight lieutenant and transfer to the Equipment Branch he left the service to concentrate on another job in which he would also excel, that of aviation artist, writer and modeller.

During Chris's tenure, the long held view that all candidates destined for FR must be second tourists from the low level, fast jet force was challenged again. After the ex-QFIs had confounded the critics by proving themselves more than adequate without this prerequisite, a first tourist was now put to the test. It is fair to say that Flying Officer Ron Elder was hardly representative of the average graduate straight out of training. He had already shown his mettle, having won the Cup of Honour at the Gnat Flying Training School at Valley and had been earmarked as the first *ab initio* student for the new RAF Phantom force. On the other hand his progress had been disrupted by delays in the formation of the Phantom force, during which time he had 'held' as adjutant of the Metropolitan Communications Squadron at Northolt, with flying available only on Sycamore helicopters, Pembroke and Valetta piston aircraft. He was then told, to his initial dismay, that his posting had been changed to that of the obsolescent Hunter FR10. Albeit with a Gnat refresher to follow, this lack of continuity was hardly ideal preparation for the FR course which he joined in November 1969, four years after first arriving at Cranwell.

Ron was the sole student on No. 52 FR Course at Chivenor, thus enjoying the full attention of a formidable team of highly experienced FR men but with all eyes on him to see whether he could make the grade. For Ron, every day started early and finished late, with the intensive ground school, two demanding trips a day (weather permitting), mammoth debriefings and more planning for the following day often continuing well after bar-opening time. His abiding memory

The Final Years. Wing Commanders Nigel Price, Ian Worby and David Thornton, Chief Instructors on 229 OCU leading from the front, ensured that the Hunters were not forgotten by the people of North Devon in their final years at Chivenor. *David Bagshaw, Tim Thorn & Jim Dymond*

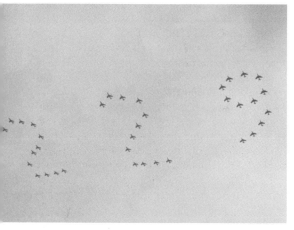

is of 'relentless pressure to keep up, get ahead, do better and do everything right.' Ron was, perhaps more than any other student up to that time, hard pressed, but he too survived to prosper later. He had broken another mould, making way for other 'chosen men' with his background to get into this elite force.

With the impending demise of Hunter FR10 squadrons in 1971, the last FR course at Chivenor finished in March 1970, the FR Flight ceasing to exist as its aircraft and men were absorbed into B Flight of 79 Squadron, with ex-II Squadron FR pilot Flight Lieutenant Geoff Hall as flight commander. Geoff had just returned from an exchange posting on recce Phantoms with the USAF and was now given the responsibility of providing lead-in training at the OCU for pilots nominated for the new Phantom, Buccaneer and Harrier squadrons, all of which would be involved in tac recce. The white-spined FR10s were then used as chase aircraft.

In its early years, FR training at Chivenor tended to concentrate on the fundamentals of low level navigation, with no means of introducing its students to F95 photography, but as the course developed it became more demanding and, with the addition of the FR10s, it ultimately provided more than a glimpse of the initial and continuation training on the squadrons. Even those students who had benefited from a previous tour on ground attack found new challenges in FR. They were more familiar with flying as part of a formation, but now they had to operate independently with very precise navigation against a variety of hostile threats with an increased workload in the target area. It follows that those who came to FR from a different role, perhaps that of air defence or instructor duties, and especially the first tourists who came later, found it more difficult, but they had been chosen with care and the great majority acquitted themselves very well.

Periodically, there were murmurs that the FR course at Chivenor demanded too much from its students but most of the instructors, albeit with their different ways and techniques, drew respect from their students and sent potentially very capable FR pilots to the front line. They too had been well chosen. Although he cannot remember any formal complaint, the author would accept that the course was optimised for the main customers in RAF Germany, with scant regard for the different tactics and techniques required for FR operations in Aden and Bahrain. That was left largely to theatre orientation. Apart from these observations and regardless of the approach, content and conduct of the courses, it is generally held that 229 OCU served the FR force very well in training the best. Few if any of the graduates were 'chopped' from their squadrons – and this speaks for itself.

Wing Commanders Nigel Price, Ian Worby and David Thornton, the OCs Flying Wing and Chief Instructors at 229 OCU, ensured that the Hunter's final days at Chivenor did not pass unnoticed on the ground or in the air. Station 'Air Days' became legion throughout the aviation community with mass formations of Hunters and Meteors becoming familiar sights in the skies over Devon in the early 1970s. It was a fitting tribute to an aircraft which had served at Chivenor for much of the Cold War.

Chapter 4
No. II (Army Co-operation Squadron)

II Squadron Crest.

No. II (AC) Squadron, Royal Flying Corps, was formed on 13 May 1912, when one of its B.E.2As and a second from No. 3 Squadron took off line abreast from Farnborough; they became the first British military squadrons to fly aircraft (No. 1 Squadron was equipped with balloons). Central to the Squadron Crest, by kind permission of Sir Hereward Wake, is the Wake Knot and the word 'Hereward', the Saxon for 'Leader of an Army', and over the years this has proved a most appropriate watchword for the squadron. 'Shiny Two', distinguished itself in two world wars, predominantly in the armed recce role with B.E.2s in WW1 and Lysanders, Mustangs and Spitfires in WW2. At the time of writing the squadron remains operational with the Tornado GR4A.

1961: A New Dawn

Conversion from Swift FR5s to Hunter FR10s began on II Squadron at RAF Jever in January 1961. During the transition the squadron continued to fly the Swifts which remained serviceable, and six Hunter F6s made redundant when Jever's 93 and IV Squadrons disbanded, until enough of the new aircraft became available. Some of Jever's F6 pilots crossed over to II Squadron, bringing with them their expertise on the Hunter, to embark on a new profession in FR. No. II Squadron then comprised Squadron Leader 'Mac' MacDonald (CO), Flight Lieutenants Benji Hives and Eric Sharp (flight commanders), Frank Sumner, Bunny St Aubyn, Bob Barcilon, 'Ben' Gunn, Phil Crawshaw, Danny Brooks, Pete Adair, Flying Officers Jock Carnegie, Dennis Fahey, Phil Holden-Rushworth and John Walker. A warrant officer, nineteen SNCOs, twenty nine junior NCOs and sixty three airmen faced the problem of harmonising the periodic servicing of the remaining Swifts and the progressive servicing introduced with the Hunters.

Nos II and IV Squadron (IV Squadron also re-equipping with the FR10), RAF Germany's (RAFG's) tac recce contribution to 2ATAF, would eventually make their home together at Gutersloh

Having watched the Swift lumber into the air and listened to the bar talk as he converted earlier from the Hunter to the Swift, John Walker admits to having been rather cynical about the departing aircraft, with its innovative reheat (afterburner) and brake boost system necessary to hold the aircraft stationary when it was engaged. He recalls a now legendary story of Swifts and Hunters launching *en masse* for a flypast, a tale which may have improved with time and might not be wholly relevant to this work but it is worth telling, if only to suggest that life at Jever would be a little less dramatic when the transition to FR10s was complete.

With II Squadron (the senior squadron) leading the fighter squadrons, thirty aircraft ran up at the end of Runway 27. The Swifts, adhering to Standard Operational Procedures (SOPs), strained in reheat with their brake boosts 'on' 'their exhausts scorching the beautiful hides of the Hunters and choking their pilots'. When all seemed well, the senior person up front nodded his head for the roll and his Nos 2 and 3 selected brake boost 'off' to rush off either side of their still stationary leader – he having failed to remember the all-important brake boost. Realising that they might be accused of desertion, the two wingman promptly cancelled reheat (assuming that after a start like that the whole show would be reassembled). Not so, the Battle of Britain spirit was alive and well in the lead Swift, as the incumbent found the brake boost switch and hurtled off between his two slothful minions – 'as only a Swift can do with its backside on fire'. The wingmen, now realising that they had misread the warrior spirit of their leader, attempted to follow him by re-selecting the sometimes temperamental reheat in the hope of a quick relight. There it was – a false start with aircraft now scattered well down the runway, leaving those in the rear confused and racked with indecision among swirling exhaust fumes as the Swift and Hunter pilots alternated between going and stopping. Above it all came a strained cry from the cockpit of one of the lead Swifts: "Barrier Barrier!" In the control tower, Air Traffic Control (ATC), all but struck dumb watching what seemed set to be the biggest single accident in the world, answered in awe that the barrier was already up. The voice came back, no longer calm or collected but that of a pilot seeing his life passing before his eyes crying, "I know it's up, get the bloody thing DOWN!" In the event 'the great fat beastie' was seen to lift off at the very end of the runway and bank at an unusually high angle of attack past the side of the barrier into the clear air – just! The rest of the story, including the formal debriefing, is best left untold.

Throughout February, FR10 availability increased markedly and by the end of the month all pilots on the squadron had completed their conversion to the new aircraft, which now carried the squadron markings. The hard work started in March with a 'fly-off' to select pilots for NATO Air Forces Central Europe's (AFCENT's) recce competition Royal Flush (Chapter Seven). Eric Sharp, Phil Crawshaw and Phil Holden-Rushworth were the pilots chosen to go on to the next round to compete against the three pilots chosen from IV Squadron (which was now also fully equipped with the FR10 at Gutersloh). In addition, the squadron had to prepare for a visit by the Instrument Rating Examiners (IREs), these various commitments accounting for thirty five hours of flying on the T7 and 154 hours on the single-seat Hunters.

All the stops were pulled out in April to meet the demands of Royal Flush training: Exercises Amled and Gentleman's Relish, the latter taking six aircraft and eight pilots to RAF Geilenkirchen for tasking by NATO's No. 1 Tactical Operations Centre (TOC). Despite this busy programme, during which the FR10s were rotating through a Maintenance Unit (MU) at RAF Laarbruch for essential modifications, all available pilots succeeded in impressing the IREs. The two remaining Swifts then departed, with Pete Adair flying the last to RAF Manston and well prepared to put on a final air display to impress his audience on this sad occasion. His efforts were to no avail, his welcome confined to a single rather miserable customs officer who charged him for his cigarettes whilst his mount (by order fully serviced and modified up to the hilt) was

Out With The Old – in With the New. Hunter FR10s replaced the Swift FR5s in 1961. *II Sqn*

'Second to None' – Men and Machines. No. II (AC) Squadron making themselves known. *Pete Rayner & II Sqn*

dragged off to an ignoble end on the fire training site. The writer of the squadron's Operations Record Book (ORB) admitted that the FR5 pilots would 'miss this much maligned aircraft with a certain amount of affection and nostalgia' and adapting a eulogy from David's lament over Saul and Jonathan thus: 'Tell it not in Goch nor in the streets of Moenchen Gladbach (local towns) lest the daughters of the uncircumcised rejoice'.

Royal Flush was held in May at the Belgian base of Beauvechain, Phil Holden-Rushworth representing the squadron in this first competition with the FR10. The short range, day team was narrowly defeated but helped 2ATAF win the Gruenther Trophy from 4ATAF in the overall results. With 174 flying hours achieved in May, the RAF and 2ATAF hierarchy announced themselves well pleased with II Squadron's achievements at this early stage of its reincarnation, 2 MFPU getting particular mention. Squadron and MFPU now began practising for the national recce competition, Sassoon (Chapter Seven), but John Walker and Bob Barcilon also found time to accept an invitation to the French Base at Mont de Marsan, only to find when they arrived overhead at the limit of the FR10's range that the only suitable runway was in use as a formal parade ground. Some very rapid calculations and best use of range options allowed them to scrape into Istres – but it was a close run thing.

In June, 'weapons tight' procedures for safe departures and recoveries at Jever were evaluated in fifteen missions controlled by the Sector Operations Centre (SOC) at Brockzetel, during Exercise Backlash. This was followed by thirty nine maximum range sorties to develop in-flight reporting in Exercise Quo Vadis. A total of 249 hours were flown in June, the highest monthly total for either FR10 squadron to date, an achievement which did much to enhance morale among the air and groundcrew. Procedures for operating the Hunters were developing apace.

Despite all its efforts, the squadron came a disappointing fourth of six competitors in July's exercise Sassoon, the photographs being particularly poor, but in the more realistic, operational and all-embracing Tactical Evaluation (Taceval) which followed all went very well. There was now concern over aspects of the FR10s ancillary equipment. The essential pressurisation and air conditioning system was failing to prevent misting and tending to give pilots periodic shower baths, while the lack of selective refuelling of external tanks was inconvenient. Also, the outboard tanks were giving rise to position errors in excess of 400 ft on the Mk19B Altimeter. Remedial action was put in hand.

In August 1961 the squadron visited Sylt for a final air-to-air Armament Practice Camp (APC).

In untypically bad weather each pilot averaged a mere eleven effective shoots for an average of 19.2 per cent which, in the circumstances, was not considered bad. Sylt will live long in the memories of all who enjoyed the many attractions there; nostalgia already setting in as the ORB scribe plagiarised Rupert Brook with 'There is some corner of a foreign field that is forever England....' The bad weather allowed plenty of time for writing the operation orders which would get the squadron back to Jever and then on to its new home at Gutersloh, offices ringing to the familiar chant, 'it's all been changed!'

The move to Gutersloh in August/September went remarkably smoothly. Once there, the squadron ran its first air-to-ground gunnery programme with the FR10, refining procedures and proving the gun harmonisation, with some 'aces' soon scoring 80-90 per cent; John Walker achieved 100 per cent on two occasions and the outcome was a very satisfactory squadron average of 35 per cent. This was followed by Exercise Treble Chance, Exercise Checkmate and routine Form Delta tasking by the TOC, all of which underlined the well-known problems in communications and tasking. The latter improved markedly when John Walker and Jock Carnegie were sent to the Forward Air Support Operations Centre (FASOC) with soldiers in the field to assist in the direct tasking of FR10s for October's exercise Spearpoint.

After many extraneous interruptions, and despite a dip in overall aircraft serviceability (one aircraft declared a 'rogue' with persistent undercarriage problems), the squadron was now able to settle down to a concentrated period of truly operational training, including very demanding performance evaluations in domestic Full House exercises. When he handed over as scribe of the ORB to Frank Sumner, Phil Crawshaw observed that this recent activity had produced a significant improvement in visual reconnaissance, but that the quality of the photographs was still giving cause for concern; it was a prophetic warning in a role so dedicated now to academic competition.

The pilot strength of ten, the lowest since the end of WW2, rose to eleven with the arrival in November of Flight Lieutenant Stan Barnes. However, bad weather led to his orientation and other flying being disrupted and resulted in the squadron's lowest monthly flying hours total for eight years. All in all, however, II Squadron's first year with the FR10 had been a success.

1962: 'Shiny Two' is Fifty

The beginning of 1962 was marred by the tragic loss of Stan Barnes when his FR10 crashed at Papenburg (near Emden) on 29 January, starting a period of turbulence amongst the pilots. Phil Holden-Rushworth departed as Flight Lieutenants Chuck Coulcher and Arthur Reed arrived, to be followed by the very experienced Flight Lieutenant Bruce McDonald. In February, Mac MacDonald handed over the squadron to Squadron Leader David Thornton. Another pilot was detached to RAF Leconfield when John Walker was chosen to join the team selected to represent the RAF in the NATO Air-to-Air Gunnery Competition, this being seen to negate the need for him to attend the Pilot Attack Instructor (PAI) course for which he had been earmarked.

The squadron was also undergoing a manpower changeover which involved some 50

Hot Shot. In 1961 Flight Lieutenant John Walker, II Squadron, was selected for the RAF team to take part in the NATO air-to-air gunnery competition, using 92 Squadron's Hunters at RAF Leconfield. *John Walker*

per cent of its groundcrew and would last for the next three months. While two replacement aircraft were awaited, those in situ continued to rotate through the modification programme, exacerbating the problem of aircraft availability. Given also a spell of poor weather, which allowed flying on only thirteen days in March, the near achievement of the flying task was most creditable. This flying was devoted largely to in-house fuel consumption and range trials in preparation for the world-wide Tactical Air Reserve (TAR) commitment, operational training and qualification of all pilots in night flying. An intensive programme of air-to-ground gunnery resulted in an average score of 37 per cent but the number of aircraft available remained at five throughout April and into May, making it very difficult to satisfy every commitment (Taceval, Exercises Backlash, Quicktrain and Playboy *et al*). Indeed, with three FR10s now suffering from 'Cat 3' damage or declared AOG (Aircraft On Ground awaiting spares), the required aircraft availability of 70 per cent in three hours could not be achieved. Flying Officer Keith Gordon arrived to face this unhappy state of affairs and take over from Flight Lieutenant Tony Strachen as the squadron engineering officer, while Flight Lieutenant Ken Tatem replaced Frank Sumner.

The squadron's fifty years of uninterrupted active service was celebrated in style over the weekend of 25-26 May with an all-ranks dance, a formal dinner night and a champagne party in

Happy Birthday. Squadron Leader David Thornton heads the celebration of II (AC) Squadron's fifty years of continuous service. *II Sqn*

the Officers Mess. At a formal lunch in his honour Lord Hives, Chairman of Rolls Royce and father of Benji, presented a magnificent silver cigar-box to commemorate the event and the squadron's long association with his company. A Review by HRH Princess Alexandra of Kent had to be cancelled because the Princess was unwell, as was a visit by squadron veterans when their airlift was cancelled, but a formal parade reviewed by the Parliamentary Under Secretary of State, W. J. Taylor Esq, a flypast and guest night went ahead to celebrate the Queen's official birthday. Mr Taylor was said to have been much impressed by the brand new, pink, frilly 'retiring room', which he thought was prepared for him but had been meant for the Princess. No. II Squadron and RAF Gutersloh (with Group Captain Colin Coulthard as station commander and Wing Commander Gordon Conway as OC Flying Wing), were good at these all important VIP events, but they would have impacted on the work-up for Sassoon had the competition not been postponed until October because of bad weather.

In August 1962 serviceability began to improve and was reflected in the number of hours flown during detachments to RAF Bruggen and RAF Chivenor while the runway at Gutersloh was being refurbished. Serviceability was particularly good during the air-to-air APC at Chivenor, with five or six aircraft on the line every day out of the seven available. These detachments seemed to have several beneficial effects at work and play, visible in the morale of the squadron. Under the able tutelage of Chivenor's PAIs and John Walker (who finished with an average of 62 per cent), the APC was completed in nine flying days, with 6,780 rounds fired on 113 sorties for the excellent average of 29.14 per cent. Mounted from the squadron's temporary home at Bruggen, the FR10s then derived great value from Exercises Night Jar and Deep South. However in another salutary indictment of the system, their success was attributed largely to the direct tasking exercised by a Brigade Air Support Operations Centre (BASOC), with squadron pilots again attached as advisers, the TOC being out of the tasking loop during Exercise Fallex.

Things continued to improve in October, with 200 hours Hunter flying, night and day, being achieved in sixteen working days. Despite Sassoon, the results of which are not known to

VIP Visit. Defence Minister Peter Thorneycroft comes to see for himself, Flight Lieutenants Bruce McDonald, John Coleman and 'Buster' Webb ready for inspection.

VIP Welcome. II Squadron flight commander holds VIP spellbound with tales of derring do. *Sam Toyne*

the author, there was also plenty of time for overdue ground training, sport and social intercourse. The squadron team was beaten at squash by IV Squadron but had success against ATC in a variety of less formal games, if at the cost of one torn muscle and two slipped discs! Flight Lieutenant Sam Jeffreys arrived and John Walker, who had made a significant contribution to the squadron, left to take up an appointment as flight commander on 229 OCU. Benji Hives followed in November, the ORB recording, 'It was very sad to see Benji go; his combination of ferocious drive and invincible good humour a rare one indeed and his absence will be keenly felt'. His replacement as flight commander was Flight Lieutenant Bob Hillman, who clearly had much to live up to.

With just eleven days flying available in November the squadron managed only 130 hours, but achieved an air-to-ground average of 36.1 per cent. The effect of four Aden cannons each firing 1,200 rounds/minute of 30-mm high explosive (HE) shells, each one equivalent to an infantryman's hand grenade, had to be seen to be believed. Ground defence training accounted for two days but it was agreed that the high standard of instruction made the course worthwhile. There was more fun but rather less intrinsic value in the driving instruction given by the Royal Dragoon Guards in their Centurion

tanks at Munster. After an excellent lunch the pilots showed more aggression than skill and the driving instructors could barely hide their feelings.

Given the generally bad serviceability at the time, the generation of four FR10s in 1 hour 30 minutes for the Exercise Quicktrain, which started at 0100 hours on 13 December, was a splendid achievement, but bad weather again limited the number of flying days that month. The time thus available to the pilots was put to good use in discussing a new War Plan and preparing the requisite target maps on up-dated low flying charts. A day's dinghy drill came as a welcome relief from frequent spells of driving Magirus snow ploughs in vain attempts to keep the airfield open. Sometimes this snow-clearing did more harm than good, and such was the case when the lead driver of three ploughs fell asleep at the wheel and drifted off the runway, taking his two 'wingmen' with him in echelon as he curved across the airfield dismantling runway lights as they went.

The ORB noted that for the Christmas festivities the Chief Matron of the British Military Hospital, Munster, very kindly (but rather unwisely) allowed six of her nurses to attend the Christmas Draw and Dance held in the newly opened Malcolm Club. No more is recorded of this event. The squadron groundcrew were entertained by the officers in the coffee bar, when Ken Tatem was presented with a highly polished, suitably inscribed but slightly worn Hunter tail skid. The story behind this somewhat unkind gesture remains unrecorded. The airmen reciprocated by inviting selected officers to their barrack block bars about which, again, no more should be said.

1963 – A Year of Fluctuating Fortunes.

January 1963 started slowly with bad weather limiting flying to seven days. Owing to the paucity of flying, with some ten hours/pilot/ month and a prolonged delay in training five non-operational pilots, the squadron commander suggested that leave might have to be curtailed when things improved. Fortuitously, the arrival of additional pilots was also delayed by the same adverse conditions affecting completion of their training at Chivenor.

Some relief came in February, with the thirteen flying days available devoted primarily to essential currency checks, an intensive work-up schedule for the newcomers and night flying, with defensive combat programmed when low flying was not possible. The squadron acquitted itself well during a Station Commander's Alert, which included operational turn-rounds and an evaluation of in-flight reporting with German units in the field.

The time had now come for Bob Hillman, Pete Rayner and Sam Toyne to go through the traditional initiation to the squadron in the Mess cellar bar. This entailed drinking a large quantity of a ritual liquid from the Squadron 'Op Pot', a highly valued two-handled pewter mug presented by the Chinese during a detachment by the squadron to Shanghai in 1927. When he recovered, Bob and engineer Keith Gordon flew to Laon AB, France, for initial discussions with a USAF Voodoo squadron on a forthcoming detachment there. Bob was also among those who took advantage of exhilarating flying over the Baltic and into the mountains of Norway, not to mention the delights of certain Danish and Norwegian towns, on the weekend forays of exercise Northern Lights. Meanwhile, the squadron was producing willing stars for a TV documentary on life at work and play at Gutersloh.

Flying increased again in March, with a total of 198 hours devoted mainly to working up the new pilots and the planned exchange with the 18th Tac Recon Squadron (TRS) at Laon, which extended 'overwhelming hospitality'. Pete Rayner remembers this only too well as a result of losing one tooth and putting another through his lip when he walked into a lamp post while he and others were escaping with what they had left

Special Relations. David Thornton and his II Squadron detachment are welcomed by Doug Brittian at Laon AB, in the exchange programme. *II Sqn*

Dusk Recce. Bob Hilman over the Baltic. *Bob Hillman*

in their wallets after a visit to the 'Crazy Horse' in Paris. The following night, as the brave walked on bottles across the slippery floor of the Officers Club, Pete did it again, with the same tooth through the same lip. Next morning they flew back to Gutersloh much the worse for wear, as Gordon Conway felt obliged to observe, but they had upheld the finest traditions of the RAF in the air and on the ground.

Having been specially selected, Bruce McDonald now began to work up an aerobatic sequence for the year's air displays. Other officers were on the move, Phil Crawshaw, Danny Brooks and Ben Gunn departing as Flight Lieutenants 'Buster' Webb and John Coleman joined the squadron.

The priority now was to prepare for the forthcoming TAR commitment and to this end the squadron deployed to an unprepared site, albeit on base, where they operated successfully in tents for several days. Shortly thereafter, Flight Lieutenant Eric Lockwood became the very welcome first incumbent of the newly established post of resident squadron PI.

With the squadron determined to outdo the American hospitality it had received at Laon, the return match at Gutersloh was equally memorable. To get the visit underway, Ken Tatem invited hosts and guests to his house to partake of a five-gall crock filled with well-stewed strawberries in brandy and topped up with champagne (one of his children causing some concern after sampling the strawberries). This was followed by what hardly passed for a golf match on the airfield's six-hole course; the crock went too, strapped to a golf trolley, and anyone playing a bad shot had to down a paper cup of the now fast fermenting brew. There were plenty of takers and few of the guests were still around that evening – but honours were even.

Close to the main gate at Gutersloh was the 'Fluggie', a German Raststatte and a home-from-home for many of the airmen from the base; it was (somewhat unrealistically) out of bounds to the officers. The inn's garden backed on to Pete Rayner's married quarter, from which he could watch a pair of huge cock pheasants and their harems strut their stuff. Having failed to tempt the birds with raisins in whisky he shot one with his 12-bore but lost the race for the stricken bird to a gentleman from the pub. Pete's wife was said to be 'livid' (whether this was for shooting the bird or failing to win the race is not known).

Voodoo Welcome. Lieutenant Colonel Doug Brittian and the Voodoo men of the 18th TRS welcomed at Gutersloh on an exchange visit in 1963. *II Sqn*

The squadron was still struggling to generate five 'combat ready' pilots, the lack of which precluded its participation in 1963's Royal Flush, but there was time to host a detachment of F-86Ds from the Royal Norwegian Air Force (RNoAF) in April 1963 and for a successful joint effort in the recce Exercise Step Out. May was another busy month. Pete Rayner introduced the squadron to 'foul line' air-to-ground gunnery very successfully; he personally adjusted the voltages of many of the gunsights and the

Norwegian Visitors. F-86K of the Norwegian Air Force. *II Sqn*

upshot was an unprecedented squadron average on the FR10 of 48.9 per cent. May's Taceval started well, with 70 per cent of the squadron's aircraft generated in one hour, but ended with relatively poor scores in one-pass shoots at Nordhorn Range in very poor visibility. Looking ahead, a number of pilots were also re-qualified and given instrument ratings on the Meteor to supplement the target towing force for the forthcoming air-to-air APC.

It was now time to celebrate the squadron's birthday again with an all-ranks party at a local hostelry and a special event 'piped in' by Sergeant Henry and piped out by Biddy Thornton, the CO's wife. In another morale raising initiative, this time in praise of husband David's laudable efforts as a tomato grower, Biddy removed the tiny fruit from his plants while he was away for a few days and tied on the best replacements money could buy – to the great (if temporary) joy of the 'boss' when he returned.

Serviceability in June 1963 was generally very good but the ORB carried a confusing story about 'an unfortunate incident' which resulted in substantial damage to four engines in the squadron hangar requiring their replacement.

The groundcrew responded magnificently, completing this task within 24 hours, only to be faced with a bird strike which caused 'Cat 3' damage to one of the aircraft. In an Exercise Northern Lights, Ken Tatem and Buster Webb attempted to reach Gardermoen, Norway, but failed to do so in bad weather and diverted without complaint to a favourite watering hole for weekenders, Aalborg in Denmark.

The squadron worked hard for Exercise Sassoon in July, but with its low experience level failed to perform well overall. However, Sam Toyne, Sam Jeffreys and Eric Lockwood did come in for special praise from the CO, who also commented formally on the excellent contribution made by 2 MFPU and thanked 468 GLS for all its efforts. For the last two years the squadron's GLS had been run effectively by the senior GLO, Major Dennis Campbell and his second in command Captain Mike Coughlin; they were replaced by Major Brian Chapman and Captain John Clark.

Most of August was spent at the Royal Netherlands Air Force (RNLAF) base, Leeuwarden, where Pete Rayner guided the squadron through a very successful air-to-air APC; his leadership, personal average score of 50 per cent and explicit debriefings being exemplary.

Perfection. On and off parade, 468 GLS Section provided II Squadron with invaluable support, Major Peter Heath and Captain John Clark (centre) in command here. *John Clar*

Professional Witness. A II Squadron pilot photographed this I Squadron pilot land 'wheels up' at RAF El Adem in 1964. *II Sqn*

In September, Exercise Lion Vert was mounted from Gutersloh with on-base dispersal to cover the full war scenario, while Triplex West took four FR10s to RAF El Adem in Libya. For this the aircraft were flown first to RAF Luqa in Malta, a non-stop flight of 2 hours 35 minutes, and then on to El Adem in a further 1 hour 50 minutes. This was reported in the ORB to be the first time the squadron had exercised outside Europe since the detachment to Shangai in 1927 – and it proved a very worthwhile detachment.

An anti-climax after such stimulating operational training, but underlining the importance now placed on the recce competitions (or rather their results) the squadron began preparing for 1964's Royal Flush in November 1963, six months ahead of the competition. With every sortie chased, eliminating rounds were flown to choose the four candidates from which a final selection would be made for the short-range team. However, some realism returned to the training programme that month with Exercise Widder, in which the FR10 pilots were tasked to find and photograph German army units in the field and on doing so to carry out strafing runs under the

enthusiastic control of German FACs. John Coleman completed his operational training, with the result that the squadron now had all its pilots combat ready for the first time in two years. December followed the usual pattern with very little flying because of the weather and much time given to ground school and extraneous activities such as a visit to the Dutch Nike Missile base at Handorf. The year culminated with a proliferation of parties to celebrate a better year for the squadron.

1964: From Strength to Strength

When weather allowed in the new year (and despite the competition rules having yet to be published) simulated Royal Flush sorties were flown into pockets of clear air where targets could be expected on the day, including forays into an extended Low Flying Area 6 (LFA 6), in North Germany. Intensive flying periods were sustained by excellent serviceability, and when a Taceval was called late in February aircraft availability hovered around 100 per cent, heaping credit on Keith Gordon, Flight Sergeant Wooley and the groundcrew. This good serviceability was maintained as improving weather encouraged training in the Ardennes, where map reading and target acquisition were notoriously difficult. The Berlin Corridor contingency plan was also exercised at Gutersloh in Exercise Quicksand IV, the FR10s supporting an offensive force of F-100s from USAF Europe (USAFE), the French Air Force (FAF) and Hunter FGA9s of No. 54 Squadron RAF. Buster Webb was sent into the field as part of the Air Contact Team and reportedly, 'returned looking like a character from a Jack London book, wearing a US-style Yukon hat'. John Coleman also 'went native' as a liaison officer for the exercise (drawing on his experience with the USAF in Korea) and was rewarded with a back-seat ride in an F-100. Bob Hillman now took temporary command of the squadron while David Thornton was in Wegberg Hospital with a problem that would keep him out of action for the next month.

Although still without the latest rules for the 'new style' Royal Flush (Chapter Seven), HQ RAF Germany sponsored intensive preview training for the exercise in March, with an Air Support Signals Unit team positioned in the field to take in-flight reports. Two high pressure rehearsals for Royal Flush followed, run by

2ATAF and said to have 'stretched everyone to the hilt', this very full programme resulted in the monthly target being exceeded by 40 hours. It was to this hive of activity that David Thornton returned to resume command, thereby releasing Bob Hillman to join Chuck Coulcher and John Clark on the RAFG rugby team (Chuck as captain).

Believing itself well prepared, II Squadron went into Royal Flush in May with great expectations, the CO recording on its completion that, 'the squadron and MFPU had put up a first class show, and that it was heartening to see everyone giving everything they had'. Things had indeed gone well; after the lay-off in 1963 to rebuild itself, Shiny Two was content with third place only 1.8 per cent behind the leaders, and it had redeemed itself after a poor performance in the previous Sassoon competition. Attention now turned again to air-to-air gunnery in preparation for another APC at Leeuwarden. The detachment itself in June did not go as well as had been hoped, with poor weather and range closures limiting the number of effective shoots and resulting in an average of 22.5 per cent (against 22.9 per cent in the previous year).

VIP Welcome, 11 Aug 64. No. II Squadron flight commander Bob Hillman presented this F95 photograph of Soviet General I P Zhuralev 20 minutes after it as taken. *II Sqn*

Had he been in the Soviet Air Force, Bob Hillman might have come in for an immediate promotion on 11 August when he presented a visiting Russian general with an excellent 9 x 9-inch air-to-ground photograph, mounted and framed, of the VIP's arrival at Gutersloh taken from a II Squadron FR10 only 20 minutes before, but this was becoming 'bread-and-butter' work for the FR squadrons. VIPs would often be treated to demonstrations such as this of the squadron's capability, but things did not always go as well as they did for Bob on that day. Normally two FR10s would be called in from a nearby orbit as the subject was expected to alight from his aircraft, hopefully to catch the guest at the door of his aircraft. On one of these occasions a tall, elegant and very senior German general decided to turn round in the confined doorway of an RAF Pembroke and bend down to thank the steward who had looked after him while airborne. It was at this *moment critique* that the Hunter pilot took the picture, flying so low that the wake from his aircraft removed the hats of the reception committee as it climbed over the hangar ahead. As if this was not bad enough for the squadron commander, he was then faced with the decision on whether to show this VVIP the photograph: nothing but his black cape filling the doorway, or to cut this piece of showmanship from the programme. He chose to show the photograph and was much relieved when the German officer saw the funny side and said he would cherish its uniqueness. In another such mishap, a VIP left a larger aircraft by a door opposite to that expected, whereupon he was asked to re-enter and leave by the other. This he did, by which time the Hunter pilots had set themselves up for a repeat run on the door he had used the first time – and of course they missed again. At this point the exercise was abandoned.

A Russian sense of humour surfaced when General Zhuravlev, clearly much impressed by the standard of the Airmens' Mess at Gutersloh, and the meal being served when he visited, asked whether he would see the same if he returned unexpectedly the following week. Group Captain David Evans, the station commander, rose to the occasion immediately by promising the general that if he did so he would be pleased to dispatch him forthwith to the Guardroom!

There was more movement among the officers of II Squadron from August to November, with the arrival of Flight Lieutenants Hugh Cracroft and Peter Riley, both old Hunter hands but Hugh fresh from an exciting exchange tour at sea with the carrier-borne Buccaneer force. Keith Gordon, the engineer who had been responsible for the marked improvement in aircraft serviceability in the previous months, also left, to be replaced by Flight Lieutenant John McGarvey.

The squadron made a welcome return to operational training in September when Sassoon was postponed until November because of non-competition weather. The weather also interfered with flying during exchange visits between the squadron and 523 Squadron, German Air Force (GAF), both for the Hunters at GAF Eggebek and the RF-84Fs at Gutersloh, where operations were also curtailed by the relatively short runway. This left plenty of time for a punishing social programme. The weather might also have taken a hand in the impending change of command when the author, then commander of 234 (R) Squadron and II Squadron heir apparent, paid an initial visit to Gutersloh in preparation for the handover in December. He now takes up the story himself:

'I decided to combine this visit with an instrument training sortie for another squadron officer in a Hunter T7, but the tailwind from Chivenor proved to be less than forecast and we were at minimum fuel for a diversion to Hopsten when we arrived overhead Gutersloh. At that point the weather was just above limits and I had no qualms about descending, but as we did so the cloud base fell to 200 ft in marginal visibility and, after the first GCA failed with nowhere else to go, I announced that we would 'ride the next one down' This message seemed to get round the station like wildfire, a great audience assembling in the gloom to witness the outcome. Fortunately all went well. Two weeks later I took over the squadron.'

Priority was again given to the training of new pilots and acquainting everyone with revised war requirements. An air-to-ground gunnery phase was completed despite appalling (but not unrealistic) shooting conditions, resulting in a reduced average for academic passes of 22.4 per cent. All this led to a total of 167 hours, which was a relatively high total for December, and the achievement of the annual task.

1965: Royal Visit and a Wedding
The December priorities continued into January 1965 with more defensive air combat training in

the upper airspace helping the squadron to get within 30 hours of the monthly target, again very acceptable for a January. It was at high level that Peter Riley experienced severe engine vibration which forced him to jettison his external tanks (fortunately harmlessly) and carry out a commendably rapid recovery to Gutersloh despite a very low cloud base.

At the end of the month the author was put to the test on the War Plan and management of squadron operations by Flight Commander Operations (Flt Cdr Ops), Bob Hillman, who had laid on a surprise squadron alert; this started badly when the hooter called the squadron to arms with a sad 'whimper' rather than the usual lusty bellow. Fortunately, the rest went to Bob's satisfaction and after an intensive flying programme under the excellent tutelage of Flight Commander Training (Flt Cdr Trg), Sam Toyne, the new CO was declared combat ready. The month ended with all available aircraft serviceable, which augured well for the new engineer McGarvey.

Grass root calls for a new coffee bar and refurbished crewroom led to an ambitious project organised by the chief protagonist Bill Armstrong (and who would argue with him?), construction beginning at once. In the air, weapons results improved markedly in February with forty-seven effective shoots raising the operational average to 28.6 per cent with a very good stoppage rate of 1:3488. A Taceval called at the end of the month followed on the heels of a Station Alert the previous day, so the squadron was well-prepared and everything ran smoothly. In a busy and sometimes difficult month the thirteen officers, thirteen SNCOs and forty airmen on the squadron strength had to work hard to achieve a monthly total of 211 flying hours.

The flying task was exceeded again in March, with high-low-high profiles and refuelling stops gaining access to the less familiar LFAs when the weather around Gutersloh was poor. All the squadron's FR training now included in-flight reporting and operational passes were standard on air-to-ground sorties while 2 MFPU was producing better quality prints within 15 minutes of camera magazine off-loading. To celebrate completion of work on the crewroom (a well-stocked aquarium now in place to steady nerves), a party was held for all the station's officers.

Inquisition. The CO faces an inquisition during the AOC's Inspection 1966 – Bob Hillman next to come under scrutiny. *Sir David Evans*

Somewhat reluctantly, the squadron returned in April to whatever non-operational Royal Flush training was possible consistent with preparations for the impending Air Officer Commanding's (AOC's) inspection and many practices for a forthcoming Royal Flypast for Her Majesty Queen Elizabeth II which, as the commander of the senior squadron in Germany, the author would lead. To this end, seven of the eight aircraft on our strength had to remain available for the final rehearsals and the flypast itself. In an additional diversion, FR10 pilots were now flying aboard RAF Argosy aircraft tasked with keeping the corridor to and from Berlin open as tensions with the Warsaw Pact increased. They benefited from close observation of MiG-19 and MiG-21 fighters harassing the RAF transports, together with sight of radar, SAM and AAA defences manned along the route. Des Watkins, who had done much to improve the performance on 2 MFPU, handed over his command to Flight Lieutenant 'Butch' Butcher.

All seemed set fair for the many commitments in May. The AOC's Inspection went well, although the photographs suggest that the squadron came under critical scrutiny. The squadron was also happy with its performance in Royal Flush, with all the required sorties flown, the targets covered well and visual findings passed successfully in-flight; it was then a matter of waiting for the results. In the final rehearsal for the Royal Flypast II Squadron led a formation of sixty six aircraft overhead Gutersloh on the right heading to an accuracy of one second but the optimism which resulted was premature. The author now takes up the story again: 'With the possibility that the Queen might be late, I had suggested that Her Majesty should be invited to review the guard of honour and static display first on her arrival at the station, to ensure that she could be escorted the short distance to the dais to match the precise timing of the flypast, but this fell on deaf ears; the Queen would travel direct from Gutersloh town to the dais, her precise arrival time being 'guaranteed'. Things did not bode well from the start, when I was asked to get our Hunters airborne in low cloud and rain (instead of the minimums of 1,500 ft and 3 nm promised), to 'see what it was like' and in the hope that conditions might improve to the prescribed minima in flight. This proved to be a forlorn hope but the seven sections of Canberras and Javelins did join up successfully during our tour of the Ruhr, and all looked well until overhead Graven, some 6 minutes out, when I was told 'the Queen was late' (Her Majesty had been mobbed by the good people of Gutersloh *en route*). Crucially, no one knew how late the Queen would be, given that

For Queen and Country. Six FR10s of II Squadron led 64 RAF Germany aircraft in a flypast for HM The Queen at RAF Gutersloh on 26 May 1965. The players: (L to R: John McGarvey, John Coleman, 'Buster' Webb, Hugh Cracroft, Bill Armstrong, Author, Sam Toyne, Pete Rayner. *II Sqn*

her convoy would now try to make up time, and with 12 nm of formation behind me in less than ideal weather, I had no sensible alternative but to continue at the slowest acceptable speed (280 kts for the Javelins). In fact, peering over the side of my cockpit without banking, I spotted the Queen's car as it careered on to the parade square as my leading section passed overhead.

So much for staff planning. The Gutersloh contingent of 12 FR10s was allowed to land 'quietly' and 'disappear' to the other side of the airfield for the rest of the day, but I did get unexpectedly close to the Queen when I met and saluted Her Majesty's car while rounding a corner (quietly) on my bicycle bound for my bachelor quarters on an unguarded road, and was rewarded with a regal wave. While the Queen enjoyed a well-rehearsed lunch with the great and the good, I and the other officers of II Squadron disappeared to the local hostelry to play bowls and drink large quantities of ale. Security remained high at Gutersloh that night, the Queen sleeping in a special Bundesbahn train in a siding normally occupied by fuel tankers behind the Officers Mess'.

In June 1965, it was off to Leeuwarden again for the annual Ω and the beginning of a long detachment from Gutersloh while the runway was refurbished once more. As usual the arrangements were excellent, starting with a welcoming party in the Dutch Officers Mess, at which three (unnamed) squadron officers consumed the beer in their host's glass boot in an average of 35 seconds – the fastest Dutch officer only managing 55 seconds. Thereafter, most officers spent agreeable evenings in the Amicitia Hotel (where they were staying), enjoying a standard fare of steak, strawberries and cream, washed down with Heineken beer.

The air-to-air firing went less well. The programme was constantly interrupted by Dutch holidays, mist, low cloud and range closures, resulting in an average of six live shoots only per pilot and a disappointing average of 22.4 per cent. The aircraft survived well, other than the author's personal mount, 'Sierra', the nosewheel of which remained firmly 'up' on one landing (Chapter Six). On 9 July, No. II Squadron

Command and Control. Flight commander Bob Hillman 'running the desk' at Leeuwarden in 1965. *II Sqn*

Royal Wave. HM The Queen bids farewell to RAF Gutersloh, having spent the night in this Bundesbahn train in a siding by the Officers Mess. *Sir David Evans*

changed places with IV Squadron from their detachment at RAF Laarbruch, the two eight-ship formations (perhaps fortunately) failing to cross paths in LFA 1 as planned, on the way to Laarbruch and Leeuwarden respectively.

The stay at Laarbruch was not a great success. There were no real problems in operating from tents in a muddy, disused dispersal, with most

host units providing the necessary basic support, but there were evident differences between the operating ethos of this tactical bomber environment and that of their guests' fighter fraternity, sometimes making relationships difficult. The author once more: 'So it was that the detachment came to a humiliating end when I, having launched into a clear blue sky at dusk, overflew the squadron dispersal at speed and executed a simple roll while climbing away to check the progress of an approaching weather front before night flying. Apparently, this was reported immediately to the station commander as 'aerobatics over the married quarters' and I

Good Living. Life was good for the II Squadron officers in Hotel Amicitia after a hard day's gunnery, here John McGarvie entertains mine host's daughter. *II Sqn*

Good Trip? Major Temple welcomes Bob Hillman and II Squadron at Laon AB for an exchange visit. *Bob Hillman*

Take Care. Major Wendle Lawrence, 32nd Tac Recon Sqn, checks Bob Hillman's flight plan. *Bob Hillman*

Where's II Squadron? 'Slash' Slaney, who arrived on II Squadron during its nomadic summer of 1965, asks the way to the squadron hangar at Gutersloh. *II Sqn*

was front and centre on landing for him to recite command regulations on aerobatics before grounding me and confining me to camp pending an inquiry. This inquisition continued throughout the following days while the rest of the squadron, led ably by Bob Hillman, departed for their next port of call, a one-way exchange with the USAFE's 32nd TRS at Laon. I was eventually released to join them, no further action being taken over this heinous misdemeanour.'

The Americans at Laon were more hospitable, even allowing 'the Brits' to take off under the inexplicable concession of 'special VFR' while all their Voodoos remained grounded by weather. Despite the constraints of flying in French airspace, useful training came from navigating with different maps over the unfamiliar 'moon country' of Northern France.

At the end of July and a wholly agreeable stay at Laon, the T7 carrying Bob Hillman and John McGarvey (whose duty it would be to change the starter cartridges and service the aircraft) led the CO to Malta, via Istres, on Exercise Southern Ranger. Never missing a chance to test his master, Bob obtained air traffic clearance to fly much of the way within a very thin but dense layer of cloud, despite clear air being within feet immediately above and below. McGarvey proved his worth when one aircraft went unserviceable at RAF Luqa and the trio arrived back at Laarbruch five days later.

On their best behaviour when they returned to Laarbruch, the squadron survived there until August 1965 without further censure, carrying out operational FR and air-to-ground training before beginning their preparation for the next Sassoon competition in the following month. The very experienced Hunter pilot Flight Lieutenant George 'Slash' Slaney had now joined the squadron and flew one of its ten aircraft back to Gutersloh on 26 August, after 10 weeks away. Already well ahead on its annual flying task, squadron engineering support was now at its best.

Sassoon training continued, the CO being caught unawares when the exercise was called without warning while he was visiting his fiancée, Margreet, the daughter of the very popular owner of the Amicitia Hotel, Jan Koops. Returning post-haste to Gutersloh, he recovered from a dentist's deep root surgery just in time to join the Sassoon team on 15 September. Sadly, the squadron did not do well in the competition itself the boss nearly colliding with a IV Squadron aircraft when they were tasked together over the same electronics target in a very misty Sauerland.

When newly qualified FR pilots arrived from 229 OCU they underwent further role training in their respective operating areas, designed to achieve operational status with minimum delay. The incumbent squadron commanders set the standards (as indeed they did for the routine training of fully operational pilots); there was

The Eyes Have It. Sandy Wilson sympathises with Slash Slaney, sitting this one out after a surfeit of visual recce training. *II Sqn*

rarely a set agenda for the content and conduct of this initial training on the squadron, the programme and pace depending on the prevailing requirements and standards set and, of course, the background, skills and progress of the newcomer. They were also the final arbiters when it came to judging when a new pilot had achieved combat ready status, themselves invariably flying qualification sorties with each aspirant. Slash Slaney was quick to pass the test and drink from the Op Pot.

Squadrons were also given discretion on the domestic organisation they thought best could meet likely commitments with the resources they had to hand. Typically, a squadron would

comprise two flights, one commanded by Flt Cdr Ops, the 'warlord' tasked with overseeing all operational matters and exercises, the other by Flt Cdr Trg, each flight balanced with an amalgam of experience.

Flight Lieutenant Alex Weiss was one of the first ex-QFIs without a fast-jet background to undergo the front line orientation process and he became operational in an admirably short time during the Laarbruch detachment. Shortly thereafter, he narrowly avoided becoming a statistic when he took off from Biggin Hill at the end of a Battle of Britain display trailing fuel in front of a very large audience and TV cameras. With great presence of mind he landed his aircraft on a straight- in approach at nearby RAF Manston and returned to Gutersloh by civil air. In the same month Bob Hillman had the interesting task of providing extensive photographic cover of a murder scene for the German CID but nothing is recorded on the value of this to the outcome of the investigation. Bob (also an ex-QFI) and Alex were in the forefront of those who impressed the Central Flying School (CFS) agents carrying out their annual examination of pure flying proficiency. FR pilots were nothing if not versatile.

The relative peace of the home base was shattered at the end of the month when 19 (F) Squadron arrived to take up residence at Gutersloh with its twelve Lightnings. A second Lightning squadron, 92 (F) would follow. From then on the noise of twin afterburners would change the ambience at Gutersloh, and make life almost unbearable for OC Ops Wg in his quarters at the end of Runway 27. None of this

Mayday! Alex Weiss takes off for an air display at Biggin Hall with his aircraft streaming fuel from a massive leak. All ended well in an immediate emergency diversion and landing at RAF Manston. *Alex Weiss*

'There it is!' Pete Rayner in the MFPU at El Adem on Exercise Dazzle

'Finals, Three Greens'. Alex Weiss turns finals at RAF Luqa. *Alex Weiss*

worried Sam Jeffreys, who left the squadron at the end of the month.

No. II squadron went to El Adem again in October for Exercise Dazzle, this operational exercise over the desert providing a welcome alternative to classic FR in the European theatre. Low level navigation, with so few features on the map, required entirely different techniques, but the squadron quickly adapted to offer invaluable information to the army and the FGA9s of No. 1 Squadron, the ground attack force in the exercise.

Oasis. II Squadron celebrates the opening of its desert garden in their dispersal at RAF El Adem, created while waiting for scrambles in Exercise Dazzle. *Author*

On several sorties FR10s led the attack aircraft to their targets and every opportunity was taken to practise the concept of recce/attack interface, with the II Squadron pilots calling in the ground attack Hunters to give immediate attention to targets they located.

Working and living conditions in the desert were rudimentary. The squadron was quite content with the tented workplace but not with the suggestion that the Hunters be dispersed on the soft sand, and the argument in favour of firm ground prevailed. All II Squadron pilots slept in one large room remote from the communal toilet facilities, and again this was no problem in itself, but the room had to be kept locked against local villains which caused some embarrassment when the remainder of the squadron officers, dutifully locking the door behind them, went off to the bar forgetting that the boss was still in the shower. Peter Riley, the keeper of the key, came in for his full wrath when the CO arrived in the bar, dressed only in a small towel, demanding the key. As with all good Cranwell-bred officers, Peter took this on the chin and showed suitable remorse,albeit short-lived when the boss was out of earshot.

Exercise Dazzle was, however, a valuable exercise in every respect; an excellent experience with great training value and a chance to work with other tactical elements in the field under a different command and control system. The squadron returned to Gutersloh from a job well done, with many hours flown and spirits high.

Back at Gutersloh the operational theme continued with single pass air-to-ground sorties flown in all conditions resulting in an acceptable average score of 27.6 per cent. Continued high spirits pervaded a guest night which, quite incidentally, preceded the author's wedding to Margreet in Leeuwarden on 22 November 1965, he remembered it well: 'Things got a little noisy, indeed somewhat out of hand, at the dinner table after the loyal toast (during which hidden bottles of wine, which had been pre-positioned covertly, were disturbed by the movement of chairs to clank noisily across the floor). Thereafter squadron rivalry began to show, leaving the station commander unamused. On the following morning, sensing trouble ahead, I sought and thought I was given some assurance that our men would not suffer for the misdemeanours of the night before, while I was on honeymoon. I then joined many others on the long trek north,

everyone driving on black ice but some not realising it! The main celebrations preceded the wedding, held ideally in the Amicitia Hotel, the wedding thereafter going ahead without a hitch under clear blue skies and with full military ceremony, although a flypast by IV Squadron FR10s, given special permission by the mayor of Leeuwarden, had to be cancelled because of snow and ice on the runway at Gutersloh. All but the bride and groom returned to Gutersloh that night, to grave retribution on the following morning for their exuberance at that guest night.

When we got back from the honeymoon in December, I found that there had been very little flying in my absence, with all the officers otherwise occupied on courts martial, summaries of evidence, boards of inquiry, duty officer and the like. Flight Lieutenant John Thomson joined the squadron in time to take part in the guest night, the wedding and the intensive staff training which might at least have stood the career officers in good stead'.

Fortunately, the annual flying task had already been completed. The squadron spirit was, however, merely dented and the newly-weds were welcomed home to a great party in their married quarter, hitherto occupied by Bob and Angela Hillman, with the tree outside festooned with bottles of Carlsberg, glistening in the winter night.

Bob Hillman had managed to defer his departure from the squadron until after the wedding but he was then seen off with due ceremony, followed shortly after by Sam Toyne. They would be replaced as flight commanders by Hugh Cracroft, already well settled on the squadron, and Flight Lieutenant Roy Holmes, who arrived from the staff of 229 OCU having completed the FR course with great enterprise and determination on an ad hoc basis within his staff continuation training there. There was, however, very sad news for Alex Weiss, who had shown so much promise but was now grounded permanently for medical reasons; he remained with the squadron until his future had been decided, his spirit and enthusiasm for all things barely diminished. So ended an eventful, interesting and productive year; albeit with some disappointments. The squadron had adjusted to every circumstance, fulfilling all that was required of it, and was now looking forward to 1966.

Inspection. Alex Weiss inspecting the Guard of Honour well. *Alex Weiss*

Guard of Honour. Officers of II (AC) Squadron on guard at the 'boss's wedding in Leeuwarden on 22 November 1965. *II Sqn*

'Now See Here'! Mrs Walpole sets the ground rules at the author's wedding. *Author's Collection*

Dining-out. flight commanders Bob Hillman and Sam Toyne were dined out in 1965. *II Sqn*

1966: A Year of Plenty

Major Peter Heath, who had taken over from Brian Chapman as II Squadron's senior GLO in command of 468 GLS, was in his element when he took the squadron officers to his old regiment, The Sherwood Foresters, in nearby Munster, to gain a better insight into the work of an infantry battalion. It might have been difficult to quantify the professional value derived from this visit but the guests remember the honour of meeting the regimental mascot, a handsome goat, before indulging in extravagant hospitality which lasted from noon until dusk. It was towards the end of this mammoth session that blue uniforms were exchanged for brown (along with their owners' names and ranks) for all to meet and greet a brand new subaltern arriving from Sandhurst. It was soon clear that his training there had not included this scenario!

John Thomson, master of the masquerade and mimic, had been at his best as the archetypal army officer in the Munster charade, but his forte was impersonating a certain station commander with a marked Canadian accent, and all had to be on their guard for the elaborate jokes for which he was responsible. One morning after the night before, when John heard that his great friend,

Army Day. Periodically, local army units brought their heavy equipment to RAF Gutersloh for recognition training and for the pilots to play with. *Sandy Wilson*

Lightning pilot Dick Leach had seen him out of the bar, John got his own back with a convincing call to Leach to report to the station commander in OC II Squadron's office (the boss was flying at the time). As quick as his Lightning, an apprehensive Leach rehearsed his lines as he crossed the airfield to II Squadron, almost ignoring the two officers standing to attention either side of the office door and throwing up the smartest of salutes on entering, without pausing to recognise officer Thomson sitting regally behind the desk. Perhaps it was because so many of John's victims were gunning for him that he wisely chose, there and then, to escape south on skiing leave. Justice caught up with him, however, when he broke an arm on the slopes and returned to Gutersloh unfit for flying and to the news that he was to become ADC to the C-in-C RAF Germany. John was so close to becoming operational on the FR10 that, having ensured that he could if necessary eject, the CO assessed his airborne performance on a unique but rigorous 'op ride' in the T7, and pronounced him 'combat ready' before sending him on his way to Rheindahlen. That was, however, far from the end of John Thomson on II Squadron. He persuaded his new master to allow him to return to Gutersloh regularly to remain current on the aircraft and well versed in the role, eliciting a promise that he would be posted back to the squadron on completion of his ADC duties. The possibility of a flight commander appointment was also mooted.

Royal Flush 1966. II Squadron celebrates the end of another competition. *II Sqn*

II Squadron Togetherness. No. II Squadron in 1966, post-Royal Flush. *Peter Riley*

In March 1966 every war mission had to be revised in accordance with a new War Plan, but Royal Flush training also began again. With competition in mind as much as the imperatives of war, identification of friendly forces being crucial in both, the squadron pilots mingled dangerously with a host of fast-moving French Army armoured vehicles and guns as they careered about their exercise purpose on a foggy Sennelager Range. Having survived that frenetic activity the CO's car was then subjected to a kamikaze attack by a German civilian in a Ford Taunus as the party was returning through Gutersloh town. This resulted in Cat 2 damage to the car and two cracked ribs for the latest arrival, and new scribe of the ORB, Flight Lieutenant Roger Wilkins. Safety was also put at risk when, at the invitation of the squadron, British armoured vehicles came to Gutersloh and the airfield thundered to their engines as the pilots demonstrated their driving skills with dubious success. A total of 245 hours were flown in March – a very good month.

It spoke well of his reputation, but was ill-timed with the approach of Royal Flush, when Eric Lockwood was loaned to the Royal Jordanian Air Force for three weeks to help resolve initial problems with their FR10 camera system. The squadron was rewarded with the coveted 'One' for its overall performance in April's surprise Taceval, but such Royal Flush training as was possible in that month did not pay off in the May competition, the squadron being greatly disappointed with its results. This was particularly sad for Alex Weiss, who was deemed to be permanently unfit medically for flying, because he had worked so hard as the overall project officer. He left the squadron pending his release from the service, but would ultimately become very successful in the electronics industry. Alex was dined out, along with John Coleman and Buster Webb, to be replaced by Sandy Wilson and Geoff Hall from the new breed of aforementioned ex-QFIs (Chapter Three). With an average of 65 hours each on the Hunter, and very little of it on the one FR10 available at the OCU during their time, the two had already shown great promise under

Full Stop. No. II Squadron FR10 at Gutersloh, drag chute deployed. *Peter Gover*

the none too tender care of John Morris - now they had to impress the front line.

Sandy Wilson takes pleasure in remembering the way his appointed mentor, Stu Penny, looked after him from the moment of his arrival. Stu met him off the 'Luton Flier' but instead of taking him straight to the squadron drove him to the hiring he had negotiated for him, in an old green Volkswagen he had also purchased for Sandy's use. Then it was off to the squadron and thereafter to the traditional welcoming beer call in the cellar bar of the Officers Mess, followed by an impromptu supper at the CO's quarters. After the meal, at the end of what had been a long day and having survived a surfeit of beer, the two newcomers faced a dilemma. Due to the exertions of command the boss fell asleep, leaving them wondering whether to wait for him to come alive again, wake him or leave; was this indeed a test? They are best able to tell the rest of the story themselves.

Despite the sceptics, Sandy and Geoff would acquit themselves admirably on II Squadron. Sandy well remembers the thoughtful help and personal attention they enjoyed, and the generally intimate atmosphere on this relatively small unit headed by a squadron leader, a rare thing given that the larger flying squadrons were commanded by a wing commander with several squadron leader executives. He flew the very high number of 106 hours in his first four months, guided rapidly but progressively towards operational status. On one long and memorable trip during his second month, a critically helpful Roy Holmes, the much respected and highly professional Flt Cdr Trg, took him on a Southern Ranger through Italy to Malta and thence to El Adem, an invaluable experience out of theatre. He also had plenty of attention from the six PAIs who vied with each other to instil their personal tactics and techniques, the amalgam clearly being so successful that the experts often had to cede to the less qualified when it came to the gunnery competitions. Incidentally, this Junta was always gunning for their boss, on one occasion spending hours proving (successfully) that the one shot on his target after an operational shoot was simply a ricochet. Apart from their specialist expertise, the ex-QFIs had one other dubious advantage over those who had spent their time on DF/GA squadrons – night flying experience. Sandy remembers that the requirement for one night

Show Me the Way Home. No. II Squadron leading a 441 Squadron RF-104 back to Marville. *Frank Mitchell*

landing a month was always programmed on a strict pecking order; the most senior pilots on the squadron would be scheduled to land on the stroke of official 'night', when it was barely dark, the new boys then sent off in the pitch black. So it was that Sandy and Geoff integrated easily and agreeably into the pool of experienced FR pilots, but the author strenuously denies that Sandy paved his way, as the squadron's IRE, by renewing his Master Green instrument rating at the first attempt.

Remember Verdun. FR10 overflies that monument to a great WWI victory. *Frank Mitchell*

NATO Exchange. OC 441 Squadron RCAF welcomes OC II Squadron to their base at Marville in France. *Pete Riley*

Squadron Exchange. II Squadron ambassadors arrive at Marville for an squadron exchange visit to 441 Squadron RCAF (CF-104s). (L to R) Frank Mitchell, Peter Riley, Author, Slash Slaney. *Frank Mitchell*

All Work and No Play… RAF Gutersloh Squash team 1970. *Tim Thorn*

With a dip in the number of squadron pilots now available to fly all the serviceable FR10s, 19 Squadron Lightning pilots Nigel Lane and Nigel Piggerskill were given a taste of flying the Hunter in the recce role, and they liked it. A welcome spell of good weather and excellent aircraft serviceability in June allowed a period of flying continuity to the benefit of all, not least the replacement pilots, and helped to exceed the monthly requirement by 84 hours. The squadron was also required to raise a team of four aircraft for limited displays, the CO leading Hugh Cracroft, Roy Holmes and Stu Penny.

July was another good month; four FR10s paid a visit to the Royal Canadian Air Force (RCAF) base at Marville, France, hosted by 441 Squadron on a one-way exchange exercise (the runway at Gutersloh was considered too short for the CF-104s). The lucky few flew sorties over terrain little known to them, the Starfighters and Hunters operated together in pairs with their pilots leading turn and turn about and learning much from the cross-fertilisation of ideas.

Those back at Gutersloh also enjoyed productive FR training with live attacks against military targets on the difficult range at Hohne.

Having done sterling work for the squadron, and finishing his time with a very profitable briefing on how to get the best out of the Vinten F95 camera's automatic exposure facility, Eric Lockwood handed over the squadron PI responsibilities to Flight Lieutenant Bill Kelly, who was transferred from IV Squadron.

Away from work there was time for sport and a multitude of social initiatives. Hugh Cracroft and Peter Riley reached the semi-finals of the aircrew inter-unit tennis tournament and Sandy Wilson played a major part on the station's squash team, but the talk of the station in August was of II Squadron's outstanding 'hoe down'. The squadron organised this party in the grounds of the Officers Mess around the lake, on which candles glittered as they floated on the surface and rubber dinghies were moored close by – just in case. The station doctor had warned that anyone tempted to test the temperature of the murky waters would be subjected at once to every precautionary injection he could think of. However, he was past caring when the more intrepid jumped in anyway claiming entirely legitimate dinghy drill; they escaped the jabs and suffered no ill effects. There was a general consensus that the senior person on the squadron, leading from rear, failed the drill dismally by attempting to enter the dinghy from the wrong end, but this version of events is hotly disputed. What had all started as a beautiful, peaceful summer's evening ended with a most dramatic storm at 0200 hours, causing the remaining party stalwarts to cram into a

We Will Survive. Dedicated dinghy drill on the Officers Mess lake, late one summer's night in 1966 *Sandy Wilson*

marquee provided for just such an eventuality and remain there until dawn. Perhaps it was a good thing that the much admired and feared Op Pot was absent at the time, taken out of service for repairs to its bottom.

Back at work, Sassoon was postponed because of poor weather, prolonging its preparation, and the four-ship display team was out of business before it began when the two displays for which it was scheduled were cancelled. Hugh Cracroft became stranded on the GAF base at Landsberg in Bavaria where his FR10 went unserviceable, as did the T7 in which Slash Slaney and airframe fitter Corporal Kitchen flew to his rescue. Whatever the defects were, all involved were required to stay in Bavaria over a weekend, both aircraft recovering miraculously from their ailments on the following Monday.

September was another very social month. At a weekend party the squadron was able to repay some of the hospitality extended by the Canadians of 441 Squadron in July. The guests were recognised as the most capable within NATO of taking on the hosts at the indoor sports of darts and billiards, not to mention volume drinking from the now

Health Check. Gutersloh's Senior Medical Officer (centre rear) 'Doc' Davies, keeps an eye on II Squadron's social habits (L to R) Joan and Bill Kelly, Peter Heath (GLO), Margreet and Nigel Walpole. *II Sqn*

Come Dancing. No. II Squadron officers and ladies demonstrate dexterity and versatility (?) on the dance floor. *II Sqn*

Security Was Tight. No. II Squadron officers were kept well clear of the VIPs. *II Sqn*

repaired squadron pot. This was followed by the ritual celebration when Roger Wilkins became operational and a typically lavish (if rather late) Summer Ball. Stung by long standing jibes from North American friends that the Brits preferred the bar to dancing (although there was no lack of volunteers among these critics to look after the wives) the squadron had begun demonstrating their prowess (or otherwise) on the dance floor. Finally there were several parties to bid farewell

Good Listener. Air Chief Marshal Sir Charles Elworthy listens intently to another of Bill Kelly's war stories. *II Sqn*

to the very popular Peter Heath and to welcome Major Reid, of the Royal Highland Fusiliers, who joined Captain Bob Arnold on 468 GLS.

With all eleven pilots on strength now operational, the monthly flying target was achieved by 21 October 1966. This allowed all hands to become involved in reorganising the hangar to relocate the GLS to more suitable accommodation, while rationalising the operational and social facilities. This went on in parallel with a restructuring of the squadron training programme and interface between flying and engineering support. Whenever possible, 'tasking meetings' were held at the end of each week to bring all elements of the squadron together for a review of the past week and to plan the next; duty supervisors were rostered to plan and oversee the 'trip of the day' and the subsequent daily debriefings. This re-structuring was celebrated with an all-ranks party organised by the social member Slash Slaney (an obvious choice) in a local hostelry, a party which also served to welcome the new station commander Group Captain David Ross and Mrs Ross. As if by reward, Slash found himself stranded again for a weekend in Bavaria, this time at GAF Furstenfeldbruch near Munich during Octoberfest with Peter Riley, when one of their FR10s burst a tyre on landing.

Deputy Supreme Allied Commander Europe (DSACEUR), Marshal of the Royal Air Force Sir Thomas Pike, visited Gutersloh in November and seemed much impressed by the squadron's nuclear dispersal facilities and approach to its primary role of post-nuclear strike. His reaction to the comment that the pilots' only protection in the nuclear playground would be one black eye patch is not recorded. The frequency of VIP visits seemed to be increasing, perhaps because of the successes the station was enjoying, but when the squadron was not directly involved in the visits they kept (or were kept) well away. Tactical symposiums were now all the rage, Roy Holmes and the CO attending one at RAF Wildenrath, given by a specialist USAF team on the implications of nuclear operations. They had not bargained for the long discussion which followed and a return to Gutersloh by T7 in the dark, thereby exceeding their monthly night flying requirement in what must have been a 'one-off'. The T7 also protested, going unserviceable for the remainder of the year. The squadron flew an unusually high number of

FR10 hours in December and ended the year well above the annual flying target.

1967: Change of Command

The excellent serviceability continued throughout the first months of 1967 with the monthly targets always exceeded. Hard and fast operational FR flying was matched by very good gunnery results, the latter thanks to Bill Armstrong and Slash Slaney who were now leading the formidable corps of five squadron PAIs, but a return to competition training lay ahead. The author takes up the story again: 'At this point I fell ill with pleurisy and had to conduct business from my bedside, Roy Holmes taking my place at the head of a NATO formation flypast over NATO Headquarters at Fontainebleau, as part of the closing ceremony. This he did with his usual immaculate planning and execution to the second. Meanwhile, John McGarvey stood in for me as chief host at an unprecedented unit party for the squadron SNCOs in the Officers Mess, to thank them for extraordinary engineering achievements over the previous year.

Disaster nearly struck in February 1967 when Flight Lieutenant Frank Mitchell's FR10 severed power cables in one of those forbidding fjords in Norway. It was on a Saturday afternoon while I was still recovering from pleurisy that I was aroused in my quarter by a call from Wing Operations saying 'one of your aircraft has crashed in Norway'. Thankfully, this was wide of the mark but within two hours I was on my way to Sola, Stavangar, in the T7 with John McGarvey, to hear the story first-hand and report back. At high level with full external tanks we were able to complete the trip non-stop and were met by two rather disconsolate FR10 pilots with cotton wool dangling from their ears where blood had been taken to confirm the absence of alcohol. It transpired that, rather than pull up as had Slash in the lead, Frank chose to turn about, and it was shortly thereafter that his aircraft struck the cables. A tortuous inquisition followed, at the end of which all involved were invited to the customary interviews at Rheindahlen. A story has it that there were two cable-cutting cases to deal with that afternoon, the second involving a Canberra crew, and that the senior person sitting in judgement got the two mixed up, thereby haranguing the Hunter pilots for the Canberra incident. He then added to their agony by refusing to accept any comment from them – and that was that!

Back at Gutersloh things continued to prosper, with a second T7 coming on strength in April and both were used very productively thereafter. Everything seemed to have gone well in May's Royal Flush, but again it was not to be (Chapter Seven).

Frank Mitchell was involved in another drama in May when a main wheel of T7 WV372 'Romeo' decided to depart the aircraft and go its own way during an otherwise normal landing; with great bounds it bounced high across the golf course and was last seen heading for Wiedenbruch, not to be found for some time. Racing to the disabled, but largely undamaged T7, already believing the worst, I demanded to know not only whether the captain had checked the security of the wheel before take-off. I also asked who had flown the aircraft on its previous trip – only to find out that it was me. An obscure

Farewell Fontainebleau. Flight Commander Roy Holmes leads NATO aircraft in a flypast to mark the farewell to the NATO HQ at Fontainebleau. *II Sqn*

Britisk jagerfly fløy mot kraftledning i Sandsfjorden

Fly kuttet kraft-linje, bygder i Ryfylke mørklagt

Dateline the 10th of March.

Picture if you can Norway, a country of 3,600,000 people most of whom are huddled round the goggle box avidly awaiting the year's big sporting event when POW - there arrives the Mad Axeman in his aluminum pursuit ship. The next moment PHUT and half of Norway is plunged into darkness (poetic license). Wrestling with his wounded bird he nurses it back to a safe landing at Sola. He reports in -

There used to be power lines here

Lights Out. Frank Mitchell made headlines in Norwegian newspapers in 1966. *II Sqn*

technical defect was subsequently found and the pilots were exonerated. Romeo suffered no long term effects and at the time of writing is alive and well, still flying in II Squadron markings (Epilogue).

In a more serious mishap at Gutersloh, a GAF F-104 pilot had his undercarriage wiped off by the runway barrier which, through some misunderstanding, was raised at the threshold of the runway he was approaching on a forced landing. The noise made in the subsequent belly landing shook the station, but the very angry pilot survived.

On the eve of my departure from an eventful command and perhaps a little 'boat happy', I sought leave of absence 'on important business' from the none too agreeable VIP I was hosting at Gutersloh's Open Day, to fly with ex-recce pilot Ray Hanna as he led the Red Arrows in what was called (rather undiplomatically) 'the biggest RAF show in Germany since WW2'. Roy Holmes, who was leading this year's display team of Peter Riley, Geoff Hall and Roger Wilkins, also led the squadron in an impressive attack on the airfield, which was marred only by the poor timing and unrealism of the prefabricated explosions designed to simulate the effects of their weapons.

C-in-C RAF Germany (Air Marshal Sir Dennis Spotswood) took this opportunity to meet Sandy Wilson, who was then summoned to appear before him formally two days later. The upshot was that Sandy left II Squadron in May for a year's duty as ADC to the C-in-C, but with the promise that he would be returned to II Squadron to resume his operational career and,

Which Way did it Go? This T-7, Frank Mitchell and John Thomson aboard, last saw the port wheel of their T7 bouncing across the golf course on its way to open country. *II Sqn*

I Shall Return. Flight Lieutenant Sandy Wilson's last Hunter flight before taking up his duties as ADC to the C-in-C RAF Germany. He would return as a squadron leader flight commander. *Sandy Wilson*

Nearly Made It! This Luftwaffe F-104 might have made a successful 'dead-stick' landing – had the barrier at Gutersloh not been raised at the approach end. *Peter Riley*

as with John Thomson before him, with the hint of a flight commander appointment.

In one final gesture, none better or more typical, 100 per cent of the aircraft were on the flight line for my final day, together with an invitation to lead half the squadron in medium level combat against the other half led by Hugh Cracroft. With most of the players ex-fighter

pilots this promised to be a memorable trip. Readily accepting, of necessity in borrowed flying kit, I returned the tribute to the engineers by taking John McGarvey with me in Romeo. Given the occasion and the T7's inadequate power, the 'best of breed' should have been queuing up at my 6 o'clock but after the first skirmish in a sky full of aircraft everyone else vanished, leaving us to come home on our own for the final flypast. There was no explanation for this in a debriefing which continued into the evening in the bar; perhaps it had been an

Final Fling. A farewell gift for the outgoing CO in June 1967, a four v four combat sortie followed by final flypasts. *Jim Dymond*

The Great Catt. A rare photograph of Puddy Catt in formal rig. *II Sqn*

unprecedented and long overdue 'be kind to the old boss' day?'

Squadron Leader Tim Barrett took over the squadron with a hand shake at about 2200 hours that evening, the now redundant person repairing to hospitality offered by John and Margaret McGarvey in their hiring – but this was not the end. At 0200 hours on the following morning the alert sounded and everyone had to report for work as usual, not knowing of course whether this was for real or simply an exercise.

Sieg Heil! Bill Norton, tank commander for a day, salutes an admiring crowd. *II Sqn*

In fact it was a Taceval, and the II Squadron officers made it quite clear that the old boss was no longer wanted on the premises.

The squadron served Tim Barrett well on his first day by gaining the highest marks possible in the evaluation, but was deprived of the ultimate accolade because of deficiencies in support functions beyond their control. This was the dramatic scene which greeted Flight Lieutenant Bill Norton on his first working day. Next to arrive was the redoubtable Flight Lieutenant 'Puddy' Catt. It was now July, and the month in which the Gutersloh Hunters began to provide a standing presence in Gibraltar to help ensure unimpeded access by RAF aircraft to 'The Rock'. The story of this on-going commitment, shared with IV Squadron, is told in Chapter Eight.

Half the squadron went to Denmark in August for an exchange with 724 Squadron, Royal Danish Air Force (RDAF), at Skrydstrup, where they stamped their mark on a Meteor found in the corner of the airfield, and on the memories of their hosts in what was claimed to have been 'the best exchange in memory'. The basis for this claim was not recorded and may be left best to the imagination, but there was mention of visits to Copenhagen, Aalborg and a brewery.

The squadron came fifth out of six in September's Sassoon competition, with no comfort taken in IV Squadron bringing up the rear.

Blow Hard. Bill Norton taking a voluntary breath test, perhaps after his tank command and before piloting Gutersloh's jet engine snow clearer. *II Sqn*

Best Behaviour. Tim Barrett shows a German General and CDS II Squadron at its best, OC Flying Wing Dave Rhodes looking unconcerned and Peter Riley telling CDS how he did it, as GLO Major Reid looks on. *II Sqn*

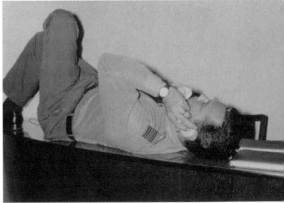

Relaxed Command. Squadron commander Tim Barrett takes it lying down. *II Sqn*

Having served the squadron exceptionally well, engineer John McGarvey departed with due ceremony; he had been liked and respected by all, his leadership reflected in the very high morale among his men and the outstanding aircraft serviceability throughout his time. He had been involved in every aspect of the squadron's life, at work and play, and was always ready to get airborne in the T7; there was little doubt that he could fly and recover the aircraft safely and demonstrated this on one occasion when his pilot suffered from serious sinus problems. John was rewarded with an MBE, and was replaced by Flight Lieutenant Dave Hill.

The ORB for October dealt almost exclusively with a 'friendly' football match between the officers and squadron groundcrew, in which Peter Riley suffered two broken ribs and goalkeeper Bill Kelly had to be carried off with a cut leg. Victors and vanquished then consumed enormous quantities of Dortmunder Pils in lieu of pain killers and it was quite incidental that three SNCOs were posted a few days later. Regular VIP visits and exchanges with local NATO army units continued apace, more often in these winter months and always resulting in a tale to tell.

It was no surprise when John Thomson replaced Hugh Cracroft as Flt Cdr Ops, but could he now be expected to refrain from his much-feared mimicry? There was equally good news for Peter Riley, who may have been sad to leave the squadron but was certainly very happy with his exchange posting to a USAF recce squadron flying Phantoms. Pete Day arrived as a replacement pilot, in the unusual rank of flying officer. The flying year finished with a whimper in December, only 81 hours being flown in the 10 days that flying was possible, but this served to help the move from Hangar 3 to Hangar 7 at the east end of the airfield.

1968: New Home, Routine and Incident.
Puddy Catt completed the Winter Survival Course at Bad Kohlgrub in January 1968, his new all-round fitness telling as he established an all-comers record of 21 seconds for draining the Op Pot to celebrate his operational status. It was still deep winter when, to its great credit, the

squadron was again awarded 'One' in a surprise Taceval, with 100 per cent serviceability and the result more impressive because it was achieved in the absence of both squadron commander and Flt Cdr Ops. By March, Royal Flush was looming again, this time with the sensible inclusion of strip searches to reflect an important aspect of the War Plan. Flying Officer Chris Bain joined as the work-up began for the competition in April. This may not have been a good time for Butch Butcher to hand over command of 2 MFPU to Flight Lieutenant Felix Leathers or Bill Kelly to be replaced by Flying Officer Dave Oxley as the resident PI, but the squadron came second in 2ATAF and fourth overall. It was not all work; in May, the officers challenged the SNCOs to a darts match, the bachelor officers held a buffet supper, four barrels of beer were consumed in the crewroom after Royal Flush and a dinner night saw off Butch Butcher and Bill Kelly in true fashion.

With nothing in the ORB on June, this seemed to have been a month for recovery before half the squadron visited an Italian Air Force F-104 squadron at Gio del Colle, while John Thomson busied himself with his solo aerobatic displays. In another big changeover, Flight Lieutenants Dave Bagshaw and Pete Atkins arrived as Slash Slaney, Frank Mitchell and Roger Wilkins returned to the UK on posting. The squadron now comprised thirteen officers and fifty seven other ranks; a four-ship display team was raised,

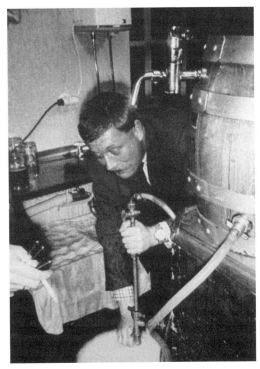

Beer Up! Puddy Catt doing what he did best. *II Sqn*

comprising Tim Barrett (lead), Pete Atkins, Dave Bagshaw and Puddy Catt and the monthly flying task was exceeded again.

In August Bill Norton had his second flame-out landing on II squadron (see Chapter 6) this time in a T7 (XL571). Bill was giving Stu Penny his instrument rating test, and it was during a steep turn on limited panel instrumentation at high level that the engine-fire warning light illuminated. Stu, well known for his rapid reaction to any situation and thinking that this was all part of the test, completed the full fire-drill to perfection, his hands flashing all over the cockpit at lightning speed, and finally stop-cocked the engine. It was considered imprudent to attempt a relight so, with the weather kind and the other aircraft systems functioning correctly, the pair joined forces in the now heavily misted up cockpit to carry out a copybook flame-out landing.

Tim Barrett felt that September 1968 was best forgotten; a month in which the guns of a II Squadron FR10 were fired inadvertently in the hangar, destroying another Hunter and coming perilously close to causing grievous bodily harm (or worse) to Stu Penny in the crewroom. With

Survival. Hackerbrau Beer at Hotel Zur Post, Bad Kohlgrub, helped aircrew on the Winter Survival School to survive. *II Sqn*

Waiting Game. Another 'Flush' over – 1968. *II Sqn*

Italian Story. No. 2 Squadron, Italian Air Force, hosts II Squadron, RAF, at Gio de Colle. *Bill Norton*

On Show. No. II Squadron goes formal in 1968. *II Sqn*

every precaution taken (usually) against such a possibility, and random defects quick to develop if the aircraft were left at the mercy of the weather, the squadron had long sheltered its operationally ready aircraft in the hangar with their guns loaded, to be ready for any contingency – but that might now change.

Nothing daunted, the squadron went about its business, enjoying a particularly good month for operational training, with missions 'chased' at 480 kts and often intercepted by 'bounce' aircraft. John Thomson's displays at Aachen, Auf dem Dumple and Werdohl were described as 'immaculate' and a season of very successful

Flame Out! Bill Norton and Stu Penny bring their T7 to a halt at Gutersloh after a copybook flame out landing. *II Sqn*

Display Time Again. Squadron commander Tim Barrett, with David Bagshaw, Puddy Catt & Pete Atkins. *II Sqn*

'Low Go'. A II Squadron FR10 overshoots on Runway 27 at Gutersloh. *II Sqn*

Southern Rangers came to an end. To all who had served at Oldenburg and Gutersloh, the dining-out of Herr Lach, mess manager *par excellence*, on his final retirement, was a very special night and eight squadron officers managed to secure a place at the table.

There was the usual spate of exercises with the army in October, several of high value to the FR10s in their war role, but again a lack of understanding of what they could and should not be required to do led to wasted effort. After this, their busy season, the squadron GLOs, Majors Reid and Arnold (Bob having been promoted during his tour) handed over to Major John Fitzgerald and Captain 'Jack' Frost. As expected, Sandy Wilson returned to the fold as Flt Cdr Trg (designate), from his ADC duties at Rheindahlen.

Group Captain Keith Williamson was now in command at Gutersloh. Having served on Hunter squadrons in Germany at Oldenburg and Bruggen, and recently helped to usher the Lightning into service, he was the ideal choice. A regular flier with all his squadrons he might remember a trip into the hills with Sandy Wilson in two FR10s which promised well at the start but soon placed Sandy in a difficult dilemma as the weather deteriorated rapidly. Should he press on at low level as the weather began to fall below limits or pull up into the dense cloud and put his master's formation skills to the test? In fact he did go below limits before climbing, thereafter anxious about the possibility of verbal retribution when they got back on the ground. He need not have worried, Keith Williamson stuck to him like a leach throughout, and made no comment on the decision to stay low as the weather deteriorated – until Sandy's farewell interview (the content of which was not revealed). Despite the usual poor weather in November and December, the flying task was achieved with ease and all alert requirements satisfied. This left nothing of significance to report in the ORB, other than the sight of Puddy Catt reacting to a call-out in his nightgown and 'bobble hat'- a deterrent indeed to any enemy!

It was during this very slack period that II Squadron carried out 'an instructional visit' to the Warsteiner Brewery in the foothills above the Mohne See, thereby unwittingly setting in train a new fashion to the benefit of all. On that cold winter's afternoon the beer went down so well that stocks had to be taken back to Gutersloh. There followed an invitation to the brewery's representative to supply the Officers Mess, then the Sergeants Mess, with ever increasing quantities. So the reputation grew; Warsteiner was soon flowing more freely locally, then nationally and internationally, the brewery forced to expand accordingly. Warsteiner is still a favourite with many FR10 beer hunters, as is a retreat (and much photographed 'target') for certain II Squadron officers at Beilstein on the Mosel.

1969: More of the Same

Unusually good weather in January enabled 'a splendid start to 1969' (ORB), but it was payback time in February with only 152 hours flown. Flight Lieutenant Derek Bridge arrived, followed by Flight Lieutenant 'Duckie' Drake, to replace Roy Holmes and Stu Penny. Duckie was soon in the news with a potentially disastrous engine problem in his FR10, but it all ended well. The attraction of weekend Blue Diamond sorties faded when the minimum height in Denmark was raised to 2,000 ft to protect young mink.

The work rate now increased as preparations began again for Royal Flush. This year, eight pilots would take part in the competition itself, each flying three sorties over static and mobile military targets. A particularly strong team of PIs was attached to the squadron, comprising Squadron Leader Fred Piper, Flight Lieutenants Jock West and Keith Garrett (all VR officers), together with Flight Lieutenant Robin Brown and Lieutenant Valerie Bennett from RAF Germany. The results of their joint efforts were not recorded in the ORB. Flight Lieutenant

Friendly Fire. FR10 'Yankee' and the squadron planning room on the receiving end of a shooting in Hangar 7. *II Sqn*

Mosel Retreat. Beilstein on the Mosel, a favourite retreat for II Squadron pilots. *Sandy Wilson*

Engine Trouble. Ducky Drake comes back on a wing and a prayer. *II Sqn*

George Lee arrived amidst this frenzied activity and was soon his usual hyperactive self in the air and on the ground.

Tasking came under fire again when the TOC sent the squadron all the way to Tranum Range in Northern Denmark for a live air-to-ground mission, to find the range closed. There was no such problem with Exercise Marshmallow, a very fruitful army exercise for the squadron in October, with the FR10s supporting the lightly armed 15 (Scottish) Para during an airborne

Blue Diamond. Dave Bagshaw's 'forward facer' shows Puddy Catt in a Norwegian Fjord. *Dave Bagshaw*

insertion into the Solling and Harz Mountains, but well laid plans to impress the army with a demonstration of the FR10 operational capability went wrong (see Chapter Two).

Tim Barrett handed over II Squadron to Squadron Leader R. J. M. 'Moose' David, in November 1969, with all the pilots combat ready and the annual flying target well within reach. Moose was soon of the opinion that his pilots were 'capable of finding any target within the FR10's range', but the squadron was unable to retain its 'One' in his first Taceval, this time because of a general failing in the Command, Control, Communications and Intelligence (C3I) support.

John Thomson left the squadron in that final month of 1969, having contributed much to its operational effectiveness as a flight commander and to Gutersloh's reputation with his aerobatic displays. He left with an Exceptional rating in his log book to take up an exchange appointment on Phantoms in the USA, putting the experience he had gained over the last four years to very good

Now Watch Me Bloggs. An intrepid George Lee shows Duckie Drake how it should be done. *II Sqn*

effect there and later in his rapid promotions to the RAF hierarchy. He was replaced by Flying Officer Ron Elder.

1970: Beginning of the End

While on his FR course at Chivenor Ron Elder had done much to show that carefully selected first tourists, properly handled, could cope with the role, but he later admitted that he faced his first squadron with some trepidation, knowing that eyes remained on him and that he had to convince his new mentors at Gutersloh of his worth. In fact, he may have felt that he was handled with undue care in his first months, with the limits of his White Card instrument rating (unique on the squadron) applied too rigidly while the other pilots plunged regularly into the perennial winter murk. This, and the consequent lack of flying continuity in role training, may have done little for his self-confidence within that aura of mystique which prevailed in the FR world at that time. Looking back at anecdotal evidence, the author now believes that there were indeed times when certain 'old stagers' on the FR squadrons did not realise the detrimental effects of this wholly

unnecessary state of mind on some of their newcomers. Fortunately, a sympathetic Pete Atkins was given the task of training Ron to operational status, which he achieved in no more than the average time, the boss handing Ron the coveted squadron badge at his final initiation in the bar in July 1970. It had been a hard eight months but the new boy had stood the pace and only two months later would be selected as the reserve pilot for the new Big Click recce competition, an unexpected accolade for a first tourist. Big Click was an Air Forces Northern Europe (AFNORTH) exercise, in which the FR10s would participate as guests – and excel (Chapter Seven).

The winter gloom persisted throughout the early months of 1970, defensive combat training at high level and the use of four external tanks for high-low-high sorties to Southern Germany and the UK again the only way by which reasonable flying continuity could be maintained and a recently imposed increase in the flying rate achieved. Whenever it was possible to remain at low level Puddy Catt did so, the culmination of one sortie making the point. According to George Lee, Puddy weaved his way home in

Watch Your Six! Over the years II Squadron FR10s caught many of their contemporaries unawares with their forward facing F95 cameras. *II Sqn*

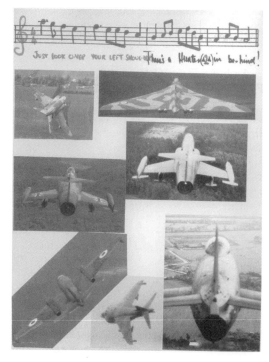

very marginal conditions, calling for a visual rejoin to break and land at Gutersloh under a low cloud base. ATC directed him to climb and recover via GCA, to which Puddy is reported to have replied, "Don't be ridiculous, the weather is far too bad for that!" That much may be true, but it seems unlikely that the Gutersloh hierarchy would have ever agreed that the FR10 pilots should be exempt from the 'mandatory GCA' flying state. In any event the time had come for Puddy to depart, destined for instructional duties in Oman. Sandy Wilson was also on the move, to convert to the Phantom FGR1 (scheduled to replace the FR10) before returning to Shiny Two and resuming his role of flight commander – as a squadron leader.

It was at about this time that a major disaster was avoided by the prompt action of men at the scene and of the Station Fire Services, all of whom reacted at once to a mighty explosion of AVPIN starter fluid within II Squadron's hangar. In the event little damage resulted but there was the inevitable, long-winded enquiry which, for reasons unpublished, led to the controversial involvement of the Special Investigation Branch.

No. II Squadron was now reinforced by four pilots released from IV Squadron when it began its conversion to the Harrier; they were Flight Lieutenants Tim Thorn, Al Mathie, Bill Sheppard and Roger Neal, who were quick to exert their already well-known individuality on the squadron. The squadron deployed to RAF Wildenrath on 1 June 1970, to operate from makeshift facilities on the south of the airfield while work was again carried out on the runway at Gutersloh. Ten days later, half the squadron flew to the RDAF base at Karup for a two-week exchange with a Danish RF-84 squadron. They were hosted royally but, with flying limited first to 2,000 ft, and then down to only 650 ft later, realistic operational training was not possible. On the other hand, the visit proved useful in preparation for Exercise Big Click to be held nearby at Aalborg in August, by allowing an insight into maritime operations around the coasts and in the Baltic. Whether the dearth of flying (Ron Elder flew only five times in ten days) could be attributed to these limits,

poor weather, unserviceabilities, or the heavy social programme, is not recorded.

Back at Wildenrath the flying effort from June to the end of August was devoted to exercise Whirlygig, more familiarisation flights over Denmark and Norway for Big Click and to the competition itself. Preparation for the competition necessitated high-low-high missions, some lasting more than two hours, or refuelling stops in Denmark, but this all transpired to be well worthwhile when the results were announced (Chapter Seven). The detachment returned to Gutersloh on 5 September, in time for the pilots to take part in a mass flypast for HRH Princess Anne when she presented Colours to RAF Germany. Bill Sheppard provided the solo aerobatic display and Tim Thorn, together with Lightning pilot Flight Lieutenant Rick Peacock-Edwards were selected to dance with Princess Anne at the Ball which followed.

Tim and Rick, neither of whom claimed to be expert dancers but who were thought by the hierarchy to be the most presentable of the bachelors available, duly reported to the C-in-Cs residence, Air House, at the appointed time for drinks before going on to the Ball in the HQ Mess at Rheindahlen. It is possible that they had already fortified themselves with the odd calming drink. At the start of this memorable evening, one of the entourage mustered by the C-in-C, Air Marshal Sir Christopher Foxley-Norris, was said to have been so overwhelmed by the beauty of the Princess as she descended

Royal Command. No. II Squadron's Tim Thorn and 19 Squadron's Rick Peacock-Edwards were specially selected to escort HRH The Princess Anne to the Rheindahlen Ball. *Tim Thorn*

the stairway of Air House, that he fainted on the spot. It then seems that, with great presence of mind, the C-in-C had him dragged behind the long curtains in front of the French windows, hoping to hide everyone's embarrassment. They had not taken account of the gentle wind which wafted through the curtains, periodically revealing two immaculately clad feet, the Hunter pilots now finding it hard to contain themselves. One of the chosen men then caused considerable consternation when, with the flourish of his arm to make a point, he upset a tray of drinks over Princess Anne's white dress. With good grace the Princess allowed herself to be mopped down but signs of the assault remained throughout the night for those who dared to look. As for the Ball itself, both Gutersloh worthies strutted their stuff and the Princess enjoyed their attention so much (their words), that despite the fact that her once pristine white shoes were soon covered in black blotches from clumsy feet, she kept the party going well after her intended departure time, arriving back in the UK by air at dawn, just in time to exercise her horse in Hyde Park.

Bachelor life had always been good at Gutersloh, notwithstanding the dearth of suitable young ladies to woo the single men off some of their dubious habits, and it was inevitable that Ron Elder should fall among thieves. Enter Puddy Catt, always in the vanguard of bachelor activity with his prodigious thirst and unique personality. Ron freely admits that he soon became a regular passenger in Puddy's Fiat 500 as they toured the local taverns looking for more 'tubes of neck oil'. Ron was rescued from bachelorhood by schoolteacher Sue, to whom he soon became engaged and arranged to marry in October 1970. Ironically, having become reconciled to the prospect of married life, he was then condemned to a thirteen-month unaccompanied tour with 8 Squadron in Bahrain (which had an FR10 element). Protests were to no avail and he left II Squadron in October 1970, only eleven months after his arrival and days before his marriage. Life could be cruel! He reminisces now that this all too short a time had nevertheless been an invaluable, character forming experience which had ultimately done much for his self-confidence.

1971. The Final Months

There was no let up for the squadron throughout the bitter winter of 1970/71 as the end of its love

Bull's Eye. Al Mathie seeks to win the 'closest photograph' competition at Ahlhorn. *Al Mathie*

affair with the Hunter FR10 drew near. There was a flurry of activity to clear inventories and hand over what was needed from the squadron to the Phantom element which had already formed at Bruggen and Laarbruch. Flying continued, but now accompanied by a heavy programme of formalities, farewells and parties to celebrate another highly successful period in the history of the squadron. Before the FR10's last operational sortie on 26 February 1971, the 'new' II Squadron was up and running with the Phantom at Bruggen (before moving to Laarbruch), with the now Squadron Leader Sandy Wilson again as a flight commander. Sandy joined two Hunter men in their FR10s for a unique photograph of the outgoing and incoming aircraft, but he unwisely bet champagne that, now with a second pair of eyes in his aircraft, he would not be caught napping in the air. This was grist to the mill for Tim Thorn who, by fair means or foul, soon had Sandy's Phantom in his sights and recorded dead ahead on his Hunter's F95 camera. The champagne tasted good.

Gin Run. Al Mathie escorts Dutch TF-104 back to Holland with a precious cargo of gin. *Al Mathie*

Second to None. II Squadron in 1970, Squadron Leader 'Moose' David in command as the FR10's days draw to a close. *Moose David*

Farewell 'Shafe'. Moose David, aided by Pete Atkins, greet Bill ('Shafe') Sheppard back from his last trip with the squadron in the traditional manner. *II Sqn*

Temporary Gate Guard. Overnight, one of II Squadron's last FR10s took up residence where the Spitfire once stood in front of Station HQ at Gutersloh – only to disappear during the following day. *Tim Thorn & Moose David*

With mixed emotions during the drawdown, the II Squadron officers decided to leave a lasting reminder of a great era for all at Gutersloh to see. On a dark and snowy night after a midnight briefing at the boss's house, they manhandled and towed one of their faithful but now redundant FR10s along the road past Flying Wing HQ and round the corner on to the sacred turf in front of Station HQ. This aircraft had been a 'hangar queen' after a fire in the fuselage; it had suffered 'Cat 4' damage, had no engine and would never fly again, but it served their purpose admirably. The journey was, however, easier said than done, because the wingspan exceeded the gap between bordering trees and roadsigns. However, two of the officers involved, believed to have been Derek Bridge and Dave Hill, had surveyed the route and were said to have very cleverly cut and hinged offending obstacles beforehand and temporarily laid some trees to the ground to enable unimpeded passage, after which they were all restored to

I'm Back! Sandy Wilson with his Phantom and the two Hunter friends. *Sandy Wilson*

Bagshaw's Privilege. David Bagshaw had the privilege of demonstrating the squadron's FR10 to the C-in-C RAF Germany, AM Sir Harold Martin. *Al Mathie*

normal. What a very sleepy corporal policeman in the Guardroom thought of this nocturnal activity, led by a squadron leader, is not known, but he let the matter pass. Much satisfied with their work, the team repaired once more to the boss's residence to celebrate their achievement in the time-honoured manner. Sadly, their euphoria was short lived; on the following day the squadron was ordered to return its trophy to the hangar, there to await an inglorious end.

C-in-C RAF Germany, the legendary Air Marshal Sir Harold 'Micky' Martin, reviewed the Handover Parade at Gutersloh (now commanded by Group Captain Mike Miller). Dave Bagshaw gave a short flying-display and joined Moose David who led the last six FR10s back to Dunsfold on 2 March 1971. There they were set upon at once by Hawker's engineers to be modified for impatient foreign customers. It was the end of an era.

Chapter 5
No. IV (AC) Squadron

No. IV Squadron Crest.

New Home Sweet Home. The Officers Mess and Officers Married Quarters, RAF Gutersloh. *IV Sqn & Pete Highton*

No. IV (AC) Squadron was formed from B Flight of No. II (AC) Squadron at Farnborough in September 1912, with Breguet Biplanes. Its badge, bearing the motto *In Futurum Videre* (To see into the Future) with the central motif of 'a sun in splendour divided by a flash of lightning' was approved by King Edward VIII in 1936. Committed mainly to tactical reconnaissance the squadron had an enviable record in WWI and WW2, in the latter with Lysanders, Tomahawks, Mustangs, Mosquitos, Spitfires and Typhoons, before converting to jets in 1950. It then served in fighter and fighter bomber roles before being firmly wedded to FR again, very briefly with the Swift FR5 and then with the Hunter FR10 in January 1961.

1961: A Very Good Start
On 30 December 1960 IV Squadron disbanded as a Hunter F6 squadron at Jever, to re-form on 1 January 1961 at Gutersloh as an FR squadron, using assets from 79 Squadron which had just disbanded and laid up its Standard. The squadron's rapid transition to the FR10 and the new role was facilitated most effectively by transferring some recce experienced pilots from 79 Squadron, converting those Swift pilots who had not flown the Hunter to the FR10, and acquainting the fighter pilots from the original IV Squadron with the FR role.

Squadron Leader 'Buck' Buchanan, the last commander of 79 Squadron, now took over IV Squadron, with a strong team of eleven other pilots, all with either Hunter or Swift experience. They were: Flight Lieutenants 'Bunny' Warren,

NATO Defenders. A IV Squadron FR10 taxys past resident Hunter F6s of 14 Squadron, visiting Javelins and Lightings at RAF Gutersloh. *Tony Buttler*

Bryan Carter, John Nevill, Kit Netherton, Eric Smith, 'Oscar' Wild, Clive Haggett, Pat King, Pete Highton and Graham Hounsell. Another pilot, Flying Officer Arthur Vine would be promoted to flight lieutenant during the tour. Three more Swift pilots from 79 Squadron, Flight Lieutenants 'Fergy' Ferguson, Glyn Chapman and 'Harv' Harvie, also spent some time with IV

Achtung Spitfire! Once based at Gutersloh, a Spitfire now stands guard between the Main Gate and Station HQ. *IV Sqn*

Squadron pending postings, proving invaluable in support. Flight Lieutenant L.J. Vickery was the engineering officer. Eight Hunter FR10s and a T7 were established and photographic support was provided by 7 MFPU commanded by Flight Lieutenant P.R. Davies.

Oscar Wild had flown the Hunter already (with the prestigious 111 Squadron and as a member of its Black Arrows aerobatic team) and had eighteen months FR experience on the Swift, so he was the ideal man to draw comparisons between the two aircraft in the FR role. He pays proper tribute to the Swift for its low level attributes and speed, which he needed when straying accidentally into East Germany, but also recalls that he nearly killed himself when trying to manoeuvre the aircraft as he had the Hunter, so he welcomed the Hunter's greater agility and range. He was one of several pilots consulted before modifications were made to the Hunter's cockpit ergonomics to optimise the aircraft for the recce role. The changes which found most favour with the FR pilots were the repositioning of the G4B compass from behind the control column to bring the instrument more into the immediate line of sight and moving the gunsight to one side to give better visibility ahead for high speed, very low-level operations. Delivering a T7 to the MU at RAF St Athan, Bryan Carter and Oscar Wild flew the first two FR10s for IV Squadron to Germany on 5 January 1961, prudently finding out first how to operate the UHF radio (the Swift had VHF) and the Automatic Direction Finding (ADF) radio compass.

Within three working days the requisite acceptance checks and air tests had been completed on both aircraft and by the end of the month a total of five FR10s were flying regularly. Meanwhile, the remaining Swifts helped maintain flying continuity while being replaced progressively by the Hunters. For this the squadron commander heaped credit upon his engineering officer and the groundcrew, as they continued to support a mix of aircraft, and proclaimed the FR10 'already a great success'.

Eric Smith flew one of the last sorties in the Swift and observed in the ORB that its departure, 'was not without some pangs of regret'. Surprisingly, this came from one of several pilots who had ejected from the FR5 and it reflected the genuine fondness among most pilots for a robust aircraft which flew so comfortably at low level.

Trail Blazers. No IV Squadron, 1961. (L to R) Flight Lieutenants Graham Hounsell, Clive Haggett, Pat King, Squadron Leader 'Buck' Buchanan (CO), Bryan Carter, Eric Smith, Oscar Wild and Peter Highton. *IV Sqn*

John Nevill, who had also ejected from a Swift, was one of the first on the squadron to have a serious incident in an FR10 when he lost his canopy on take-off, one rail causing 'Cat 3' damage to an engine intake – but he landed safely. The brake parachute mechanism also gave trouble at the start, leading to eight Special Occurrence Reports (SORs) in this first full month of FR10 flying.

This start was followed by another splendid achievement in February when the squadron overflew its already ambitious target of 220 hours, helped by the many sensible range trials carried out in the early days. These revealed that low-level range could be increased by 63 nm if two 100 gall drop tanks were carried on the outer wing pylons in addition to the two 230 gall tanks inboard. From Gutersloh in this configuration, the

End of an Era and Start of Another. OC 79 (Swift FR5) Squadron becomes OC IV (Hunter FR10) Squadron, as the outgoing and incoming Standards were paraded at Gutersloh. *Peter Highton*

FR10 could reach the Polish border, fly high-low-high to and from East Anglia or at high level non-stop to Malta, these ranges being well beyond the Swift's capabilities. Hawker submitted plans for extending the 230 gall tanks by 3 ft, increasing their fuel capacity to 330 gall with the same frontal area, but this was rejected on the grounds that lower 'G' limitations would result.

There had been very little night flying in the Swift at Gutersloh, the 2,000 yard runway being considered a little short for safety, but there was no such constraint with the FR10 or the T7 (which were equipped with brake parachutes) so night flying became part of the training syllabus. The FR force would now be better trained to carry out dawn and dusk sorties (to obtain information visually if not with cameras), night survival scrambles and deployments.

The new capability offered by the Hunter was soon recognised in changes to the war tasks, Oscar Wild recalling that his Hunter would indeed take him almost to the East German/Polish border. *En route*, he would be required to photograph that most formidable Reichstrasse 1 road bridge over the Elbe at Magdeburg, which connected Russian-held Berlin with the Ruhr, a potential strike target for NATO's bombers. When Oscar crossed the bridge by road in 1976, on the only route open then to Berlin for British forces, the exhaust on his car broke loose and his temporary repair understandably attracted much attention from the East German police (VOPO). This was not how he had expected to recce the bridge The Gutersloh FR10 pilots knew something about the corridors to Berlin, taking part in the annual British, French and American tripartite contingency exercises aimed at keeping them open to Allied traffic if closure was ever threatened by Warsaw Pact forces. In this year the Hunters would be joined at Gutersloh by F-100s of the FAF and USAFE.

In March, the squadron began a six month detachment to Jever while the runway at Gutersloh was refurbished. Even with this turbulence, leaving only thirteen days to fly 210 hours, the target was again achieved with the few pilots who remained available as a bout of sickness and extraneous commitments began to bite; leave now had to be monitored closely and sandwiches became the order of the day for lunch. The T7 was also busy, adding 12 hours to this total for important instrument training and proficiency checks. It was now time to select

three pilots for the first Royal Flush competition with the FR10, to be held in May at Beauverchain in Belgium. Kit Netherton, John Nevill and Eric Smith were finally selected to represent the squadron in the run-off against II Squadron, with veteran Swift pilot and former Royal Flush 'ace' Harv Harvie as the Hunter team manager.

Sceptics might say that political pressures and demands from the strongest voices to benefit national interests were responsible for the ever changing rules for Royal Flush, rather than any review of operational considerations. Certainly there was no joy in the British camp when this year's crop of new conditions called for stand-off photography of large target areas, tasks which required the FR10s to fly at very vulnerable heights of at least 500-1,000 ft. This again showed a lack of understanding of the optimum use of the aircraft.

Notwithstanding these rules, operational training was now being carried out at speeds of 540 kts and as low as was allowed. Turbulence affected the Hunter more than its predecessor and its new finish was soon showing signs of wear and tear, while struts between the mainplane and tank pylons were jumping from their sockets. Harv Harvie lost both inboard tanks in flight, one causing damage to his pitot tube which required a precautionary landing at Laarbruch. Thereafter, all drop-tank supports were strengthened. Brake parachutes continued to give trouble, one streaming inadvertently in the air, and undercarriage defects led to a temporary grounding of FR10s in May, but this did not affect the forthcoming Royal Flush.

Royal Flush was the highlight of that month with Eric Smith representing IV Squadron and the Hunters coming second only to the more experienced French Mirage team. In the overall results, 2ATAF beat 4ATAF. However, it was Exercise Gentleman's Relish which stretched the squadron's resources to the limit, with dawn to dusk missions mounted from detachments at Bruggen against unrealistic targets at maximum, sometimes excessive ranges, again raising questions as to the efficacy of the tasking and targeting agencies.

Less frustrating and certainly more enjoyable was the 10 day exchange visit to the RCAF at Baden Soellingen which followed in June. Training over largely unknown terrain and countryside was always welcome and the natural affinity between the two air forces at work and play made this a particularly agreeable detachment. When fuel was available after an operational training exercise the Gutersloh pilots enjoyed a little sightseeing, practising their photography with 'happy snaps' over the Black Forest and the captivating state of Bavaria.

Back at Jever, IV Squadron performed very well in its first NATO Taceval with the Hunter, having all available FR10s on the line within 50 minutes of the 0400 hours start on that July morning, after which the pilots excelled in the subsequent, realistic tasking. They were not so successful in the Sassoon competition which followed, coming a disappointing fifth among the six contenders, but things would get better. With the aircraft now cleared for gunnery, initial air-to-ground sorties preceded an air-to-air APC at Sylt. Three weeks on the holiday island of Sylt in August was every FR pilot's dream and with 24 hours on duty followed by 24 hours off, it was all they could have wished for. Buck Buchanan was in his element, being a good shot in the air and on the ground he was often seen with a 12-bore under his arm, his dog to heel, off for a bit of game shooting. Eric Smith remembers that when the AOC came to visit them at Sylt and asked how the shooting was going, Buck replied "Not too bad sir, two grouse and a partridge last time out". This first squadron shoot with the FR10 was not encouraging; without radar ranging, the guns were fired at pegged ranges using as yet unproven harmonisation patterns at 12,000 ft and the 20.5 per cent average over 99 effective sorties fell below expectations. Little can be found in the records of the squadron's extraneous activities during what would be its last APC at Sylt before the *Luftwaffe* took over the base, and personal memories seem rather vague, but perhaps that is just as well. At the end of the APC Eric Smith was detached to RAF West Raynham to attend the Day Fighter Combat School (DFCS).

When the squadron returned to Gutersloh and a new runway in September, only seven pilots remained available (Eric Smith being detached and Kit Netherton on leave in his native South Africa), so they had all the flying they needed. Excellent operational training was derived from the autumn Exercises Panzer Grenadier, Treble Chance, Extra Dry and Spearpoint, but pilot fatigue was now beginning to tell and there was little respite ahead. In November's Exercise Quicktrain, the squadron had two aircraft at the runway threshold within 30 minutes and flew five of the seven available continuously throughout the exercise.

At the height of this activity, on 7 November 1961, Buck Buchanan relinquished command to Squadron Leader Ray Bannard, and Flight Lieutenant C.L. Burke took over 7 MFPU; the outgoing incumbents surely well pleased with this excellent start for the squadron in its new incarnation.

As this first year with the FR10 drew to a close, Ray Bannard had every reason to conclude in his monthly report that the squadron was in good heart. Despite much turbulence and some teething troubles with the new aircraft the transition had gone smoothly, the aircraft and pilots were fully operational and the flying task had been exceeded. Looking to the future, Ray declared his intention to prioritise a re-examination of crucial penetration and egress profiles and evasive tactics against the increasingly formidable Warsaw Pact defences. He announced that IV Squadron would provide the RAF's short range team recce for Royal Flush at Ramstein in 1962, but warned that, with the projected postings plot, there would be a shortage of pilots in the spring. On extraneous activities, he confirmed that the squadron expected a Royal visit in 1962 but that the intended celebration of its 50th birthday might be at risk because of a fifteen month break in service at the end of WW1. There was another busy year ahead.

1962: Consolidation

Eric Smith, who had returned from DFCS to the squadron in December, now had plenty of opportunity to rehearse his newly acquired skills to the benefit of the squadron and to prepare himself for his impending appointment to the DFCS staff, as winter weather forced the squadron into high-level combat training. The first months of 1962 passed quietly but the predicted movement of squadron officers soon began. Bunny Warren (now a squadron leader) and Bryan Carter were posted, John Nevill and Kit Netherton replacing them as flight commanders, while Flight Lieutenants Bo Plummer and Bob Price filled the vacancies. Pete Highton was detached for an indeterminate period to Leconfield as a contender for the RAF's gunnery team and Flying Officer Shaw took over as squadron engineering officer.

By April, things were hotting up; Royal Flush training had begun again in earnest for the competition in May, with Eric Smith as the team manager; 7 MFPU would provide support for the RAF's team and 244 Signals Unit the in-flight reporting facility. In parallel, the squadron detached six pilots, four aircraft and twenty groundcrew to the RNoAF base at Rygge on an exchange exercise and completed a very successful air-to-ground gunnery programme which resulted in an average of 43 per cent and stoppage rate of 1:1295. As expected, the shortage of pilots now required the squadron to co-opt pilots from II Squadron to fulfil all these commitments.

Half the squadron was detached to Ramstein in May, first for the process of selecting the final team and then for Royal Flush itself, but it all proved worthwhile when the squadron won outright in the short range event. Very few resources had been left at Gutersloh for routine training or other commitments, but one of the squadron's FR10s took to the air first in a no-notice Taceval. The successful Royal Flush team returned to intensive preparation for exercise Sassoon, stimulating a renewed debate on the relative value of these academic exercises *vis-a-vis* more realistic operational training. There was little time left for the latter with another surprise alert in Exercise Quicktrain, a Royal visit and the Queen's birthday parade which, as always, involved numerous rehearsals and an inevitable 'spring clean' of the station. This had indeed been what Ray Bannard called 'a truly magnificent month for the squadron', but he also warned of the dangers inherent in any anti-climax which might follow.

In fact, there was no need to worry; soon it was all hands to the pump again to prepare for the squadron's 50th anniversary, now sanctioned officially after deliberations on the fifteen month 'hibernation'. Bachelor Flight Lieutenants Stanford Howard and John Owen arrived, both with previous Hunter experience and useful musical talents, while Pete Highton was covering himself in glory gaining the highest score within the RAF's gunnery team and coming second overall in the NATO competition. Eric Smith, in the wake of his success on the squadron and particularly his achievements in the 1961 and 1962 Royal Flush competitions, was posted to the staff of DFCS. Individuals were making their mark on IV Squadron.

With Sassoon postponed until October because of unsuitable weather, IV Squadron now

had the respite it needed. The 50th birthday was celebrated in style on 11 July and its Hunters were now being scheduled regularly on Exercise Blue Diamond to Norway and on the 1,135 nm trip to Malta on Exercise Southern Ranger.

In August, the whole squadron deployed to Chivenor for its first APC in the UK. This may not have been Sylt, with all its social attractions on the beach and in Westerland, but at least there was no need for dugouts, windbrakes or protective baskets on the warmer sands at Braunton and Croyde, and there was always the 'Willy's Arms' and 'Three Tuns' for refreshment and to find new friends, so the squadron was content. The Hartland Point range and radar provided the means to complete 162 effective sorties, during which 6,178 rounds were fired to achieve a most creditable squadron average of 30.6 per cent. John Nevill claimed the highest score of 98.1 per cent and Pat King the remarkable average of 58.6 per cent, but for the squadron the icing on the cake came with a win against a team selected from the best of the highly experienced staff on 229 OCU. The chosen men of the FR force were indeed 'all-rounders'. It seems surprising that, with so many recreational opportunities away from home, there were no reports of misdemeanour among officers or men of this 50-year old squadron. No wonder the squadron commander was well pleased in his report on the detachment.

The New Breed. Squadron Leader Ray Bannard (second left) with Flt Lts (L to R) Stanford Howard, John Owen, Bo Plummer (intake), John Heathcote (on wing), Barry Stott, Jock Beaton, Mike French and Ron Price – the cream of IV (AC) Squadron, 1962. *IV Sqn*

Going Places. High/Low/High profiles were always an operational option but here two IV Squadron FR10s were stretching their legs on a 'Blue Diamond' to Norway. *Peter Highton*

No sooner had the squadron returned to Germany in September than four of its aircraft, with supporting groundcrew and an element of 7 MFPU, were sent to Ankhialos Air Base in Greece for 8 days to support No. 54 (Hunter FGA9) Squadron, 16 Para Brigade and 2nd Hellenic Division in Exercise Falltrap, part of Exercise

Tourist Attraction. Marble Arch, Libya, was a popular attraction for Gutersloh's FR10s on 'Southern Rangers'. *IV Sqn*

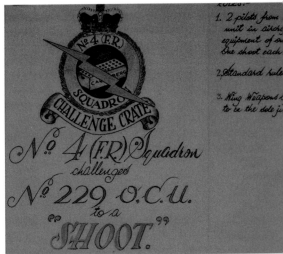

Sharp Shooters. IV Squadron went to RAF Chivenor in 1964 for their annual air-to-air gunnery camp, took on all-comers and won. *IV Sqn*

FLT LTS. J OWEN, S. HOWARD, R PRICE, P. KING, G. HOUNSELL. FLT LTS. B. PLUMMER, C. HAGGET, W. NETHERTON, SQN LDR R. BAN... FLT LTS. J NEVILL, M W...

Fallex. Living and working 'alfresco' in frequent heavy rain meant that this was no picnic, improvisation and self-help was the name of the game. Those who remained at Gutersloh had time to regroup and return to some sort of normality before a busy programme of exercises (Desert Rat, Silver Dollar, Canada Cup, Autumn Double and Playboy) in October, which generated 208 useful flying hours. Two experienced FR pilots, Kit Netherton and Graham Hounsell, departed and were replaced by Flight Lieutenant Ron Glynn and Flying Officer John Heathcote. Such intensive activity now began to take its toll, leading to very poor serviceability in November which limited flying

Can I Have a Helmet Too? Flight Lieutenant John Heathcote about to ride in the back seat of a USAF F-100. *IV Sqn*

Greek DIY Holiday? IV Squadron's 'DIY' detachment at the Greek base of Nea Ankhialos was no picnic in ten days of almost continuous torrential rain, Ron Price and Mike French dealing with their own F95 prints. *IV Sqn*

to 114 hours, but this released time to catch up on a rather neglected groundschool programme and target study. The Berlin corridor contingency exercise was held at Gutersloh again, John Heathcote taking the opportunity to fly in the back seat of a USAFE F-100.

Worse was to come when classic Gutersloh weather in December reduced flying to a mere 79 hours. However, 1962 had been a very fruitful and satisfying year overall, with much flying achieved and many accolades recorded. Ground training had also been satisfied and so attention

now turned to celebrations. The squadron officers gave the Officers Mess a party and enjoyed an equally memorable all-ranks dance; they also served the airmen with Christmas dinner in the time-honoured fashion and the more resilient accepted several invitations to sup ale in the barrack block bars.

1963: A Nomadic, Satisfying Year
The appalling weather persisted into 1963, in what was said to be one of the most severe winters in many years; the temperature rose above freezing point on only 3 days in January and a mere 72 hours were flown. For the first two weeks of February the airfield was again snow-bound but when conditions improved, with plenty of aircraft now serviceable, the squadron flew intensively for a total of 165 hours. Flight Lieutenant Pat O'Connor took over as squadron engineering officer and a new post of squadron PI, long overdue, was filled by Flight Lieutenant Eric Adamson. This was the state of the squadron when Flight Lieutenants Brian Meadley and Jock Beaton arrived to add further invaluable experience in the air and on the ground, and they were followed by ex-FGA pilot Flying Officer Barry Stott, as all thoughts now turned to Royal Flush scheduled for May.

The better weather and good serviceability persisted into March, resulting in the achievement of an unprecedented 282 flying hours; primarily, effort was devoted to

Showing The Flag. IV Squadron pilots looking for those elusive holes in the flag during their Armament Practice Camp at Leeuwarden in August 1963. *IV Sqn*

Fearsome Few. IV Squadron pilots on an exchange visit to 52 Wing, German Air Force, at Sylt in September 1963. *Mike French*

Those Were The Days. While on an exchange visit to a German Air Force squadron at Sylt, Brian Meadley and one of the hosts exchanged aircraft, Brian flying the RF-84F. *Brian Meadley*

Bannard's Nomads. The FR10 squadrons were rarely at home for long. *IV Sqn*

preparation for Royal Flush but 25 hours were also flown at night. This trend continued into April and May, enjoyed mainly by those pilots progressively down-selected to compete in the

Dress Code. Sweaters were definitely not de rigueur in the 1960s! *Mike French*

Lethal Brew. The contents of 'Pimms 79' displayed (perhaps unwisely) before a memorable IV Squadron party, but the mix was classified. *IV Sqn*

competition itself , in which the squadron again did well (Chapter Seven).

As the competition fervour subsided, Clive Haggett and Oscar Wild departed the squadron, Oscar none too enamoured with his ground appointment as a flight commander at RAF Locking. Flight Lieutenants Mike French and Mike Milner arrived, the latter soon to be detached to DFCS. All this continued to underline the pilot turbulence which Ray had predicted. The other ranks strength remained fairly steady at fifty-eight.

The successful APC at Chivenor in 1962 was not to be repeated in 1963, an alternative venue having been found at the RNLAF base of Leeuwarden, using the ranges on the northern Dutch islands in August. Nothing is recorded in the ORB on this detachment but personal memories suggest that, while Leeuwarden could not be compared at a social level with Sylt in the summer, or even Chivenor, everyone found plenty to do at work and play, with perhaps a little more time to concentrate on gunnery.

It was back to Sylt in October, not too late for the ritual soirees with late holiday makers at the

At the Helm. Wing Commander 'Pinky' Mandeville, OC Flying Wing (centre) and Group Captain David Evans, Station Commander, sharing IV Squadron's hospitality. *IV Sqn*

Good Show. Ron Price was one of many FR10 pilots who received official accolades for the manner in which they dealt with emergencies in the air. *IV Sqn*

Copper Kettle, Witte Haus or Chez Katrinas, and not this time for an APC but for an exchange with a GAF RF-84F squadron, living in their very different messes. Guns were also the order of the day in November, with an intensive air-to-ground programme at Nordhorn which raised the squadron average to 56.6 per cent. Bannard's nomads were rarely at home for long.

The month culminated in a final celebration of the squadron's 50th year on the 30 November 1963, with the eminent Marshal of the Royal Air Force Sir John Slessor as the principal guest, beginning the traditional run of parties over the Christmas period. There was plenty to celebrate at the end of another very good year. Bo Plummer, one of the architects of IV Squadron's excellent weapons performance, became the Wing's PAI, he being replaced on the squadron by Flight Lieutenant Tony Richardson.

1964: Change of Command

After a successful command, Ray Bannard handed over IV Squadron in January 1964 to the newly promoted Squadron Leader Mike Milner who had recently returned from DFCS. Uncharacteristically, the winter weather was kind and the squadron was able to fly 376 hours during the first two months of the year. At the end of February, Gutersloh did well in the NATO Taceval, the squadron adding the final touch with all its eight aircraft carrying out an operational shoot at Nordhorn. It then went from strength to strength by flying 277 hours in April, in preparation for the 1964 Royal Flush in its new format (Chapter Seven).

Royal Flush in May was followed by the annual AOC's Inspection and Parade, with all the rehearsals adding to an already busy programme, after which the squadron detached to Leeuwarden for another APC. This year, after muted suggestions that the Officers' Mess was not anxious to offer hospitality again after previous visits by the FR10 squadrons, the officers stayed in the Amicitia Hotel downtown. May was also the month in which 'IV's Four' was born, officially as a 'flat' aerobatic display team, led very ably by Brian Meadley and for which there would be a great demand throughout northern Europe. The team performed first at Borkenberge on 31 May and next at Hunsborn in July.

The six aircraft required for Quicktrain in June were generated in an impressive 2 hours 30 minutes despite Sassoon training being in full swing. The competition itself was held in September and then it was back to more realistic operational training in support of the army's autumn exercises.

Flying low and fast carried the risk of bird strikes, often without causing critical damage but sometimes placing both pilot and aircraft in jeopardy. An increasing number of these incidents would result in 'Birdtam' warnings and to the curtailment of specific flying operations in particular areas during periods of bird migration.

Plentiful flying during the summer, with 245 hours achieved in May and 231 in June, came to an abrupt end in October when, for the first time since March, the squadron failed to reach its target; age and operational demands on the aircraft were now beginning to tell.

There was even less flying in November and December, initially with half the squadron away on an exchange with the Danes at Karup. Meanwhile, the social programme at Gutersloh was intensifying as the now Squadron Leader Eric Smith (the very able and experienced Swift and Hunter FR pilot and former member of the squadron) replaced Mike Milner as squadron commander. Flight Lieutenant Doug McDermott took over 7 MFPS from Pat Burke and Flight Lieutenant Pete Headley, with a previous Hunter tour behind him, joined the squadron. The December Quicktrain again went well, starting at the unusual time of 1730 hours and including an unprecedented vertical dispersal at night, which proved the ability of Gutersloh's radar operators to marshal the Wing into the requisite survival pattern safely.

1965: The Pattern Established
No. IV Squadron started 1965 with only six aircraft available but managed to fly 158 hours in typical January weather. Tony Richardson represented RAF Germany on the Cresta Run, promptly breaking his ankle, and Flying Officer Johnny Baines joined the squadron. On special occasions (or whenever there was an excuse) IV Squadron perpetuated a 79 Squadron tradition, very unwisely imbibing a lethal concoction known as 'Pimms 79' from a huge silver tankard, presented by ex-79 Squadron pilot Roger Pyrah. One such occasion was Eric Smith's renewal of operational status and welcome to Gutersloh's new OC Flying Wing, Wing Commander 'Pinky'

Going North. Four FR10 of IV Squadron over Norway. *IV Sqn*

Mandeville. As an ex-member of 79 Squadron, Eric knew what he was in for and survived the ordeal, as did Pinky, but the latter's crepe-soled shoes melted and disintegrated when exposed to the Pimms! Perhaps concerned by the sight of this, Eric exercised his prerogative as squadron commander and true Scotsman, by revoking the tradition and introducing a new celebratory drink – a quaish of whisky. However, old traditions die hard and Pimms 79 soon returned to IV Squadron's social agenda.

The squadron earned a 'One' overall in February's Taceval, called at 0530 hours. Seven of its eight aircraft were put to good use despite poor weather and completed thirty sorties in the two days, including eight effective air-to-ground shoots. Ron Glyn was now manning the tower at Nordhorn Range, having been posted from the squadron medically unfit. Bob Price, who had been rewarded recently with a 'Good Show' for bringing back an FR10 in difficult circumstances was also posted, followed by the squadron's engineer, Pat O'Connor, who was replaced by Flight Lieutenant Peter Scott.

Royal Flush training began again in March, interrupted when increased tension with the Eastern Bloc committed several FR pilots from the Wing to flying on sorties in RAF Argosy aircraft demonstrating NATO's right to pass down the corridor to Berlin. This enabled them to see inquisitive Warsaw Pact fighters at close quarters, sometimes rather too close for comfort.

April and May were full months, with a Royal Visit by Her Majesty the Queen to Gutersloh in May, preceded by many rehearsals for this and the associated flypast. The visit itself had its moments (Chapter Four), but great credit for its success overall must go to Gutersloh's OC Administrative Wing, Wing Commander Claude Rennie. One of his many responsibilities was the Royal luncheon, for which several practices resulted in an apparently flawless event. That said, not everyone could be served simultaneously and lesser mortals at the table ends had their plates whisked away as soon as the Royal party had finished eating, long before many were empty. Nor could Claude Rennie be blamed for a problem at breakfast on the Royal train, which was parked in the grounds behind the Officers Mess; the potential disaster avoided when a cup of milk for the Royal tea was 'borrowed' from Pinky Mandeville's nearby residence.

This momentous event was followed by an AOC's Inspection and Royal Flush. The new home based concept for Royal Flush persisted (Chapter Seven), albeit with some rules again modified to placate the strong and requiring more PIs to cope with the increased volume of work.

This year the squadron was reinforced by Flight Lieutenants A.C. Smith and J. Lister, Sergeant P. Timpson and J/T F. S. Nixon from the Joint Air Reconnaissance and Intelligence

Fit For A Queen. Several full scale dress rehearsals perfected a lunch for HM The Queen during her visit to Gutersloh. *Sir David Evans*

Centre (JARIC), while Flight Lieutenants K. Garrett and W.G. Luty RAFVR were there to observe. Eric Adamson saw the exercise out before being replaced as resident PI by Bill Kelly, a one time Stirling bomber pilot who also belonged to that exclusive club of F-86 Sabre pilots who served at RAF Linton-on-Ouse. Bill had many a good tale to tell and was responsible for some himself. The present C-in-C RAF Germany, Air Marshal Sir Denis Spotswood, then the station commander at Linton, remembered that Bill had a prodigious thirst and was a natural selection for bar officer there. As such, Bill took his duties seriously, spending many hours monitoring service in the bar himself. With this sense of duty it was clear that he could not contain his bar bill within the then regulation £7 a month and generated a second, attributed to a fictitious 'Flying Officer Crockett D'. This did not go unnoticed; when he invited Dennis Spotswood to take a farewell drink with him, the station commander thanked him but said: "If you don't mind, Bill, I'll have this one on Flying Officer Crockett". Bill Kelly had little fear of senior officers, many of whom he had served with as contemporaries, and he enjoyed the opportunity to keep his younger brethren in line.

With the new style Royal Flush the GLOs and 261 GLS had also assumed a new importance, the incumbent Major Brian Cobb,13/18 Hussars, giving way to Major Michael Wise, Grenadier Guards (only the best for IV Squadron). In May's competition the squadron` covered 162 targets in fifty four missions and were well satisfied with their collective performance.

After this hectic month, the squadron began a nomadic existence as work began again on Gutersloh's runway. After first operating in field conditions (duck boards essential) from a disused dispersal at Laarbruch, IV Squadron went north in July for another APC at Leeuwarden, taking over from II Squadron and again staying in the luxury of the Amicitia Hotel. Unexpectedly poor weather reduced the number of live firings to five/pilot and the squadron's air-to-air average to 18.4 per cent. It was then back to Laarbruch and preparations for a two week exchange exercise for a fortunate half of the squadron, led by Eric Smith, to Norway and the base at Rygge again. Aware of how to be popular from the start, the visitors secreted two cases of whisky and copious quantities of other drink into their baggage, to be produced for joint

Captain Mike Nuttall, IV Squadron GLO, captained RAF Gutersloh's rugby team in 1966. *Mike Nuttall*

consumption at opportune times. During the first party, Jock Beaton told Eric that one Norwegian pilot had been to the drink table frequently, each time to fill his tumbler with neat whisky before disappearing outside again. The next time he appeared for a refill, Eric congratulated him on his choice and capacity, and suggested that in true Scottish fashion they down the next one together – in one. His guest could only comply, but vanished immediately thereafter.

Flight Lieutenant Jim Dymond, fresh from the recce flight in Aden, had now arrived to replace bachelor John Owen who departed on an exchange posting to the USAF's RF-4C Phantom recce force at Shaw AFB, South Carolina. The squadron also welcomed Flight Lieutenant Iain Weston, already a seasoned Hunter pilot, who would contribute much to the squadron's future success. Away from the domestics of home life, there had been plenty of flying for the nomads with monthly totals all well above 200 hours in the three months before everyone returned to Gutersloh at the end of August, straight into Sassoon training.

No. IV Squadron came second in September's Sassoon, and then returned to operational training in October's army exercises. When weather permitted, Autumn Handicap allowed pilots into the normally prohibited Air Defence Identification Zone (ADIZ), on the border with East Germany, while Double Deal provided a great number of good military targets in the field and Right Foot involved many very useful line searches. The air defence Exercise Co-op, in which the FR10 provided targets, was not so welcome. In a year when major incidents had been mercifully few, Barry Stott was commended for an excellent flame-out recovery into the busy USAF base at Wiesbaden.

It was all change again in November, with the squadron's second GLO, Captain Mike Nuttall leaving and Flight Lieutenants Colin Richardson and John Osborne, both experienced fighter pilots, joining. The industrious Mike Nuttall had also found time in the winter months to captain the station's rugby team, although he failed to seduce many volunteers from the squadron to join him. In his final report on 1965 Eric Smith was upbeat, remembering the many successes of the past year. He reported that the flying target had been exceeded by 100 hours (an improvement on the previous year) and noted that the upper air work carried out when the weather was poor at low level was reflected in their air combat performance.

1966: Triumph and Tragedy

There was more turbulence among the officers in early 1966. The departure of Barry Stott and Mike French was followed by that of one of the squadron's most colourful characters, Brian Meadley, while Flight Lieutenants Hoppy Granville-White (pilot) and 'Steve' Stephens (PI) joined the squadron. With winter sports always high on the agenda for FR pilots, Pete Headley earned a place on RAF Germany's ski team which, perhaps surprisingly, beat USAFE on its home ground at Garmish. Peter's need for speed was reflected in his choice of cars, an E-Type Jaguar – red of course. Sadly this beautiful car was slightly dented when it came into conflict with an immovable object one night as Peter, probably tired from the day's work, sought a little fresh air in it after leaving the bar. On the following morning the station commander, David Evans, discussed the incident with Peter and prescribed a rest from driving for a month, taking care of Peter's driving licence to help him avoid any temptation. After a decent pause, Peter pleaded for this sentence to be reduced on the grounds that what he really needed was a little female company and some exercise at a nearby dance. Needless to say, this was refused and Peter left the group captain saying: "I thought you would say that, but I hope you didn't mind me asking". No comment!

This was typical of Group Captain David Evans, whose time in the service stretched back to WW2 and who clearly preferred to curb high spirits sensibly rather than have to encourage them. Equally welcome was the latitude he gave to his unit commanders. Throughout, there was a refreshingly old fashioned attitude towards orders and instructions, according to the well established adage 'rules are for the guidance of wise men and the total obedience of fools'. Given their head, the executives did their best, knowing that they were being relied on to produce results and that attitudes might change if they did not. David Evans claimed to have been even-handed in his administration of justice, which included some jurisdiction outside the station. He pointed to the manner in which he dealt with no fewer than fourteen parking and driving offences in Gutersloh town, believed to have included one involving his wife, but he failed to reveal the

punishments he awarded. With command and leadership now becoming increasingly intolerant elsewhere, Gutersloh thrived on this mutual understanding of how things should be and this resulted in a happy station which earned plaudits on many fronts.

Back on the flight line, another Taceval in April interrupted the work-up for Royal Flush, but the squadron was up to it, with a 'One' being awarded for the forty six sorties it flew in two days.

Then in May came a more visible accolade, when IV Squadron was named the 'Outstanding Reconnaissance Squadron in 2ATAF' and placed third overall (after two French squadrons) in Royal Flush XI. Eric Smith claimed, with every justification, that morale was now 'at an all-time high'. Flight Lieutenant 'Taff' Wallis was also named 'top day pilot' and 7 MFPU, under Doug McDermott, was given a special mention for its performance. Colin Richardson had been the team manager and the six reinforcement PIs were Flight Lieutenant Hood, Sergeants O'Neill and Hollis from JARIC, Flight Lieutenants Luty and Swift of the VR and Flight Lieutenant Watt from RAF Germany (Chapter Seven). The NATO celebration of this splendid achievement was held at Strasbourg in June.

IV's Four Re-born. In 1966, Flight Lieutenant Iain Weston led Flight Lieutenants Peter Headley (No.2), Johnny Baines (No.3) and Peter Gover (No.4) in another successful season for IV's Four. IV Sqn

Perhaps all this inspired the newly arrived Flight Lieutenant Peter Gover, another of that new breed of university entrants with only one QFI tour behind him. Eric Smith admitted that he wondered whether Peter would be able to cope with the exacting low-level role, but later said: "It was with great relief and indeed pleasure that he proved to be totally dedicated and a first class recce pilot".

In June, quite out of the blue, the Secretary of State for Defence, the Rt Hon Dennis Healey, forecast that the FR10s would be redeployed to Celle by the end of 1967. The men at the sharp end thought this far too close to the border for comfort, and indeed it never happened. The only other fact worth recording that month was the extraordinary air-to-ground gunnery score of 79 per cent by Hoppy Granville-White on a first run attack. Thereafter, it was back to operational training mixed with preparation for the Sassoon competition and several appearances by Iain Weston on the display circuit, both as the Hunter solo aerobatic pilot and new leader of IV's Four.

Then came tragedy, when John Osborne was killed at Gutersloh aboard a Zlin light aerobatic aircraft from a local German flying club. Watching from ATC, a IV Squadron colleague remembers: 'It was with total horror that we watched the aircraft flick over at low altitude and crash back on to the runway, bursting into flames. We raced to the scene but there was nothing we could do'.

Exercise Link West was mounted out of RAF West Raynham in September, the highly competent FR pilots again having cause to criticise a targeting and tasking system which failed to understand what the force could do and should not be asked to do. Until these agencies were staffed by able and dedicated men with the right background, properly rehearsed within the full system to be used in war, much up-to-the-minute and potentially invaluable intelligence would continue to be wasted.

Towards the end of 1966 Peter Gover took over as scribe for the squadron's ORB and described December as a 'lost month'. Prudently, he did not record then the story he tells now of the hush which descended on the usually noisy flight planning room when Eric Smith entered and harangued Peter loudly on his choice of 'non-tactical' IPs for his next sortie. It was only when he left that the minions came to life again and confided that the boss was enduring another of his non-smoking spells. Later, it was revealed that contingency plans existed for these dark times, with Eric's wife, Sheena, ready to hand Jock Beaton a packet of Eric's favourite brand to 'lend' to Eric when things got really bad. Peter also recalls a day when Eric, perhaps suffering another period of abstinence, ordered a programme of high-level cine weave with him, as squadron commander, 'towing' first at around 50,000 ft and the shooters starting on the 'perch' 2,000 ft above, 'as we did at DFCS'. In FR10s carrying two 230 gall drop tanks this was a very tall order indeed for the most accomplished fighter pilot and for lesser mortals it was nigh impossible, as Eric found when his turn came on the perch in his own aircraft 'Alpha', which was known to have the best performance on the squadron.

Most fast-jet pilots are unable to resist a challenge and those in the FR10 force were no exception. Peter Gover was among several who encountered a WW2 Sea Fury, painted red and used for towing aerial targets, in the air near Cologne. He took an F95 photograph of this rare aircraft before its pilot manoeuvred into his six o'clock position, clearly looking for a fight. Unable to out-turn this powerful piston-engine fighter in the horizontal or in a vertical scissors to port, he eventually found he could do so in a

Easy Prey? Peter Gover (and others) found that this German registered Sea Fury was no easy match in a turning fight! *Peter Gover*

Career Change? Senior ranks of 5 Field Regiment RA, Mansergh Barracks, who cared for their fighting vehicles, recommended that these IV Squadron pilots did not give up their day jobs. *IV Sq*

starboard scissors, attributing this to the effects of the piston engine's torque. There are two sequels to this tale. The first was that, as a result of the fight, Peter had run himself so short of fuel that he had to divert to Wildenrath where, to avoid censure, he pleaded a possible hydraulic leak which, to no-one's surprise, turned out to be spurious. The second came later in the year when Peter met his adversary at a Dumple Flying Club party. This worthy man turned out to be an ex-WW2 *Luftwaffe* pilot, who commented that it had been a long time since he had been beaten in combat – and never by a jet.

The poor winter weather now kept the aircraft on the ground for long spells, but when Hoppy Granville-White was posted unexpectedly to become ADC to the Chief of the Air Staff, there was enough flying for all with a pilot strength of only eight. Advantage was taken of spells on the ground to carry out war training of a different kind, courtesy the NATO armies. Flushed with their apparent (to them) success in driving (not firing) the British Cavalry's Chieftain tanks, the pilots then accepted an invitation to the German Panzer Brigade at nearby Augustdorf to extend their experience to Leopard tanks, a variety of armoured personnel carriers and tracked artillery pieces. It was through exercises such as these that the GLOs promoted a better understanding among their pilots of military tactics and techniques in the field, information

vital to recce pilots in war and valuable in peacetime competitions. For instance, it was due to their GLOs that the IV Squadron pilots could often identify the nationality of units under camouflage solely by the set of any netting used.

Eric Smith discovered a downside stemming from this new found confidence in driving unorthodox army vehicles: 'Just before one AOC's Inspection I found that some of the squadron officers, allegedly led by Johnny Baines, had finished off a Friday evening's drinking by test-driving a bulldozer, left unwisely outside the squadron hangar over the weekend. This had caused major damage to a grass patch over which the great man would pass on the following Monday'. Eric read the riot act and needless to say the whole area was immaculate on the day of the inspection.

On that day, the squadron's FR10s were lined up on the apron, each with an NCO and two airmen in attendance, and to ensure that he introduced them correctly Eric had secreted a list of their names in his glove. He remembers: 'All seemed to go well until I realised that my list did not tally with those in the line and I noticed a slight grin when an individual was addressed incorrectly. Later, as I began to remonstrate with Peter Scott, our engineering officer, a couple of sergeants took the wind out of my sails by confessing to an unkind plot, just to enjoy my reaction'.

This did nothing to stop 1966 ending on a high, Eric Smith being appointed OBE for his leadership of the squadron, as exemplified in Royal Flush XI; this was a rare honour for a squadron leader and a just reward for the squadron's achievements during his tenure.

1967. Mixed Blessings

Tragedy struck again in January 1967 when Master Pilot Tom Radcliffe, an accomplished pilot who had once landed a Hunter successfully on a beach in the East Friesland Islands and was now serving on the Gutersloh Wing staff, was killed when his IV Squadron aircraft hit a hill in the Sauerland. Peter Gover took the call at the squadron's operations desk, to be told by the German police that the pilot was a Flight Lieutenant Peter Gover, the name on the nose of the aircraft. Eric Smith took Tom's brother to the scene and ferried the family car back to the UK in time for the funeral, at which IV's Four flew an evocative last salute.

Open House. Gutersloh Open Day in 1967 was declared: "The biggest show by the RAF in Germany since WW2". *Peter Gover*

Flight Lieutenants Mike Seyd and Al Cleaver joined the squadron at the beginning of the year, followed by Flight Lieutenant Ken Petrie and Flying Officer Chris Shorrock in February. This brought the squadron back to a full strength of eleven pilots for the first time since the previous August. March heralded the renumbering of 7 MFPU to 4 MFPU, a more appropriate title given the squadron it served.

Perhaps the importance of realistic tasking and targeting was now getting through to battle management, with the introduction of a more collective approach to war fighting; the TOCs would now task targets for Royal Flush training and in the competition itself, mirroring their *raison d'etre* in war. Although undeniably sensible in principle, the flying men viewed this move with great apprehension, fearful that such involvement in the competition would deny them their rightful accolades. Time would tell.

Jim Dymond, the project officer for the Royal Flush in May 1967, became a father on the second day of the exercise. He denies now that, on the spur of the moment, he vowed to call his daughter 'Eye Pee' (IP) – and she did escape that fate. Chris Shorrock ran the in-flight reporting cell provided by the Royal Signals and Steve Stephens headed the usual able team of reinforcement PIs. No. IV Squadron was the only participating squadron to avoid a camera failure and all seemed to go well, but no official record can be found of the results.

At the end of May came 'British Week' at Gutersloh, with a memorable open day and air display in which Iain Weston went through his aerobatic repertoire before a crowd of 150,000.

Peter Gover wrote in the ORB that he took the plunge and got married: 'joining the others in the water and beckoning the remainder to join him'. Thus warned, the bachelor Pete Headley piled all his worldly goods into his E-Type Jaguar and departed the squadron.

By June 1967 the squadron was short of pilots again, but all went well in the annual Taceval. This might not have been so in the case of the Queen's Birthday Flypast over the Joint Headquarters (JHQ) at Rheindahlen when Iain Weston had to abort the lead and hand over to a somewhat alarmed No. 2, Taff Wallis. This is Taff's edited story:

The plan was for Iain to lead eight Hunters at the head of a formation of all the other flying squadrons in RAF Germany over JHQ just as the reviewing officer arrived on the saluting base, and to this end preparations had been meticulous, with timing to the second marked on the maps. Despite being Iain's deputy, Taff had expected to go along 'just for the ride'. The Hunters were to launch from Geilenkirchen, picking up sections of Lightnings and Canberras

Ignore Him! There was an ugly rumour that II Squadron's John Thomson was 'spoofed' on to these 'friendly' USAFE F-100s by IV Squadron during the Berlin Corridor Contingency Exercise 'Shooting Star' at Gutersloh. *IV Sqn*

The Blame Game. Who was responsible for this laudable effort to relieve the parking problem at the Officers Mess? II & IV Sqn

at selected points *en route*, and all this went like clockwork in the rehearsals. So it was on the appointed day, the 10th June, right up to the point where the Hunters were rolling down the runway. Then it all went wrong. Iain had reached about 110 kts when, as Taff said 'he seemed to stop dead and go backwards', calling as he disappeared that he had engine problems and adding 'It's all yours, Taff'. To this day Taff wonders how Iain got off the runway with other aircraft all roaring down on him at 15 second intervals but he did and, with the spare slotting in as Taff's wingman, the Geilenkirchen contingent was airborne. Taff then regretted that he had given the route map little more than a cursory glance during the briefing, but from that moment on he gave it his scrupulous attention as they continued around the route, fortunately in excellent weather, collecting the rest of the formation. In his bed at Wegberg Hospital, Colin Richardson, who had been nominated the original leader before Iain but was now *hors de combat*, noted with great satisfaction that the formation passed overhead precisely on time and on track, not knowing what drama had gone before. Taff then led the fray over the saluting base within seconds of the appointed time. There was a well worn expression in the RAF at the time, 'I learned about flying from that', and Taff certainly learned something from that event. Let him have the last word: 'It took me much longer than the flight itself to get over that shock, a shock that I could well have done without, and when Iain and I eventually got back to Gutersloh I had a few choice words to say to him'.

This very full month of May also included the AOC's Inspection and it was not surprising that the squadron fell just short of its flying target, but it would soon recover as new pilots were rushed through their operational training.

In June 1967, Squadron Leader Tony Hopkins took command of IV Squadron. Eric and Sheena Smith were sent on their way after a lavish squadron dinner night with a difference. The boss and several officers from II Squadron dressed as waiters and with proper humility, emerged from the kitchen to serve the last course and say farewell to their friends with a final round of brandies for the whole squadron. Rivalry may have existed but during Eric's tenure there was also enduring friendship. Indeed squadron pilots were exchanged to learn from their opposite numbers (other than competition ways). Pilots from each squadron sometimes flew together on Blue Diamond and Southern Ranger exercises in comradeship as it should be.

July was another busy month, but one devoted more to flying. Exercise Sky Blue called for fifteen sorties by midday on day one and forty sorties, including many on air-to-ground gunnery, in the remaining two days. An exchange with the 51st Squadron, Italian Air Force followed, the squadron dispatching four aircraft, eight officers and twenty airmen to Istrana, from where many useful sorties were flown at low level over terrain new to the pilots. In an interesting departure from the norm, the FR10s also exercised jointly with the hosts' F-86Ks in radar interceptions and air combat. Needless to say, the exchange involved unhealthy sessions with Pimms 79 and Pyrah's Pot. This was also the month in which IV and II Squadrons began a continuous two aircraft presence in Gibraltar (Chapter Eight).

For every good reason, Iain Weston was now promoted to squadron leader; he had been a powerhouse in IV Squadron's operational and competition training, a highly effective leader of IV's Four and RAF Germany's Hunter display pilot. Flight Lieutenant Bill Sheppard and Andy Sharp (PI) joined the squadron as Colin Richardson left, temporarily unfit medically, to become Range Safety Officer at Nordhorn, Ken Petrie taking over as Flt Cdr Ops, all credit to an officer on a supplementary list commission. The squadron also said farewell to Taff Wallis, the Royal Flush 'ace', destined to take up an

Anything II Can Do IV Can Do Better! But where II Squadron could do it with one FR10 – IV Squadron needed four! *Bob Hillman and IV Sqn*

appointment as a Phantom test pilot on the MU at Aldergrove. He was replaced by Flight Lieutenant P.A.D. Williams, known generally as 'Pad'. Despite all this turbulence, and having two Hunters in Gibraltar, the flying target was exceeded by 30 per cent.

In the ever varying fortunes of competition, the squadron came a very unexpected last in September's Sassoon, but this disappointment

Blame Game. There is no knowing why this quip appeared in the IV Squadron scrapbook *IV Sqn*

was offset by the great operational training value derived from the British 4th Division Exercise Rob Roy, and the flying task was again exceeded by 20 hours in October. More useful experience was derived from Exercise Overdale, mounted from Geilenkirchen, which required the FR10s to react rapidly to recce requests from British paratroops in the field, and in-flight reports to be passed to them direct. All this was grist to the mill for the FR pilots, who enjoyed and excelled in the challenge. Tony Hopkins was now operational and the man who had done so much to raise the standard of photography and help IV Squadron acquit itself so well, both operationally and in competitions, Doug McDermott, left 4 MFPU.

The squadron now began its move into Hangar 6, recently vacated by No. 18 (Wessex) Squadron, but in the ORB Mike Seyd recorded that the squadron's aircraft had to spend many winter nights outside while the hangar floor was rebuilt 'causing many to develop colds'. Nothing was written about the social activities over the Christmas period.

1968: More Accolades

When he took up his pen again in the New Year, Mike reported that the move into 'good' accommodation in Hangar 6 was completed in early January 1968 and that this was celebrated

Try Landing On That! Pete Rayner, II Squadron, photographed IV Squadron's Tony Richardson, who accompanied him on a Southern Ranger Exercise, against HMS Ark Royal in Valetta Harbour, Malta. *Peter Rayner*

Party Time. No. IV Squadron treated their hosts at the Italian Base of Istrana to large quantities of 'Pimms 79', Iain Weston doing the honours. *IV Sqn*

The Morning After? The IV Squadron guests look a little happier than their Italian hosts. *IV Sqn*

by a squadron Open Day, static display and party for members of the German aero clubs at Werdol, Hamm, Werl and Dumple, in return for their hospitality during the previous year. Iain Weston provided a disco, Messrs Shorrock and Williams were responsible for the imaginative

Togetherness. F-86Ds of 51 Sqn IAF and IV Sqn's FR10s. *Jim Dymond*

decorations and early flying dress was de *rigueur*. This was the very social scene which greeted Flying Officer Sam Goddard when he arrived to bring the pilot strength up to ten operational and two non-operational pilots.

Tony Hopkins was the inspiration behind the next social extravaganza, a cocktail party for the Officers' Mess which required each of his officers to exhibit a 'piece of art' for the decor. Cartoonist Chris Shorrock and oil painter Pad Williams were in their element, while Sam Goddard rose to the occasion with his nail sculpture and Jim Dymond excelled with his evocative painting of an FR10 heading for a gap

The Sound of Freedom. VI's Four, turning hard and low (with 20 deg of flap) add noise to their overall impact. *Peter Gover*

Tell Me Another! Jim Dymond may be a little sceptical at Pete Padley's tale but everything was allowed at this celebration of yet another IV Squadron win in 1968's Royal Flush XIII, for which Jim was the project officer. *IV Sqn*

No Escape. For the privilege of becoming 'operational' Tony Hopkins drinks the prescribed brew from Pyrah's Pot. *IV Sqn*

in the hills under a thunderstorm. Even Al Cleaver, who laid no claim to artistic talent, produced a very effective 'After the Night Before' montage from a cornflake packet surrounded by 'fag ends' and a spilt coffee cup, set on a black hardboard base. All this contributed to an outstanding evening.

In February, IV Squadron earned high marks in a Taceval, despite flying only ten sorties. The newly arrived Flight Lieutenant Ken Jones completed the 1,250 nm trip back from Gibraltar to Gutersloh in 2 hours 45 minutes (which may have been a record) and an air-to-ground gunnery phase produced academic and operational averages of 29.7 per cent and 24.4 per cent respectively. Then it was off to Rygge again for half the squadron in March, while the other half entertained Norwegians and their five RF-84Fs at Gutersloh. Al Cleaver remembers their stay in Norway well, having enjoyed the excellent flying but not the staple fare of stew in the combined Mess, the main ingredient of which 'looked like beef but tasted like fish and was actually whale'. Then it was back to Royal Flush training again and another season for IV's Four.

IV's Four Again. The new IV's Four in 1968 comprised Tony Hopkins, Ken Petrie, Bill Sheppard and Chris Shorrock.

The Team 'At Home'.

We're Clear.

Watch that mast!

Now for the Party. The team at Itzehoe, North Germany. *IV Sqn*

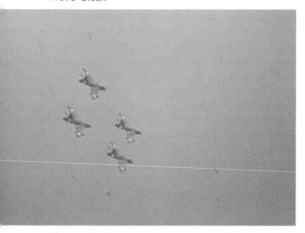

Led now by Tony Hopkins, IV's Four performed regularly in 1968 with a schedule of seventeen airshows throughout Europe, including those at Seppe in the Netherlands, Balen in Belgium, Siegerland, Itzehoe and Hamm in Germany. The programme would end on Battle of Britain Day at RAF Coltishall in September, this display drawing a compliment from the station's highly respected OC Flying Wing, Wing Commander George Black, that he had never seen four Hunters flying so close together.

May produced the most cherished accolade of all for a recce squadron, at least in competition terms, outright victory in Royal Flush, with twenty nine sorties flown by the nine pilots competing. Understandably, the squadron stole the limelight at the awards ceremony, hosted by

the RCAF at Lahr in June, the month when a new zenith was reached with a monthly total of 420 flying hours.

It was on this high note that Iain Weston left the squadron; Jim Dymond followed and Flight Lieutenant Derek Whitman was posted in. Derek was already well known in the FR world from his successful tour with 1417 Flight in Aden and 8 Squadron in Bahrain, but particularly to Al Cleaver, who had been his Radar Observer in Javelin Vs of No. 151 Squadron at RAF Leuchars in 1958-60, after which Al decided to become a pilot. How things had changed for both of them since then.

In July the Gibraltar Commitment came to an end, freeing up aircraft for exercises Playboy and Whirlygig to test the FR10 pilots against gun and missile units dispersed and concealed in the field. There was a welcome emphasis on in-flight reporting through the NORTHAG/2ATAF system and the Hunters acted as targets for the all-weather fighter force. In the wash-up, the

Anybody There? Jim Dymond inspects the inside of a very tall chimney. *Jim Dymond*

squadron was credited with finding five of the six well camouflaged units deployed and escaping all attempts by the fighters to carry out successful interceptions. Continuity in air-to-ground gunnery was paying off, with averages for two and four-pass shoots now hovering around 30 per cent.

When made deputy leader of four aircraft tasked to escort a Valetta carrying Air Marshal Sir Christopher Foxley-Norris to his new appointment as C-in-C RAF Germany, it was Ken Petrie's turn to be reminded that things do not always go as planned. Tony Hopkins was to have led but his aircraft and that of his No. 4 went unserviceable on start-up and he had to hand over to Ken, who admits that he was not as well prepared as he should have been for this eventuality. However, he left it to Clutch Radar to effect the join-up and everything seemed to go well. A subsequent signal from the new C-in-C thanked all concerned for the welcome but commented that the leader needed a shave, a nice way of saying that Ken was flying a little too close for his liking.

Group Captain Keith Williamson took over command of RAF Gutersloh from David Ross in mid-1968. As mentioned in Chapter Four, he was eminently suited to the job, having served on Hunter squadrons in Germany in the 1950s and he became thoroughly acquainted with the Lightning while commanding No. 23 Squadron at RAF Leuchars. He comments now that he knew from the start that he would be dealing with two distinct groups of officers, born of different cultures and with different attitudes to work and play. On the one hand, he had two Lightning squadrons comprising largely young and inexperienced pilots, mostly straight out of training but fortunately led by highly competent, experienced and properly responsible executives. These were privileged men and they knew it, flying the RAF's most sophisticated fighter with very limited endurance, frequently in marginal weather, having to interpret their own air intercept radars and work out the geometry of an interception, albeit under radar control but without the help of a 'back seater'. All this could be achieved effectively and safely only with close supervision in the air and on the ground at squadron level, and with a great deal of self-discipline.

On the other hand, the two Hunter FR10 squadrons were, as a matter of policy, manned predominantly by experienced fast-jet pilots or at least ex-QFIs, a policy justified by the demands of the low level operations in Germany's perennially poor weather, invariably by single aircraft over long ranges. Once they were airborne, there could be no further supervision; FR pilots were on their own and the results of their missions were there for all to see from the photographs and reports they brought back. It followed that those who succeeded had developed particular skills, of which an innate ability to think and act rapidly for themselves was of crucial importance; they were 'loners'.

The difference between these two groups of pilots was very evident to the new station commander. All four squadrons had their fair share of highly spirited men, and this he welcomed, but the FR men exuded understandably greater self-confidence and this was sometimes reflected in their behaviour in the air and on the ground. Most had also been brought up in the less responsible era of the 1950s, an anachronism in the necessarily more regulated environment of the host country in the late 1960s, but the station commander remained ever conscious that some might be a little slow to change their ways.

Not that the group captain had any complaint when he flew as wingman during a particularly demanding FR exercise through the Sauerland in weather which could best be described as marginal. His leader saw nothing of their target, and neither perhaps did he, but it transpired that he alone among the several pilots given that task had brought back the required photographs.

For some time now IV squadron had been evaluating 'trip-of-the-day' training, practised regularly by II Squadron, but it had become very unpopular in some quarters for its alleged lack of flexibility, together with lengthy and acrimonious end-of-day debriefings which sometimes extended the working day to 1900 hours. In an attempt to keep it going, Tony Hopkins suggested that the first wave should have its own met briefing at 0600 hours and launch when the Low Flying System opened at 0730, but this foundered when it was realised that most of the airmen shared scheduled, off-base transport with the rest of the station personnel, who would clearly not welcome the idea of coming in much earlier. So the 'trip of the day' succumbed to a do-it-yourself 'target system of the week' (bridges/airfields/storage et al), which gave rise to some interesting initiatives. This reverted to the popular latter day modus operandi which allowed every pilot to choose his own targets, areas and weather etc, with a collective system debriefing at the end of each week.

In August, 4 MFPU celebrated twenty-five years of service since D-Day, although having served IV Squadron under its present number plate only since March 1967. However, there were mixed feelings rather than celebrations when the C-in-C announced that the squadron would be re-equipped with Harriers in early 1970.

As for competition, it was now rumoured strongly that in 1969 Royal Flush would involve representative teams flying from the same base (Spangdahlem), each group covering the same targets in the same weather and thus returning to the format of the 1950s. This had the advantage of similar opportunities and problems for all participants, but would put only those chosen few from each squadron to the ultimate test.

Meanwhile, IV Squadron undertook its fair share of Southern Ranger and Blue Diamond exercises, often with a story to tell on return. Derek Whitman remembers that in September 1968 he and Mike Seyd set off on what was intended to be 'a four day gallop' to Luqa and El Adem, back to Luqa and a return to Gutersloh via the low-level routes around Calabria in Italy. However, it started to go wrong at Luqa on the return leg, when one FR10 refused to take fuel from its rear saddle tanks and the other was found to have sustained severe Foreign Object Damage (FOD) damage to its engine compressor. The two pilots enjoyed the delights of Malta while awaiting help, becoming a little richer each day at the expense of the Dragonara Casino. Help came three days later in the form of a terse signal ordering Derek to return, by stages if necessary, in the aircraft with fuel feed problems and Mike to do so by the first available civil flight; this was necessary to maintain established NATO pilot manning criteria. Derek set off accordingly with empty rear tanks on a maximum range profile 'equipped with spanners, locking wire and graphic instructions from the engineers on how to refuel the aircraft in this configuration should he have to stage through Istres in France'. In short, he would have to undo the access band around the rear fuselage, switch the fuel cocks to refuelling and then back again afterwards before wire-locking them, 'generally performing as a flight line mechanic-cum-powder monkey'. Fortunately, the winds were kind and overhead Istres Derek calculated that he could reach Gutersloh with sufficient reserves to divert to Hopsten if necessary. He landed (much to the relief of Tony Hopkins in ATC) after a flight of three hours exactly, perhaps a record without rear tank fuel. Mike Seyd returned to Luqa three days later to recover the other aircraft, with orders not to dally at the Dragonara.

It was back to army games in October, with much good training in Exercises Playboy, Iron Hand, Blue Devil, Keystone and Eternal Triangle. In the latter, fifty-six very useful tasks were flown in six days, the ORB noting the value of having Peter Gover attached to the Forward Air Support Operations Centre (FASOC) to enhance the tasking. Derek Whitman remembers that this involvement became a sine qua non for future exercises of the type, the results having so impressed army commanders and civilian analysts, particularly when the FR10s completed their tasks in weather thought by the army to be too poor for flying.

In the on-going spirit of innovation, improvisation and determination, Messrs Petrie and Williams were credited with repeating and improving on the procedures developed in Aden (Chapter Nine), to expedite prints to customers in the field by parachuting photographs from the Hunter's airbrake. They claimed to be able to drop their packages within 20 yards of positions required.

A Taceval Part 1 (No Notice Phase) was called at the unkindly hour of 0330 hours on a dark November morning, but the squadron rose to the occasion to have its first aircraft available by 0414 hours, the second by 0500 hours and the required 70 per cent by 1054 hours, well inside the 12 hour requirement. The early winter darkness encouraged night flying, but it was daylight when a fellow pilot attempted to ascertain the position of the nose wheel on Pad Williams' aircraft which had an 'unsafe' indication and the two FR10s collided. Damage was limited to 'Cat 2' on both aircraft and the normally very careful pilot responsible got away with a 'wigging' by the station commander. Such incidents were rare in the FR force.

In a seemingly ironic reward for continually achieving their prescribed monthly and annual flying hours, but in fact to conform with NATO's Allied Command Europe standards, the official flying rate for the two FR10 squadrons was now raised from 23 to 25 hours/month/airframe, and from 17 to 18 hours/month/pilot. This was of no concern to two new pilots on the squadron, Flight Lieutenant Bill Langworthy, who took over as scribe for the ORB, and Flying Officer Al Mathie; they were happy to fly whenever they were tasked. Al was accompanied by his faithful Irish Wolfhound, Kanga, who became a source of endless pleasure, amusement and sometimes embarrassment on the squadron, perhaps in equal measures. This large animal never tired of chasing the paper balls thrown across the floor by Bill Sheppard, invariably crashing into the changing lockers.

1969: A Very Busy Penultimate Year

Al Mathie started his time on the squadron and 1969 well, by nursing a Hunter home after its engine had shed compressor stator and rotor blades from the fourth stage and then locked solid during a well-executed emergency landing. He was one of many who had cause to be grateful to Rolls Royce and the Avon engine for getting him back safely. There were more bird strikes, Peter Gover suffering a head-on attack by two buzzards in the Frankfurt area but able to

bring his aircraft back to Gutersloh at a steady throttle setting to complete a successful precautionary landing before the engine seized on run-down. Both engine intakes were found to be partially blocked and the compressor badly damaged.

No. IV Squadron now took over the Tactical Air Reserve commitment from II Squadron, which now meant being ready to deploy anywhere in the world in four days to support thirty eight Group operations and to be self-supporting for 28 days. Realistic pressure was also being increased by NATO, which now declared that future Tacevals would include assessments of ability to survive and operate in both conventional war and in nuclear, bacteriological and chemical (NBC) conditions. On the competition front a return to the single base concept of the 1950s, anticipated for 1969's Royal Flush, was finally rejected in favour of the more recent, multi-base model. Unusually for a January, the squadron flew the remarkably high total of 223 hours.

Winter returned with a vengeance in February, with only 148 hours flown in seasonal ice and fog while Tony Hopkins was representing Gutersloh in the RAF Germany ski championships. He was soon rendered *hors de combat* for several weeks with a broken leg, during which time Derek Whitman acted as squadron commander. Flight Lieutenant Pat Kiggell joined the squadron in time for Exercise Prologue, in which the FR10s were tasked to find simulated Harrier sites dispersed tactically in the field under various degrees of camouflage; this was primarily an evaluation of their concealment and deception plans. As was so often the case in such trials the test parameters did not conform sufficiently to realistic operational practices, either on the ground or in the air, so the exercise was said, at least by the pilots, to have been of limited value. On the other hand, those involved on the ground claimed to have derived much benefit from having Sam Goddard with them to give an airman's perspective on site selection, concealment of the men and materials deployed, and the need for disciplined movement in and around the sites.

There was good news from a weapons training phase in which the squadron achieved an average score of 36.6 per cent on operational/semi-operational strafing, with an improved stoppage rate of 1:1444. Peter Gover

Shall We Dance? Ken Petrie uses all his 'charm' on the boss's wife. *IV Sqn*

The Odd Couple. A rather coy Tony Hopkins escorts a well dressed Peter Gover, Bill Kelly (right) studiously ignoring the pair. *Roger Wilkins*

was chosen to represent the RAF on the Cresta Run and Tony Hopkins, who had graduated to 'clomping about the squadron on his full-arm crutches', was suddenly 'casevaced' to the British Military Hospital Munster with a collapsed lung and a dire prognosis that he might not return to duty until the end of May.

In March, Ken Petrie took half the squadron to Karup on a squadron exchange, during which their Danish hosts were introduced to the evils of Pimms 79. No one of those involved seems able to remember anything more of the evening but when flying resumed after they had all recovered, the FR10 pilots found their host's role to be very different from that with which they were familiar. Ship recces in the Baltic were often the order of the day and on one such sortie Ken remembers flying over the sea at low level in a veritable 'fish bowl', suddenly realising that the strange disturbance behind his leader's aircraft was in fact the jet efflux. Fortunately, his call to 'pull up' came in time and the experience was no more than a salutary lesson. Seeking a little light relief,

the Hunter pilots cancelled flying on the Friday afternoon, declaring their intention to sample the delights of Aalborg town, but the Danes demanded that they stay put for 'ground school'. This turned out to be a pornographic film show.

Meanwhile, back at Gutersloh the Danish guests responded to the welcome they had received by offering their hosts seemingly endless supplies of Aquavit and soused herrings, cooled in transit within the voluminous bodies of their RF-84Fs. All was far from well in the Sergeants Mess, however, a distraught Danish officer announcing to Derek Whitman that his sergeants, members even then of a powerful union, were wholly dissatisfied with the accommodation and were threatening an immediate sit-down strike if a better alternative was not found forthwith. In the flurry of activity which followed, now involving the station commander and Chairman of the (Sergeants) Mess Committee, a solution was found to the satisfaction of all and the sergeants got down to some serious socialising.

In The Lead. Derek Whitman leads the Gutersloh Hunters and Lightnings in a mass flypast to celebrate the Queen's Birthday in 1969. *Derek Whitman*

Nasty Turn. No. IV Squadron's Keith Holland lost much of the tread on an FR10's tyre on take off and then had multiple brake failure recovering to Gutersloh. *IV Sqn*

The detachment at Gutersloh ended with simultaneous parties in the Officers Mess and for the other ranks in the squadron crewroom. Derek thought it prudent to have one officer on duty in the crewroom (rotating on an hourly basis) in the hope of ensuring that things did not get out of hand, and nominated Al Mathie to get the ball rolling. Meanwhile, both nations' officers were getting into their stride in the Officers' Mess, with numerous speeches, toasts and incomprehensible Norwegian limericks all greeted with great and general approval. It was at this stage that, having completed his duty, Al joined his peers and set about catching them up. This he did without delay and in great style until, well satisfied, he fell asleep on the carpet. Unaccustomed to this style of drinking, or the drink itself, few of his colleagues were able to go to his assistance and it was left to a few resilient Danes to cart him off to his room, where Kanga supervised his recovery. What remained of the party then petered out, followed in the morning by an unexplained bout of influenza among the pilots!

Whether it was because he had had enough of bachelor life, one too many incidents with Kanga, or the obvious attractions of married life, Al Mathie seemed to conclude that he now needed a wife to take care of him and his hound, and hopefully keep them both out of trouble. An intensive search led successfully to Dot – the future Mrs Mathie.

The very busy period came early in 1969, with nine rehearsals for the AOC's Parade, a long Easter grant and an intensive work-up for Royal

Flush again exposing shortcomings in the TOC tasking system, typically with one target misplotted by some 40 km. Under pressure from

For Services Rendered. IV Squadron flight commanders Ken Petrie and Derek Whitman were both promoted to squadron leader at the end of their tours. *Ken Petrie*

one of the major players and alleged to be demanded by flight safety, the all-important in-flight reporting would no longer be included.

To his credit, Bill Sheppard was selected to be RAF Germany's solo aerobatic pilot for 1969; he is also said to have promoted aerodynamic braking in the FR10, contrary to official SOPs but proving very effective in certain circumstances.

Meanwhile, in the spirit of Wing solidarity if not to demonstrate his prowess in formation, Chris Shorrock flew Flight Lieutenant (Doctor) Tony Erlam in the T7 to make up the number in 92 Squadron's diamond-nine flypast of otherwise blue-finned Lightnings for the departing AOC, AVM John Aiken. Knowing that the AVM would not read the ORB, the scribe commented wryly on the commitment of ten bodies and seventeen engines to the event.

Justifying a massive effort on Royal Flush in May, IV Squadron came top of its class in 2ATAF, but 4ATAF won the Gruenther Trophy.

On 14 June Derek Whitman led Gutersloh's contribution to the Queen's Birthday Flypast at Rheindahlen, a 'vic' of five FR10s from IV Squadron and a 'box 'of six Lightnings from 19 and 92 Squadrons. Derek claims that 'after four practise runs in the preceding days we were able to slide neatly into a gaggle of Canberras and I'm sure those at the international cocktail party below thought it all very impressive'. Who knows? There was no comment in the ORB on the resources consumed on this occasion.

Operational FR in June's Exercise Summer Sales showed the British Army how easily its helicopters could give away the positions of important units, albeit well camouflaged, when they hovered and landed close by. This mutually productive training contributed to the high monthly total of 268 hours which was followed by another good month in July, a month which included useful recce against an artillery brigade in Exercise Whirlygig and an air-to-ground gunnery phase producing an all-

Going Home. Bill Sheppard got this FR10 down in one piece at Bremen Civil Airport in an epic emergency landing in 1969 – but it came back by road. *IV Sqn*

Starhunter. IV Squadron found this hybrid during their exchange visit to the Dutch airbase Eindhoven, in the winter of 1969. *IV Sqn*

And Another Thing! Officer Commanding IV Squadron, Tony Hopkins, telling Air Marshal Sir 'Gus' Walker all about it – his GLO wishing he was elsewhere. *IV Sqn*

round average of 40.6 per cent. There was also a demanding in-house operational training phase run by Chris Shorrock which called for minimum target-run speeds of 480 kts, each sortie to be disrupted by 'bounce' interceptions, diversions and rapid in-flight tasking. With this programme, and a Southern Ranger, it is not surprising that Sam Goddard's log book records a monthly total of 31 hours.

Derek Whitman and Peter Gover were forewarned of their impending promotion to squadron leader at the end of June, Ken Petrie having received the same good news some six weeks earlier but pledged to secrecy while he signed an 'extra-regulatory transfer' to the General Duties Branch. The good times came to an end for Pad Williams and Ken Jones, now time expired on the squadron, just as they began for Flying Officer Keith Holland who arrived from the OCU. Not of his making, Keith would soon have an 'off-runway' experience from which both he and his aircraft would escape to fly again.

Carnival Time. No. IV Squadron thespians tread the boards for the Officers' Mess in February 1970.

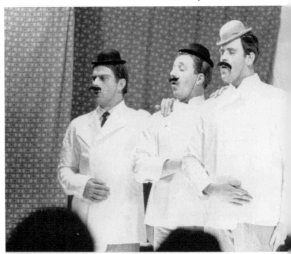

Tony Hopkins doing his thing. *Sam Goddard*

'I Look Up To Him....' (Al Cleaver, Tim Thorn and John Grose(GLO). *Sam Goddard*

Barber's Shop Trio (Bill Langworthy, Sam Goddard & Keith Holland). *Sam Goddard*

This is Your Life. Some heavily disguised worthies of IV Squadron take Wing Commander Dickie Dickinson (centre) through his life. *Sam Goddard*

A second phase of the controversial Harrier site trial, Exercise Prologue (this time targeting nine sites on Sennelager Range), was flown in August, but again it was unpopular with the FR pilots for its lack of operational realism. Exercise Playboy, tasking the Hunters against AAA and SAM sites defended by Lightnings, was better value.

On the social side Squadron Leaders Whitman, Gover and Petrie celebrated their elevation and impending departure. They were finally seen off with the ritual dining out, for which they reciprocated with a Pimms 79 party in the Alpine Bar followed by a lavish dinner at a local hostelry. No. IV Squadron did it in style.

The autumn programme of exercises started with Exercise Shooting Star, rehearsing again the Berlin Corridor Contingency Plan with six FAF F-100s, six USAFE F-100s and four FR10s. The exercise was mounted from Gutersloh in a scenario simulated on Sennelager Range. Then came Exercises Dress Rehearsal, Top Twenty, October Fest and Playboy, followed by an air-to-ground phase in which there were mixed fortunes. The scores of 48.8 per cent academic and 26.6 per cent operational were considered good but there was near disaster when a ricochet passed through an engine intake, piercing a fuel pipe and causing 'Cat 3' damage which grounded the aircraft for three months.

Flight Lieutenant Tim Thorn now arrived on IV Squadron, fresh from a tour on FR10s and FGA9s on 8 Squadron in Bahrain. Tim hailed from East Africa, another typical bachelor fighter pilot, complete with a red E-Type Jaguar. In Germany he would continue to fly anything, anywhere and in any weather, and he would do it well, but he too was beginning to think that he needed a wife. Inevitably, he soon set his sights on the very attractive Rosi, an air traffic controller serving at RAF Wildenrath, where the 'Tower' then became a well-photographed FR target. Tim would marry Rosi – but not yet.

Pat Kiggell, now writing the ORB, reported extensively on nine excellent air/ground exercises in October, the best involving camouflaged and dummy targets, direct tasking from the ASOC in the field and in-flight reporting. All this in turn led to the flying task being exceeded again with a laudable total of 246 hours. The only drama of the month occurred on 6 October, involving Al Mathie and XE580 again, when engine vibration caused him to divert into Bremen civil airport where a first stage rotor blade was found to have sheared. A new engine and six groundcrew were dispatched from Gutersloh at once, only to find that there was no suitable crane at Bremen to make the change. The requisite machinery was dispatched forthwith from Gutersloh, only to fall into a ditch near Osnabruck. The British Army then came to the rescue, providing the necessary equipment from 7 Armoured Brigade Workshop. Despite all this, the work was completed in time for Al to fly the aircraft back to Gutersloh, only two days after he had diverted.

A Taceval was called on 24 November, again during the evening rush hour and only two hours after the departure of HRH The Duchess of Gloucester from Gutersloh. The squadron responded well with all available pilots and six FR10s (plus a T7) on state within an hour. Squadron and MFPU were then dispersed on this dark and frosty evening, in what was described as the worst weather for months, to the west end of the airfield to operate (without live flying) in full NBC protective clothing. When flying was possible on the following day, the squadron mounted nineteen sorties before the end of the exercise. Despite this excellent performance, the Taceval team could only award a 'Two', because the operations bunker had no air filters and inadequacies were noted in the Wing Operations Centre.

Bremen had another visitor from IV Squadron in December, when Bill Sheppard made an emergency landing with severe engine vibration in very poor visibility and no navigation aids. His undercarriage failing to lock down, he left the runway for the grass and wrote-off two runway lights. The aircraft, which was recovered to Gutersloh by road, required a new wing and engine. It could have been worse.

A very full year ended with the squadron having completed all that was asked of it and again exceeding its flying task; in addition to all the exercises already listed, there was an exchange visit to the Dutch base at Eindhoven and a surfeit of VIP visits.

1970: The Final Months

That winter, Tony Hopkins and the highly talented Keith Holland provided the inspiration behind another great social success, a cabaret staged by the squadron in the Officers Mess. This included among other acts Keith's imitation of the comedian Al Reid, Sam Goddard on the catwalk as a fashion model and 'I look up to him', dialogue with Al Cleaver as a pilot, Tim Thorn as 'the boss' and John Grose (GLO) as a staff officer; the show ended with 'This is Your Life', featuring OC Flying Wing, Wing Commander Dickie Dickinson.

All Together Now – For The Last Time. A T-7 leads IV Squadron's FR10s into retirement from the RAF in June 1970. *IV Sqn*

With Tony Hopkins leading from the front again, the squadron officers and wives visited a night club after a dinner night. A stripper soon spotted the rowdy group and their leader and invited Tony to wash her all over in a small bathtub made for two; he readily joined her and complied. Two other squadron officers (who might prefer to remain anonymous) then agreed with alacrity to dry her down.

In its last Royal Flush, at the Dutch base of Deelen in May 1970, the squadron had mixed fortunes; it did not achieve its usual greatness but Sam Goddard was named best pilot in his class and 2ATAF recovered the Gruenther Trophy (Chapter Seven).

On 2 June 1970, IV Squadron paraded for the last time as a Hunter unit and handed over to its Harrier successors. The Deputy Commander RAF Germany, took the parade and the squadron's last Hunters were flown to Dunsfold on the following day. So ended the FR10's nine years of sterling service in another highly successful phase of the squadron's history.

This had been a happy breed.

March On! OC IV Squadron, Tony Hopkins, flight commander Chris Shorrock and the Standard Party led by Roger Neal, lead the Hunter Stand Down Parade, 2 June 1970. *IV Sqn*

Chapter 6
Sierra

There was nothing particularly unique about 'Sierra', indeed the aircraft bearing that tail letter could be said to have been typical of most FR10s which served on the front line or at Chivenor – except that on II (AC) Squadron it was the CO's personal aircraft. Aircraft XF432, 'S', started life as a Hunter F6 but no record can be found of it entering service in the fighter role, and it is assumed that the aircraft went straight into storage at 5 MU, Kemble, from where it was retrieved by Hawker in 1960 and converted to an FR10. It first flew in this configuration in November 1960, with Don Lucy at the controls, and was delivered to II Squadron at Jever on 21 December. It seems likely to have been the personal mount of the then OC II Squadron, 'Mac' MacDonald, and would certainly bear the name of his successor, David Thornton, and all the squadron commanders who followed him throughout its active service with the RAF. Sierra was their first choice whenever they were on the flying programme together for routine training,

detachments and squadron exchanges. Lesser mortals seemed to choose it more frequently than others on the many weekend Blue Diamond and Southern Ranger exercises, perhaps on the unlikely premise that it bestowed some prestige and would be accorded extra privilege. The author does not recall being consulted over the aircraft's transfer to his name in 1964 but he was wholly content that it should be. It was right and proper that Sierra should lead the Royal Flypast for Her Majesty the Queen on 26 May 1965 (Chapter Four).

Sierra may not have had any particular attributes in the way that other aircraft of a particular mark were believed to have (all other things being equal), such as a slightly better performance; these differences were only apparent when and where comparisons were possible, for example on full throttle air combat training at high level on the air defence fighter squadrons. In the way of FR operations, opportunities for such definitive comparisons

On Show. Seen here on static display, Sierra carried the squadron commander's pennant and the name 'Squadron Leader David Thornton' from 1962 to 1964. *Roger Lindsey*

Sierra Goes Visiting. David Thornton (centre) took Sierra with him to USAF Air Base Laon, France, in 1964, accompanied by Bob Hillman, Bruce McDonald and Ken Tatem. *Bob Hillman*

were rare so there was no apparent reason why Sierra should have been deemed to have been 'better' in this way.

Nor was Sierra any less troubled by the technical problems which beset all FR10s to a greater or lesser degree. After one air-to-air

How Do You Start This Thing? Tim Barrett seeks advice from his groundcrew. *II Sqn*

gunnery exercise off the Friesland Islands, with the author aboard, its nose wheel failed to extend when selected down during recovery to land at the Dutch base of Leeuwarden. None of the published (and unpublished) emergency procedures (including negative 'G' in inverted flight below a low coastal cloud base) solved the problem as the low fuel state demanded some quick thinking. Thankfully Bob Hillman, flying on Sierra's wing, called on the Dutch to clear the circuit and lay a strip of foam with all speed under his direction, he himself then landing

Snap! Banking port to photograph an electronics site on the hill with the starboard F95, Tim Barrett uses terrain masking over the Sauerland. *Tim Barrett*

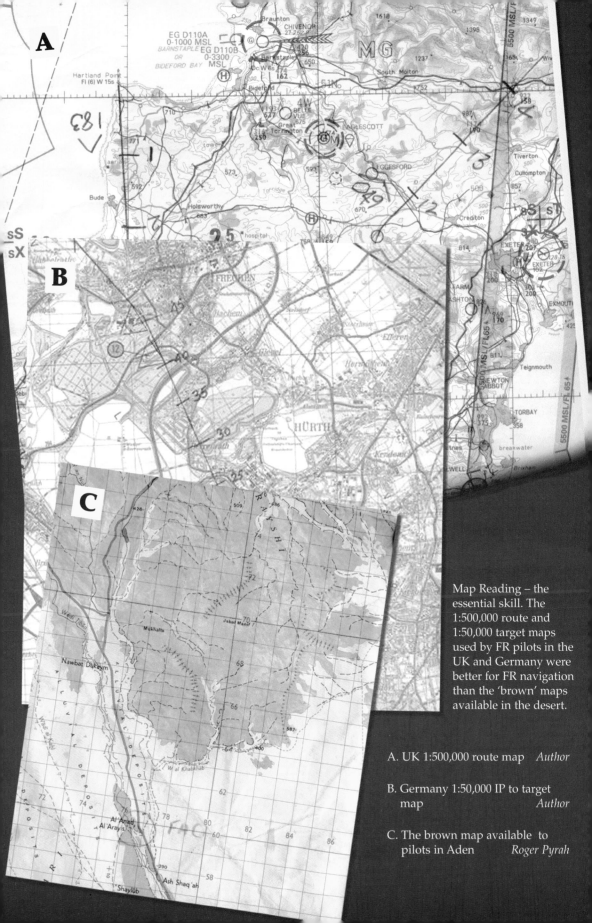

Map Reading – the
essential skill. The
1:500,000 route and
1:50,000 target maps
used by FR pilots in the
UK and Germany were
better for FR navigation
than the 'brown' maps
available in the desert.

A. UK 1:500,000 route map   *Author*

B. Germany 1:50,000 IP to target
   map   *Author*

C. The brown map available to
   pilots in Aden   *Roger Pyrah*

II Squadron Crest

HEREWARD

Old Friend. II (AC) Squadron, at Leeuwarden in 1967, left its mark on a veteran Meteor, a variant of which it flew in the 1950s. *II Sqn*

Puddy's Back. Puddy Catt, relaxed as ever, signing in after a Royal Flush training sortie. *II Sqn*

Royal Flush 1966. II Squadron celebrates the end of another competition. *II Sqn*

Team Workers. Officers, NCOs and airmen of II Squadron in 1969. *II Sqn*

IV's Four Re-born. *Above*: In 1966, Iain Weston led Peter Headley, Johnny Baines and Peter Gover in another good season for the team. *Peter Gover*

Terrain Masking. *Left*: Peter Gover stays well hidden in the contours and against the mountains of Norway during a Blue Diamond exercise. *Peter Gover*

Parade With Pride. *Left and below*: Mike French parades IV Squadron's Standard with pride – for the 1964 AOC's Inspection.

A

B

C

No Room For Error.

A. No. II Squadron goes Rock climbing
Peter Rayner

B. No. IV Squadron steers well clear.
Peter Gover

C. Burst tyres, poor brakes and
unsympathetic winds could make life
difficult. *Peter Gover*

Empire Outpost. Controversy with
Spain over Gibraltar brought
Hunters to the peninsular in the
late 1960s. *Peter Gover*

The First Team. The resurrected 1417 Flight including (*L to R*) Roger Pyrah, Johnny Morris, Peter Lewis, Jim Dymond an d Geoff Timms. *Ken Simpson*

Evidence On Camera. With great expertise, the photographic personnel at RAF Khormaksar produced excellent results from these rudimentary facilities. *Ken Simpson*

Kill! *Above:* Two hits on this one pass was far from typical of 8 Squadron's shooting at Sharjah Range – but those on the second (*below*) might be enough against some targets with the Hunter's mighty 30-mm cannon.

Coasting In/Coasting Out. 8 Squadron FR10s in 1969 trained hard over land and sea. *Mike Barringer*

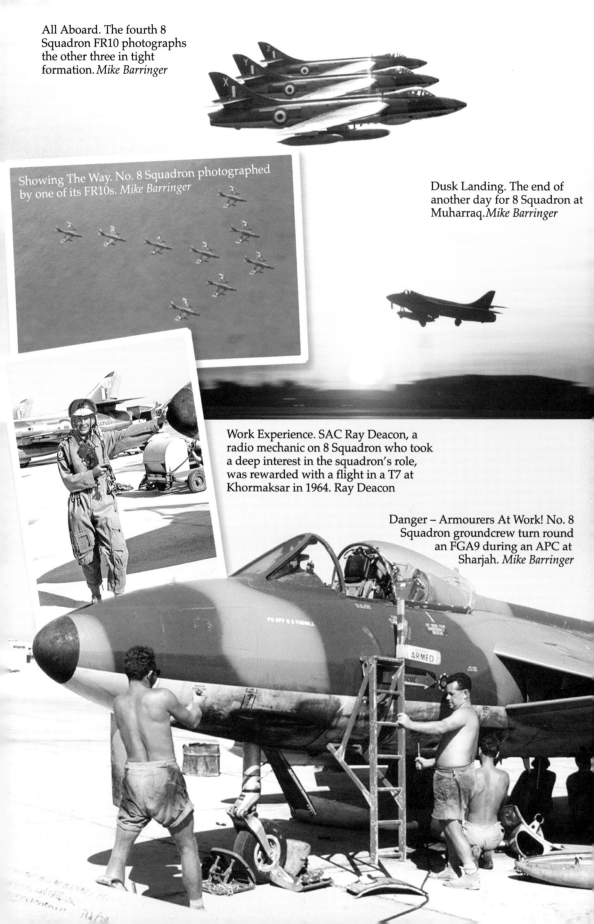

All Aboard. The fourth 8 Squadron FR10 photographs the other three in tight formation. *Mike Barringer*

Showing The Way. No. 8 Squadron photographed by one of its FR10s. *Mike Barringer*

Dusk Landing. The end of another day for 8 Squadron at Muharraq. *Mike Barringer*

Work Experience. SAC Ray Deacon, a radio mechanic on 8 Squadron who took a deep interest in the squadron's role, was rewarded with a flight in a T7 at Khormaksar in 1964. Ray Deacon

Danger – Armourers At Work! No. 8 Squadron groundcrew turn round an FGA9 during an APC at Sharjah. *Mike Barringer*

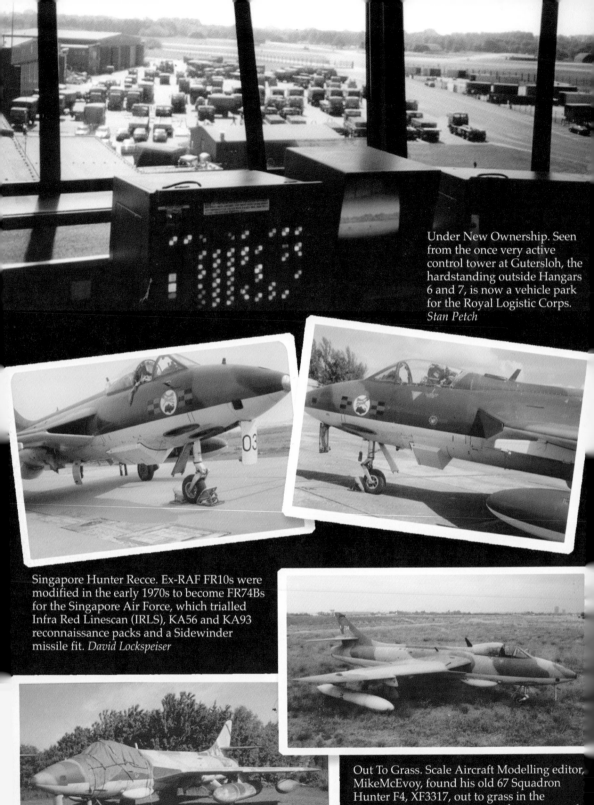

Under New Ownership. Seen from the once very active control tower at Gutersloh, the hardstanding outside Hangars 6 and 7, is now a vehicle park for the Royal Logistic Corps. *Stan Petch*

Singapore Hunter Recce. Ex-RAF FR10s were modified in the early 1970s to become FR74Bs for the Singapore Air Force, which trialled Infra Red Linescan (IRLS), KA56 and KA93 reconnaissance packs and a Sidewinder missile fit. *David Lockspeiser*

Out To Grass. Scale Aircraft Modelling editor, MikeMcEvoy, found his old 67 Squadron Hunter F4, XF3317, out to grass in the Santiago Aviation Museum, it having served its time in Chile as an FR variant with the number 734. *Mike McEvoy*

Hybrid. A worthy attempt to resurrect the memory of a once great Cold War warrior, this hybrid FR10 was last seen by the author on the disused airfield at Long Marston.

North and South. During its good service with II Squadron Sierra was a frequent visitor to Denmark and Norway on Blue Diamond exercises and to Malta, Libya and Italy, overflying France, on Southern Rangers.

Above the snow somewhere in Norway. *II Squadron*

Checking activity over Mount Vesuvius, Sicily. *Tim Barrett*

Recovering to RAF Luqa, Malta. *Sandy Wilson*

before they did so. The procedure Bob prescribed, although common and found to be invaluable in the RAF, seemed new to this Dutch base but they complied with great dispatch allowing Sierra to nose down precisely along the foam strip with very little damage. Squadron engineer John McGarvey was on the spot at once to oversee the aircraft's equally rapid removal from the runway, his immediate action once the nose had been jacked up being to administer a well-aimed blow just where it was needed to dislodge the wheel; ground locks were then fitted and the aircraft towed to a hangar. The fault was diagnosed, easily remedied and Sierra was soon airborne again to rejoin the rest of the squadron. A good team effort by all involved.

Undercarriage problems of various sorts, often involving the sequence valves, were far from uncommon on the Hunter and, as luck would have it, many led to, or were associated with, other incidents. Such was the case with Sierra on a day when the weather was too poor for low level training and Bill Norton, Flight Commander Operations, was leading Geoff Hall in a high-level cine weave exercise. For no good reason, Sierra's engine suddenly complained volubly and with an explosive bellow flamed out. Fearing the worst, Bill stop-cocked the engine and set up a classic flame-out pattern, selecting manual control and making ready to blow the flaps and undercarriage down with the emergency air at the prescribed time. Low cloud

was not the problem at Gutersloh that day, but the visibility was so poor that flares had to be fired from the runway caravan to help Bill find the threshold, which he did. All went well until Sierra's port wheel failed to lock down, and what would have been a perfect flame-out landing ended when the aircraft inevitably slewed off the runway. Bill's handling in the final stages and retention of the empty drop tanks probably confined damage to the port tank and flap. He escaped without injury, although whisked off by the Senior Medical Officer to Sick Quarters for

Nosy! Sierra makes friends with a Bristol Freighter of the RCAF at Marville, France. *II Sqn*

Home Again. Sierra taxis in at Gutersloh from a routine sortie in 1968. *Geoff Cruckshank via Roger Lindsey*

the usual checks, and the faithful aircraft was flying again within a few days.

Aircraft XF432 was not the only 'Sierra'. Having served continuously for eight years but now tired and due for a major servicing, XF432 was withdrawn from the line, its tail letter, squadron commander's pennant and name transferred without delay to XJ633. The new Sierra was known to have had a life before arriving on II Squadron. Part of the fourth production batch of forty-five F6s built by

Hawker at Kingston (the first Hunters to be fitted with the leading edge extensions from the outset) it took to the air with David Lockspeiser at the controls on 4 December 1956. In the following February it was delivered to 5 MU to serve in the air defence role, first as 'F' with 93 (F) Squadron and later as 'Z' on 65 (F) Squadron. Converted to an FR10 in 1959, it completed its operational life in the RAF on II Squadron.

Both Sierras were purchased back by Hawker in 1971 for modifications pending delivery to

Ready in the morning, Sir! No. II Squadron engineers made short work of the minimum damage to Sierra when the nose wheel failed to lower at Leeuwarden AB, Holland. *II Sqn*

Welcome Back. Recovering quickly from its landing at Leeuwarden without a nosewheel in June 1965, Sierra rejoins II Squadron at Laarbruch. *Peter Riley*

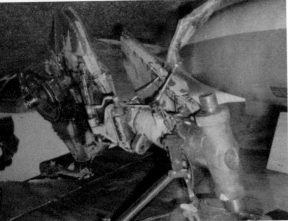

Legless. Sierra's port mainwheel failed to lock down during Bill Norton's emergency landing at Gutersloh. *Bill Norton*

Reincarnation. After loyal service, XF432 went for a major health check, and XJ633 took over Sierra's mantle. In 1970 Moose David, the last boss of II Squadron in the FR10 era, ordered the external tanks removed in those final days for the pilots to enjoy the exhilaration of a 'clean' FR10. *Moose David*

the Republic of Singapore Air Force (RSAF) as FR74Bs; XF432 as No. 526 in 1972 and XJ633 as No. 534 in 1973. Tim Barrett, who remembered XF432 well from his days in command of II Squadron, was delighted to find and fly his old mount again in its new guise in Singapore in the 1970s. By now a wing commander, he had accepted the temporary rank of lieutenant colonel while seconded to the RSAF as OC Flying Wing at Tengah, where his command included two Hunter squadrons.

At that point the trail goes cold and the ultimate fate of the Sierra sisters is not known. RIP.

Chapter 7
Trophy Hunters

They were loved by some (usually the winners) and hated by others (usually the losers), but competitions were a fact of life in NATO's tactical reconnaissance community before and during the Hunter era; indeed, they dominated the lives of most of the tac recce squadrons. Repetitive mention of these academic exercises in the diaries of events contained in Chapters Four and Five underlines this fact. The realists recognised that competition results were used, at least by politicians and many in the military hierarchies, as definitive comparisons of national, unit and individual operational capabilities in the role, thus according them every priority. Purists claimed that they could be detrimental to realistic operational training and thus wasteful in time, expensive national resources and flying hours. Of course the truth lay somewhere between the two opinions, depending on personal interests but also on the pattern and rules of the competitions at the time, which were constantly changing. The only enduring factors were disagreement and acrimony, within and between national units and air forces. Inevitably with some repetition from previous chapters 'Trophy Hunters' is a *résumé* which considers some of the issues already raised by these competitions, bringing together

threads which were common to both RAFG FR10 squadrons.

The photographs produced in a reconnaissance competition might seem to some to offer a fair comparison of performance, even a measure of individual and squadron operational recce effectiveness. However, Chapter Two reveals many other aspects in the employment and potential of tac recce in war, which allow honest practitioners to argue that 'pretty pictures' alone were not enough on which to pass such judgments. Visual sightings and immediate in-flight reports were also very important to war fighting and, with survivability imperative, operating tactics and techniques had to be taken fully into account. Arguments that international competitions were unfair because of differences in national equipments, concepts, regulations and modus operandi were less

GENERAL GRUENTHER

The Gruenther Trophy, which symbolises excellence in aerial reconnaissance, is presented each year to the ATAF obtaining the highest score in the Royal Flush competition. Donated by the Republic Aviation Corporation the trophy is named after United States Army General Alfred M. Gruenther, a former Supreme Allied Commander, Europe (SACEUR).

Royal Flush. The prestigious tactical reconnaissance competition Royal Flush started during General Gruenther's tenure as SACEUR, with the Gruenther Trophy awarded to the ATAF with the best overall success rate. *IV Sqn*

In the 1960s FR10 pilots participating in Royal Flush had to compete primarily against the RF-84Fs, and RF-101s. *IV Sqn*

viable; if specific differences were seen to influence results that was a matter for the nations themselves. All these factors came into play.

Within NATO's AFCENT there was Royal Flush, and in AFNORTH Big Click, while the RAF had its own national competition for the Sassoon Trophy. Royal Flush was a strictly recce competition held annually between 2ATAF and 4ATAF, primarily for the Gruenther Trophy (named after the United States Army General Alfred M Gruenther, SACEUR in the mid-1950s). Within the main competition there were also other accolades to be won, between and within each ATAF, in the day, night, short and long range classes, for squadrons and individual pilots, and for the 'best' army target. The first Royal Flush was held at the FAF base of Lahr, Germany, in 1956.

In the early days, the two Swift/Hunter FR squadrons held eliminating rounds to select three pilots, the six then competing against each other to provide two pilots and a reserve for the RAF's short range, day team. They then joined their Canberra colleagues in the long range/night class and similar representations from the Dutch and Belgian air forces to make up the overall 2ATAF team. The opposing 4ATAF competitors came initially from USAFE and the FAF until the French opted out to participate thereafter only as 'guests'; the GAF and RCAF then joining the Americans. For the next nine years the FR10 would compete primarily against the RF-84F, RF-101, RF104 & RF-4C, with the French guests flying the Mirage. Royal Flush itself was then held on one base, rotating between the nations, and there was much to

commend the single-base concept. The simplicity of the model lent itself to most productive and enjoyable professional and social intercourse, resulting in a cross-feed of how, why and with what the various participants went about their business. Fierce rivalry there may have been on the day, with some nations perhaps more secretive than others on competition practices, but when flying with the Swift team the author did not sense that potentially beneficial recce ideas were being hidden from NATO Allies.

Mounted from a single base, the early Royal Flush exercises had the great virtue of fairness; all competitors within each category overflew the same targets within the same time window and therefore in more or less the same weather. Moreover, because relatively few targets were needed, they could be the best available and most representative of those which might be tasked in war, with sufficient well briefed airmen to act as ground umpires at each target, in order to judge the weather, log the times over target of each player, assess tactics and, if necessary, report violations. In the case of mobile, military targets, the umpires could also verify location, consistency of disposition and state of camouflage. Given so few targets involved in each category, the same PIs could be used to assess the resulting photographs and reports, with on-the-spot arbitration by judges if necessary; the whole process completed in short order. All the photographs, aircrew and PI reports, assessments and final results were posted for players to see when the bar opened at the end of each day's flying. Every team member was assumed to be among the best his squadron

Early Days. In only its second year with the FR10, IV Squadron did well in Royal Flush VII at Ramstein Air Base

Kit Netherton leaving the cockpit in a hurry. *IV Sqn*

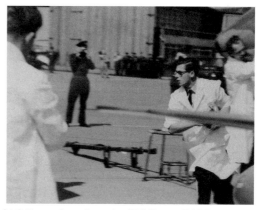

SAC Kennedy rushing the F.95 film to 7 MFPU. *IV Sqn*

Eric Smith receiving the 'Outstanding Day Squadron' trophy. *IV Sqn*

Eric Smith flanked by team members Oscar Wild (L) & Kit Netherton. *IV Sqn*

could produce, but it was well recognised that even he was capable of a random misfortune or of making a human error. To lose was particularly painful for him and a matter of regret to his squadron and air force, but this form of competition was quite rightly not seen as a measure of overall effectiveness in wartime conditions and professional reputations were, at worst, only dented. Above all, there were few opportunities for the many unethical practices which developed in later formats, which could be detrimental to the truly operational training to which all NATO nations should have been firmly committed.

After the eliminating rounds two pilots from II and IV Squadrons took part in the first Royal Flush competition with the FR10 in May 1961 at Beauvechain, Belgium. Eric Smith, who would be highly successful in many a Royal Flush, was

part of this team. He recalls: 'I overflew one target, designated a 'communications centre', at about 500 ft but couldn't see anything; this worried me because I knew I had taken a photograph of the exact location, but as I dropped my height and looked back over my shoulder I saw a single guyed pole-aerial silhouetted right on the position given. The target did not even show in 3-D on the negatives but the PI circled the spot and we put in our claim. We were the only ones to gain top marks and we watched with amusement as the French studied the print with a magnifying glass in the hope of challenging our reports'.

The newly formed Hunter team contributed markedly to overall victory for 2ATAF over 4ATAF for the Gruenther Trophy and was defeated only narrowly in its short-range day event. The ORB records that Eric managed the

Hunter team in the following year's competition, Royal Flush VII at Ramstein AB, IV Squadron going from strength to strength with Eric, Oscar Wild and Kit Netherton representing the two FR10 squadrons and winning outright in their class.

No. IV Squadron began its preparations for Royal Flush VIII, scheduled for May 1963, early in the year, given new impetus when a resident PI was established and Flight Lieutenant Eric Anderson arrived in February to fill the post. After a highly competitive selection process, five pilots were chosen to proceed to the next stage of the competition, the ORB recording: 'The limit of perfection in the subsonic visual recce role has surely been reached, which means that the competition turns largely on temperament, gimmicks and luck. Morale is good and our tricks cupboard is bare – so all we need now is the good offices of Lady Fortune.' This time Bob Price managed a team of four pilots, comprising Oscar Wild, Pat King, John Owen and Clive Haggett; Stanford Howard looked after the in-flight recording cell and Eric Anderson was joined by fellow PIs Eric Lockwood and Ian McGregor, while Pat Burke ran 7 MFPU. With the French not playing, IV Squadron competed against the 4ATAF RF-84Fs of the GAF's Immelmann Wing at Ingoldstadt. All team members flew two sorties, each comprising one pin-point target and a line search. No. IV Squadron won the day with 767 points against 507 for the Immelmann Wing. Summing up, Ray

Two Heads. Pat King, IV Squadron, and a photographic interpreter pool their expertise in planning a sortie in preparation for the Sassoon Trophy competition. *IV Sqn*

Bannard recorded: 'The competition is very expensive in aircraft hours and manpower and very few pilots benefit from it. Nevertheless the atmosphere and spirit of competition permeates throughout the whole squadron and much is learned by those who observe. I hope to see the competition continue, but in a form which will encourage an exchange of views and techniques.'

Competition was now all-pervading on IV Squadron and, with no pause after Royal Flush, intensive training began in June for the Sassoon Trophy, fully utilising the six aircraft which remained available on the squadron (two being on the modification programme). The exercise was flown on 15 July but this time best efforts were to no avail, the squadron team of Ray Bannard, Oscar Wild, Clive Haggett, Bo Plummer and Stanford Howard coming fourth out of the five squadrons competing.

The major downside to the single base concept for Royal Flush was that, other than in the eliminating rounds, too few could play and those who went on to the later rounds took a disproportionate part of a squadron's total assets (the best aircraft and reserves, equipment and men) if they were to stand a chance of defeating their opponents. This could leave little for the remainder to work with during the long run-up to and during the competition. The solution adopted in 1964 put all the operational elements of each eligible squadron to the test collectively and simultaneously on a common Royal Flush pattern but at their home bases, weighing the individual and aggregate results within each ATAF to identify the best pilots/crews, squadrons and ultimately the winning ATAF. There was clearly great merit in testing this overall capability, the outcome of which was dependent not only on the aircrew but also all the support agencies in the overall organisation and employment of resources; in short it would now embrace whole squadrons, their wing and national back-up. So every measure was considered to enhance domestic organisations and systems to best satisfy competition requirements, but which would hopefully also meet the demands in war. Typically, although it was not available for this first 'new look' Royal Flush, a dedicated teleprinter was purloined by IV Squadron to provide continuous updates on airfield colour states, and thus a reliable indicator of the prevailing weather in those areas. This was a very good example of an entirely legitimate improvement in capability for use in peace and war. Royal Flush did inspire innovation.

There were, however, major criticisms of the multi-base concept from the start. As with all other competition rules and procedures, the methods by which targets were chosen and allocated changed over the years, ranging from selection at squadron level using competition dossiers to assignment by the tasking agencies which would perform the same role in war. Unrealistic scenarios and potential inequalities abounded. If the choice of targets was left to the squadrons or national staff they would clearly choose those closest to their recce bases, the easiest to find, access and recce, and/or those already known to their players, rather than simulate as closely as possible the demands of a war scenario. It has since been said that some squadron target libraries, which should have been placed under lock and key before the competitions, were hidden away and used covertly on the day. It is also possible that some army units which provided mobile targets ensured that they favoured their national recce forces, perhaps even leaking the essential details (This was later found to have been the case). Most importantly, competitors within each class no longer flew over the same targets within the same timeframe and weather, so there was no longer a 'level playing field'. Clearly there would no longer be enough qualified, unbiased umpires to cover the vast increase in the number of targets involved, even if they were predictable, to confirm that each was in place and could be acquired visually from the air at or close to the position given, and that any violations of prescribed rules were properly reported.

Supporters of the new format claimed that this full cover was not necessary because good photographs of the map reference could attract full marks, while many (very visible) airborne umpires would lurk in the target areas to see fair play.

Few denied that a brand new 'tricks cupboard' had been opened, with more opportunities for 'gamesmanship' and the gimmicks which were considered fair game by some (usually the winners) and grossly detrimental to operational practices by others (usually the losers). With squadron reputations now very much on the line, certainly more so than when representative teams played against each other, it was very tempting to resort to the unethical.

In this first year of the 'home-based' Royal Flush, II Squadron came second in its class, only 1.8 per cent behind the leaders, giving them some authority to comment on the new format. Officer Commanding II Squadron, David Thornton, wrote in the ORB: 'Competition flying is looked upon as a means to an end, but naturally everyone wants to do well and thus considerable working-up time is devoted to the two annual competitions at speeds and heights that are not operational and could have a long term adverse effect on the operational capabilities of the pilots. I am sure that it would be preferable to have just one competition a year.' He spoke for many but his words fell on deaf ears; not only did the nation's Sassoon competition prevail, but its 'par time' for the routes to be followed was reduced to 330 kts, greatly favouring the Canberras and adding

Hard at It. Flight Lieutenant Pete Rayner, II Squadron, prepares for a Royal Flush sortie in 1964, under the watchful eye of a USAF umpire. *II Sqn*

Can't Stop! Hugh Cracroft and II Squadron photographers waste no time in getting the information to their customers in this practice for Royal Flush in 1965. *II Sqn*

The Nerve Centre. No. II Squadron Royal Flush project officers Sam Jeffreys (left) and Alex Weiss were meticulous in their planning for the competition. *II Sqn*

further weight to the argument that the competition was not rehearsing operational practices for those aircraft which should be making the best of their potential.

In 1965 and 1966 Royal Flush followed the 1964 format, except that certain rules were changed to placate the strongest voices. In both years II Squadron worked hard and thought it had done well but it lagged behind IV Squadron, now commanded by Eric Smith, which was at its best in 1966 (See Chapter Five) and Taff Wallis became the squadron's hero. He himself takes up the story: 'I see from my log book that I flew three sorties on the 10 May and two on the 11th

before having trouble on the final one necessary to complete my commitment on the 12th. After getting airborne on that third day my engine ran down to and stayed at 6,800 rpm, regardless of throttle position (this was later attributed to a failure in the fuel control unit). I returned to the airfield and loitered overhead while the squadron debated the rules in these circumstances with the Royal Flush umpires.'

This sort of thing had always been a contentious issue and where some previous missions had been aborted for similar reasons they had been awarded 'nil points', effectively depriving them of any chance of heading the order of merit. Fortunately for Taff and IV Squadron common sense prevailed on this occasion and he was allowed to land and complete his sixth mission in the spare aircraft. Taff continues: 'No one was more surprised than I when the overall results showed that I had been placed third in the individual pilot order of merit (behind two French 'non-NATO guest pilots') – and best individual pilot in 2ATAF. Needless to say, there was a lot of champagne about that night and no flying for me for the next day or two.'

A contingent from II Squadron, led by the author, joined the victorious IV Squadron at FAF Strasbourg on 16 July for the prize giving ceremony, to congratulate its sister squadron and

Rehearsal. The author debriefs a photographer after a Royal Flush practice sortie, as the magazines are rushed for processing. *II Sqn*

Duty Carried Out. Eric Smith debriefs a Royal Flush sortie with PI Eric Adamson (foreground), under the watchful eye of a NATO umpire. *IV Sqn*

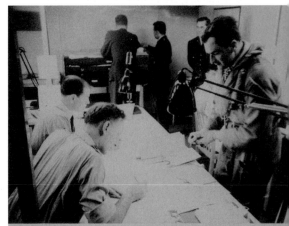

They Also Serve Who Stand and Wait. No. 2 MFPU, led by Flight Lieutenant 'Butch' Butcher' is ready and waiting. *II Sqn*

Help! Taff Wallis, ready to fly, sees his Royal Flush target for the first time – while PIs and Ground Liaison staff prepare to brief him. *Mike French*

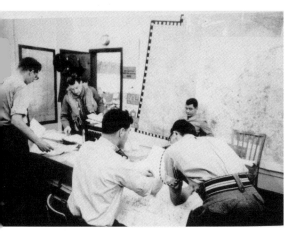

celebrate this great achievement. It would not be their last.

The results of the Sassoon competition which followed in September were very different, the Hunters losing out to two Canberra squadrons. However, IV Squadron claimed a moral victory, its ORB recording that 'some Canberras blatantly disregarded the rules but suffered no penalties and our FR10s had better prints.' So much for the much vaunted spirit of competition.

As Royal Flush developed in the Hunter era, with a proliferation of umpires in the air and on the ground but no knowing which targets were covered, it was wise to stay within the rules of the day, to approach each target at 'normal operating speeds' below 1,000 ft and not turn 'significantly' within 5 nm of the target to have more time for visual surveillance. Weather, time and fuel permitting, however, there was nothing to stop orbits at height outside the 5 nm exclusion zone in order to locate the target early, refine the approach and have a long look at the target to improve the visual report. Armed with a pair of binoculars, Peter Gover tried this tactic at a safe height during a work-up and found that it had its limitations. On his first orbit, as he moved his glasses from abeam to ahead, he came suddenly upon an unmarked, guyed aerial, frighteningly close through the magnification. On his second attempt he swung them from ahead to abeam to come face-to-face with a GAF pilot in an F-104 who had crept up unnoticed to formate on him. What the German pilot thought of this NATO colleague who needed binoculars to see him that close can only be imagined. Dropping his glasses for a second time Peter called it a day, conceding that this was probably an impractical expedient.

Umpires would sometimes help the players, albeit unwittingly, as the following story on Royal Flush in a IV Squadron commemorative booklet reveals. As the pilot approached his IP to find, photograph and to report on a military unit deployed in a military training area 10 nm west of Wetzlar in Germany, he heard the following transmission on Guard frequency:

Voice: Aircraft over Wetzlar, are you going to remain orbiting?
Aircraft: Yes.
Voice: Are you a Royal Flush umpire in a T-33?
Aircraft: Yes.
(Now forewarned that there is an umpire in the area the pilot immediately reduced his

Serious competition planning and scanning on IV Squadron.

Barry Stott. *IV Sqn*

Brian Meadley and Mike Nuttall. *IV Sqn*

Mike French. *IV Sqn*

Tony Richardson. *IV Sqn*

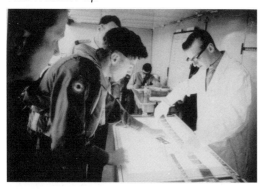

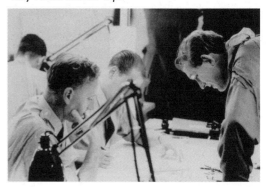

(Top, L to R) Mike Seyd, Iain Weston; (Below, L to R) Jim Dymond, Pete Headley, Eric Smith and Peter Gover. *IV Sqn*

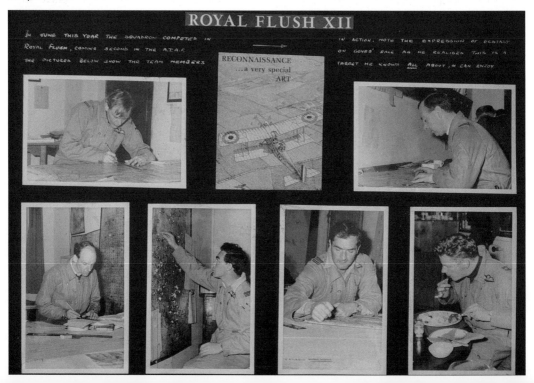

Semaphore. Mike French, IV squadron, signals the groundcrew as he taxis in from a Royal Flush sortie. *IV Sqn*

On the Record. IV Squadron excelled in Royal Flush XI, 1966, as the 'outstanding day reconnaissance squadron', with Taff Wallis as the 'outstanding day reconnaissance pilot'. *IV Sqn*

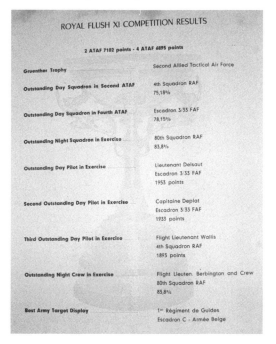

ROYAL FLUSH XI COMPETITION RESULTS

2 ATAF 7102 points - 4 ATAF 6895 points

Gruenther Trophy	Second Allied Tactical Air Force
Outstanding Day Squadron in Second ATAF	4th Squadron RAF 75,18%
Outstanding Day Squadron in Fourth ATAF	Escadron 3/33 FAF 78,15%
Outstanding Night Squadron in Exercise	80th Squadron RAF 83,8%
Outstanding Day Pilot in Exercise	Lieutenant Delsaut Escadron 3/33 FAF 1953 points
Second Outstanding Day Pilot in Exercise	Capitaine Deplat Escadron 3/33 FAF 1933 points
Third Outstanding Day Pilot in Exercise	Flight Lieutenant Wallis 4th Squadron RAF 1893 points
Outstanding Night Crew in Exercise	Flight Lieuten. Berbington and Crew 80th Squadron RAF 83,8%
Best Army Target Display	1er Régiment de Guides Escadron C - Armée Belge

The Winners Taff Wallis (centre) and a victorious IV Squadron celebrate their awards. *IV Sqn*

height from 2,000 to 500 ft and increased speed from 250 to 420 kts.)

Voice: Could you go to 288.2?

T-33: Roger.

(Pause as voice, T-33 and recce pilot change frequency to 288.2 mcs and the voice reveals that he is a ground umpire at the target location)

Ground Umpire: The Honest Johns and tank regiment haven't arrived yet, all we have here are a few tanks, jeeps and some infantry dug in.

T-33: Roger.

Ground Umpire: When is the next player due?

T-33: Anytime now.

Ground Umpire: Ah, I see him! (spotting the FR10 pilot, now at competition height and speed).

T-33: Roger – looks OK to me. (Hunter pilot cackling with insane glee, spots Leopard tank, APC and a few Jeeps, takes photograph, doesn't see infantry but knows they're there so includes in his in-flight report: 'Suspect infantry in area' and resists temptation to ask for exact location of infantry and returns to base giggling uncontrollably, with the expectation of being awarded very high marks.

Luck could be a major factor in Royal Flush.

In 1967, II Squadron again believed it had done well in Royal Flush, with only one camera failure. Apart from that, its pilots and PIs were confident that exact target locations had been photographed well but, crucially, nothing was seen of several mobile, military targets which were said to be there. Were they indeed there, too well camouflaged for even the cameras to see, not there but unseen nearby, or had they just gone home to tea (two of those at issue were in Belgium and they were tasked close to the end of a day's play)? Queries to the judges failed to produce satisfactory answers and to its dismay the squadron found itself placed 5th out of 12 participants, 1 per cent behind IV Squadron. Those pilots who had competed in the single base exercises, where results were posted for all to see by the end of each day, came to regret the fact that with this exercise format there could be no such post-mortem. Regardless of disappointment, the senior person on II Squadron felt able to write in the ORB: 'I would like to record my complete satisfaction with the squadron; the honest endeavour of everyone involved in the exercise, individually and collectively, exceeding anything I have seen in my long experience of this competition'. Such pride underlined one of the main benefits of this form of competition, that of

bringing together all those involved in the total recce process and melding them into an effective team with a common purpose.

At the start of 1969 it seemed that those who favoured a return to the representative team, single base concept, had convinced the establishment that it was the better option overall, but subsequent political pressures or louder voices won the day to retain the multi-base pattern. There was also a laudable attempt to replicate the modus operandi in war by involving everyone within the established battle management organisation, with respective ATAF tasking agencies brought into the loop to allocate targets to their squadrons as they would in war. Regrettably, this quickly proved that some of those who matched targets to missions lacked the necessary expertise or currency in their roles to be sufficiently judicious in their tasking. The fliers were now very uneasy, believing that mistakes would be inevitable and costly, and that they would be penalised in competition (and worse in

The Last 'Flush'. Hunter FR10s flew their last Royal Flush competition from Deelen Air Base in Holland in 1970.

The Aircraft. *IV Sqn*

Sam Goddard arrives at N°4MFPU (known as "The Muff") on completion of his 4th sortie in "Royal Flush XV" RNLAF Deelen   14 MAY 70

Just Desserts. Sam Goddard, named 'best individual pilot' needs a helping hand into the limelight. *IV Sqn*

Good Sortie? Sam Goddard looks content as he hurries to debrief his final sortie of the competition. *IV Sqn*

A Very Royal Flush. His Royal Highness Prince Bernhard of the Netherlands, graced the Awards Ceremony for Royal Flush at the Dutch Air Base of Deelen, where Peter Gover accepted the Gruenther Trophy on behalf of 2ATAF and Sam Goddard the accolade of Best Individual Pilot. *IV Sqn*

'When Do We Get To Keep It?' Officer Commanding IV Squadron counts the number of times IV Squadron has won the 'Best Day Squadron' trophy – more than any other squadron in NATO. *IV Sqn*

war) for ineptitude or poor judgment beyond their control. With such concerns rampant, this well-intentioned objective to improve the simulation of war was short lived. Thereafter, each participant would be required to fly three sorties from a list issued by the TOC for final selection by the squadrons and, for some inexplicable reason, the valuable expedient of in-flight reporting was excluded from the competition. All this may have satisfied some but it did not reflect realities and said little for the organisation which would come into play in war. The new look exercise also prompted Derek Whitman, IV Squadron's acting CO, to comment: 'I do think the concept is spoiled because the competitive element of pilot skills in the air, together with the effectiveness and efficiency of the squadron's supporting elements on the ground, such as the MFPU and the GLO briefings, is substantially undermined by the universal pre-knowledge of the static targets assigned to each mission'. That said, his squadron put every effort into the 1969 Royal Flush, at the expense of all else, and came top of its class in 2ATAF with 73.36 per cent, closely followed by II Squadron with

Big Click – Aalborg, Denmark, 1970.

The Rewards. Moose David guards the Overall Winners Trophy, Dave Bagshaw the Best Individual Pilot Cup. *Moose David*

Welcome Home. The Station Commander, Group Captain Keith Williamson, welcomes Dave Bagshaw and the Big Click team back to Gutersloh. *Moose David*

72.11 per cent. No. IV Squadron competed in Royal Flush for the last time at Deelen AB in Holland in 1970, Sam Goddard carrying off the 'Best Individual Pilot Cup'.

Not to be outdone, II Squadron entered the 1970 AFNORTH Big Click recce competition, an exercise optimised for NATO recce forces in the region, the Germans in Schleswig Holstein, the Danes and Norwegians on their home grounds. Although unlikely to be tasked there, the Hunters were invited as guest players and readily accepted the opportunity to fly over very unfamiliar terrain and targets, typically route recces in very mountainous areas and shipping searches in the open sea and the many inlets and fjords. In preparation, the pilots carried out many high-low-high and land-away sorties before deploying with their groundcrew and 2 MFPU to the Danish base of Aalborg in Jutland for the competition in August.

Unaccustomed as they were to tasks of that sort in that region, the II Squadron team of Dave Bagshaw, Tim Thorn and Bill Norton, managed by their new boss, Moose David, were all experienced men and they excelled. They won Big Click outright, Dave Bagshaw being named 'Best Pilot', with Tim Thorn coming a close second. The MFPU took the Best Photo Lab award and the PIs the Best PI/Int trophy. It was a fitting finale for the trophy hunters.

However logical the arguments in favour of competition, in whatever form, the sceptics were never appeased. The purists remained implacably opposed on the grounds that there would always be ways of circumventing the rules and that any rules acceptable to all (always with reluctance by some) would be inconsistent with certain operational practices. Moreover, they deplored the often excessive time devoted to competition training, the results of which were no true measure of a squadron's or nation's operational tac recce capability and might bring out the worst in some players. So it was that dissension, acrimony and conflict within and between the NATO air forces over the benefits, realism, operational value, flight safety implications and price to pay for competitions persisted throughout the Hunter era. Be that as it may, and whatever the pros and cons, the tac recce squadrons had no choice but to live with the competitions which were so dear to the heart of hierarchies and to many at lower levels in the participating nations. The overall winners in peacetime were those who learned the facts of life, and some RAFG squadrons did very well from them, the Hunter FR10 itself earning an enviable reputation in competitions throughout its operational life.

Chapter 8
Gibraltar Duty

When a 'no-fly zone' was imposed by Spain around Gibraltar in the summer of 1967, the Gutersloh FR10 squadrons were required to take it in turns, with the 38 Group Hunter FGA9 squadrons, to provide a continuous presence of two aircraft in the colony. Their task was to safeguard the sovereignty of British airspace and to allow free access to civilian and military aircraft against any harassment by the Spanish Air Force.

The new restrictions made operations at the airfield difficult, particularly for civilian airliners in bad weather. All aircraft using Runway 27 were required to make an offset approach on a heading of 300 deg until approximately half a mile and 200 ft from the threshold before turning on to the runway heading to land. Runway 09 had to be approached via the centre of Algeciras Bay on 350 deg before turning starboard to the runway heading.

Flight Lieutenants Frank Mitchell and Geoff Hall of II Squadron took the first two RAFG FR10s to Gibraltar to relieve a pair of FGA9s from 54 Squadron on 11 July 1967, flying initially to Decimomanu to refuel and team up with a Canberra tasked to navigate them safely to their destination. After take-off from 'Deci', the Canberra suffered an electrical fire in the cockpit which the captain, Squadron Leader Paddy English (well known to the two Hunter pilots from earlier QFI tours) and his very competent navigator dealt with successfully. Although the Canberra was then left with no navigation facilities it was decided to press on to Gibraltar, making good use of such bearings as the FR10's were able to provide from their radio compasses, an ironic turn of events since the Canberra was there solely to navigate them to their destination. Visibility at height was excellent and the peninsula was sighted 100 nm out, with the trio coming under radar control thereafter. Unaware of recently introduced air traffic restrictions, the three aircraft flew several passes over the airfield with the Hunters in close formation on the Canberra, first in 'vic', then in line astern and finally in echelon starboard, all aboard satisfied that they had 'shown the flag' well. Those on the ground took a very different view. The requirement existed to report any violation of the restricted area to the Foreign Office in detail and in writing, and this flag waving initiative had generated more infringements than had occurred since the zone had been created several weeks before. So it was not surprising that the station hierarchy was there in force to meet the first aircraft on to the chocks – Geoff Hall hurriedly pointing to Frank, the detachment commander, who was still taxiing in. Frank in turn pointed to the Canberra following him and it was left to Paddy English to explain. Why had the flight not been warned off by ATC as soon as its intentions became clear?

The Hunters remained on alert throughout the daylight hours, one or both aircraft (the number

Shipping Watch. Airborne from Gibraltar, Peter Rayner spots two Russian ships, a Kresta class cruiser and J-Class Submarine. *Pete Rayner*

Alternative Transport. Despite the combined efforts of the Gutersloh pilots when off watch, this man-carrying kite failed to come up to expectations. *Peter Gover*

depending on other scheduled air movements) permitted to get airborne for whatever training was possible, including simulated attacks on RN ships to test their defences. Otherwise, they

Unique Rendezvous. Quite accidentally, aircraft and aircrew of Nos I (Hunter FGA9), II (FR10), 3 (Canberra) and IV (Hunter FR10) Squadrons meet in Gibraltar. *Frank Mitchell*

Welcome. The indigenous population of Gibraltar made the FR pilots welcome. *Peter Gover*

would spend their time looking for other shipping, always with the prospect of sighting Soviet vessels of interest: II Squadron's Pete Rayner finding one of the new Russian Kresta warships some way out in the Mediterranean

Unlikely Bedfellows. A Fiat G91 joins a Royal Navy Sea Vixen and Buccaneer somewhere over the Mediterranean. *Roger Wilkins*

and a 'J' Class submarine in the Straits of Gibraltar.

Off duty, water sports abounded, with a motorboat available from the Officers' Mess for water skiing or less active pursuits. The boat came in useful when the FR10 pilots flight tested a man-carrying kite known as 'Crab 1' (in deference to RN vernacular). This project hardly got off the ground, even when unwisely tested in front of a visiting team from the Empire Test Pilots (who presumably took one look at it and thought better of interfering). Surprisingly, no-one recalls any thrilling exploits with this potentially dangerous venture or what happened to the kite.

Then there was the challenge of the 'Rock' itself, owned by the apes who were welcoming enough but took little interest in the exertions of the more physically inclined visitors. To some, the Rock had to be climbed, walked up or run up, but again there are no great stories recorded of derring do or records broken by the men from Gutersloh.

What the Hunter pilots got up to after the sun went down, with all the social opportunities on the 'Rock', is another matter. They often met interesting people and aircraft in transit through the station and the down town Casino drew them like a magnet to play roulette or simply take drink while listening to music. On one such occasion, in what Geoff Hall called 'something akin to a Hollywood comedy', Frank Mitchell tripped on the stairs into the Casino gardens, sprawling below as the sound of clanging tray and shattering glass filled the void while the band took a rest. Of course this earned little sympathy from his peers who led the laughter as an uninjured Frank dusted himself off. While they were arguing who should pay for a replacement round, a tray of champagne arrived unannounced, said to have been paid for by a wealthy and immaculately dressed punter who, having just lost a great deal of money on the tables, quickly regained his sense of humour at the sight of Frank's antics.

There were mixed feelings among the Gutersloh pilots and supporting groundcrew when their presence was no longer deemed necessary and they were released from the Gibraltar commitment in July 1968. This had been an enjoyable diversion from the routine in Germany, but it was costly and contributed little to realistic, operational training.

Chapter 9
Action in Aden

No 8 Squadron Crest.

Empire Outpost

Centred on Aden, British Forces Arabian Peninsula (land, sea and air) were responsible for a vast area extending from East Africa through Somalia and the Aden Protectorates to the Persian Gulf, including Muscat and Oman and Masirah Island. The main air base at RAF Khormaksar in Aden offered staging facilities for civilian aircraft and the RAF's strategic transports, while accommodating a resident force of tactical transports, (including helicopters), fighter bombers, reconnaissance and maritime aircraft. The Hunter FR10 force would be the main source of near real time information on activities throughout the area, joining the Royal Navy's organic air support in offensive action, offshore surveillance and search and rescue operations.

Long-standing tensions between the forces of the Crown and indigenous factions in the Protectorates, supported by the Republic of Yemen, persisted throughout the 1950s. Timely information on potentially hostile movements was essential and much of this requirement had been met by PR Canberras of Nos 13 and 58 Squadrons deployed from RAF Akrotiri in

Cyprus and RAF Wyton in the UK respectively. However, there was also a need for a resident unit of faster, armed reconnaissance aircraft and, initially, four Meteor FR9s of C Flight No. 8 (Venom) Squadron, equipped with cameras to supplement the pilots' visual reports, served this purpose.

In August 1959, the FR9 force became a separate entity known as the Arabian Peninsula Reconnaissance Flight (APRF): Flight Lieutenants Fred Trowern, 'Porky' Munro and 'Manx' Kelly (all ex-FR9 pilots from RAF Germany) and the four Meteors coming under the command of Flight Lieutenant Tai Retief. This new unit remained heavily committed to diverse support of Venom operations, flying pre-strike recces for targeting purposes, marking targets with their 20-mm cannon for a strike force and taking post-strike photographs. They were also involved in dropping leaflets to warn dissidents of imminent attack and in the delivery of Christmas cards (to friendly forces!) by air. Having talked his way out of his last appointment as a flying instructor, Fred Trowern remembers these as 'halcyon days', but the operational tasks were not easy and one replacement pilot who failed to make the grade was posted out.

The pilots of 8 Squadron and the APRF completed their conversion to the Hunter at Chivenor in September 1960, the two units merging again on their return to Aden, with B Flight now established as a recce element within the squadron. In order to retain their special expertise pending the arrival of the FR10s, and indeed while the new aircraft were 'settling in' during periods of poor serviceability, the recce pilots continued to conduct operations with the Meteors and were allotted additional flying time on the squadron's new Hunter FGA9s. Middle East Command (MEC), with its HQ in Aden and Air Marshal Sir Charles Elworthy in command, assumed the responsibilities of British Forces Arabian Peninsula in 1961, Air Forces Middle East (AFME) being the air element, with Air Vice-Marshal F.E. Freddie Rosier as the AOC. MEC would orchestrate all operations and

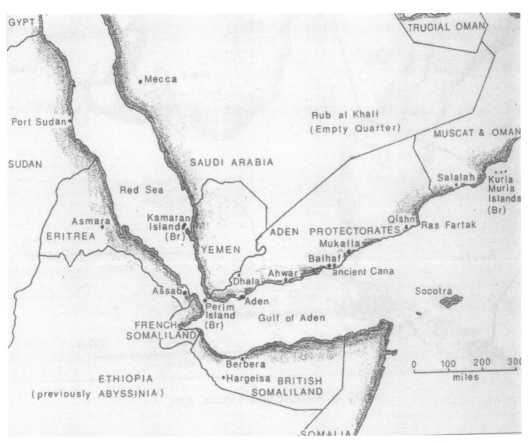

Area or Responsibility. HQ MEC had responsibilities from Kenya, through the original Aden Protectorates east to Muscat and Oman. Colin Richardson & Author

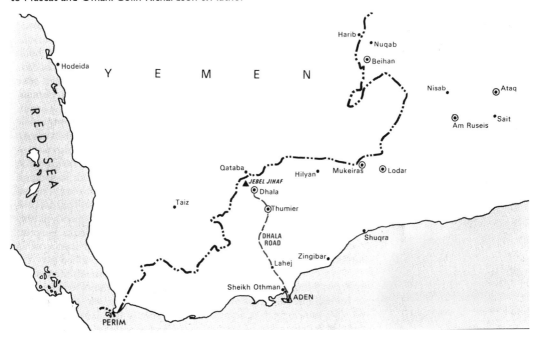

Me and My Shadow. Flight Lieutenant Fred Trowern and his Meteor FR9 of the APRF cast their shadow over the deserts of Aden – to which Fred would return in a reincarnation. *Fred Trowern*

administrative support for the three armed services in Southern Arabia from 1962.

Four FR10s (plus a Command reserve) arrived to equip B Flight in April and May 1961, but they were given scant attention in No. 8 Squadron's ORB. 8 Squadron's engineering officer, Flying Officer Owen Truelove, threw some light on this when he recalled that Hunter serviceability was appallingly low and that much time was taken up on aircraft acceptance checks, together with

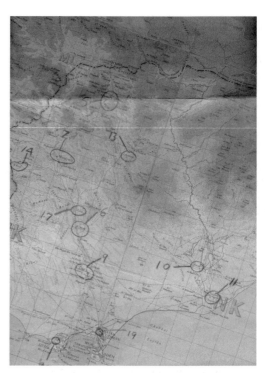

Aden Hinterland. The 'brown map' showing significant locations in Aden's hinterland. *Dave Bagshaw*

groundcrew, photographic support and pilot training. Some pilots flew as little as four hours/month in the FR10s. The flight suffered its first minor casualty in September 1961, when an

Top-Down. Roger Pyrah used his F95 oblique cameras for this vertical shot of Aden, Shamsan Mountain in the centre. *Roger Pyrah*

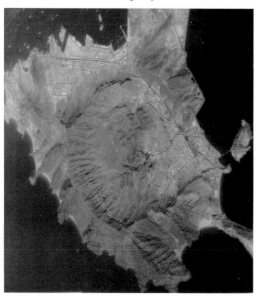

Transport Support. Part of the transport force of Argosies, Beverleys and Hastings at Khormaksar. *Roger Pyrah*

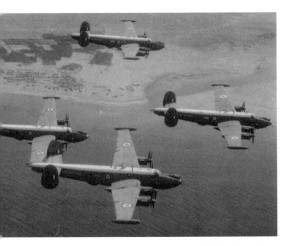

The 'Heavies'. The Shackletons of 37 Squadron provided Strike Wing with more fire power and a limited night capability. *Author's Collection*

Out With the Old. Meteor FR9s of the APRF retired from Aden in 1962. *Fred Trowern*

FR10 was struck by hostile fire in the Yaffa region and returned to Khormaksar with 'Cat 3' damage.

The problems facing both FGA and FR pilots over the very variable desert terrain were unusual, requiring quite different techniques from those used in Central Europe and which dominated operational training at 229 OCU. For many areas the flying maps available were simply inadequate; the large scale 'white maps' surveyed in the late 1940s were of little use now, while the smaller scale 'brown maps', reproduced from aerial photographs, relied on shading rather than contours and incorporated very few spot heights or place names. Furthermore, given the nomadic nature of the indigenous people, the positions of villages which were marked could not be relied upon.

Eyes Over Aden. FR10 XE599 of 8 Squadron approaching Aden in 1962. *Sandy Burns via Ray Deacon*

Ma'alla Straight. Home to many married servicemen and their families in Aden. *Sandy Burns via Ray Deacon Ray Deacon*

In With the New. The Meteor FR9s of the APRF were replaced by Hunter FR10s, which initially became part of No 8 Squadron, joining the FGA9s, both variants shown here with the squadron. *Ray Deacon*

With few opportunities to regain track by reference to the map, adherence to carefully planned headings, speeds and timing, was of the utmost importance. Where they could, the FR pilots corrected the positions of landmarks inaccurately plotted on their maps and added others for future use.

As aircraft serviceability improved, the FR10s were employed in wide-ranging support of ground and air forces in operations against rebel tribesmen, infiltration of supporting forces from the Yemen and their supply columns. In addition to working with the FGA9 squadrons, their main 'customers' were the infantry, Royal Marine, Parachute Regiment and Special Air Service (SAS) units, all of which wanted photographs to supplement or confirm any in-flight or subsequent visual reports. Khormaksar's Tactical Wing Photo Processing Section met this ever-increasing requirement with commendable

B Flight, No 8 Squadron. By 1962, the Hunter FR10s were flying in 8 Squadron's colours. *Derek Whitman*

Into the Radfan. An FR 10, bearing Geoff Timms' initials 'GT', heads for the hostile Radfan in 1962. *Ken Simpson*

Radfan Recce. Ralph Chambers' FR10 XE589 'RC' over the Radfan mountains. *Ralph Chambers via Ray Deacon*

Follow-My-Leader. Sandy Burns takes a 'nose facer' of Johnny Morris as they pass over a village on a flag waving mission. *Ralph Chambers via Ray Deacon.*

Lone Pioneer. An FR10 gives one of Khormaksar's versatile Twin Pioneer aircraft 'top cover' on its lonely mission up-country. *Ken Simpson*

efficiency, working from antiquated caravans said to date back to D-Day in Europe. In the absence of dedicated PIs, the pilots analysed the photographs themselves, poring over light tables to annotate the negatives and adding the grid references of targets they had covered.

1963: The Federation of South Arabia and Rebirth of 1417 Flight

On 1 January 1963, the British colony of Aden merged with the ten members of the Federation of the Emirates of the South to form the Federation of South Arabia. This British-sponsored federation would be heavily opposed by the people of Aden, with two rival nationalist groups emerging: the National Liberation Front (NLF) and the Front for the Liberation of Occupied South Yemen (FLOSY).

Pilot Officer David Baron, who arrived on 8

Head of the Line. A 1417 Flight T7 and two FR10s, head this line up on the pan at RAF Khormaksar in 1963. *Ray Deacon*

Workhorse. In 1963, 1417 Flight was made responsible for all T7 workhorses supporting the Hunter force at Khormaksar. *Ray Deacon*

Squadron fresh from Chivenor in that month, converted to the FR10 on the squadron. He remembers an initial check-out in the Hunter T7 with Flight Lieutenant Ernie Powell before being 'let loose' in the FR10, on which he flew 14 hours in that month on visual and photo recce sorties, with a further 10 hours on the FGA9. In February, March and April his flying included 7, 4 and 1 hour respectively on the FR10. This including two sorties on Operation Jacknife, in which he flew as a wingman patrolling the disputed border between the Western Aden Protectorate (WAP) and the Yemen at Beihan

Hunter Force. The Hunter FGA9 and FR10 Flight Line at RAF Khormaksar. *Roger Pyrah*

with loaded guns (given special dispensation because he was not 'combat ready').

The increasing importance attached to the FR10s was recognised in May 1963 when No. 1417 Flight, which had made a reputation for itself during WW2, was resurrected from 8 Squadron's B Flight and established as an independent unit with the five FR10s, five recce trained pilots and fifteen groundcrew (four of whom were photographic tradesmen). The flight would also be responsible for the Wing's Hunter

'Prussian Pete'. Flight Lieutenant Peter Lewis, the first flight commander of the No 1417 Flight when it re-formed with Hunter FR10s. *Peter Lewis*

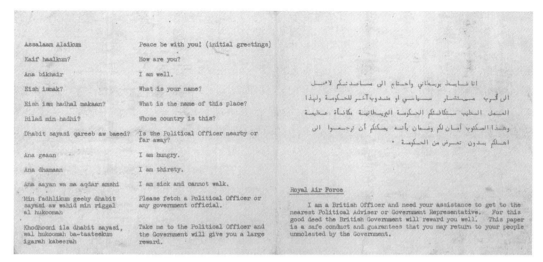

Assalaam Alaikum	Peace be with you! (initial greetings)
Kaif haalkum?	How are you?
Ana bikhair	I am well.
Eish ismak?	What is your name?
Eish ism hadhal makaan?	What is the name of this place?
Bilad min hadhi?	Whose country is this?
Dhabit sayasi qareeb aw baeed?	Is the Political Officer nearby or far away?
Ana geaan	I am hungry.
Ana dhamaan	I am thirsty.
Ana aayan wa ma aqdar amshi	I am sick and cannot walk.
Min fadhlikum geeby dhabit saysai aw wahid min riggal al hukoomah	Please fetch a Political Officer or any government official.
Khodhooni ila dhabit sayasi, wal hukoomah ba-taateekum igarah kabeerah	Take me to the Political Officer and the Government will give you a large reward.

Royal Air Force

I am a British Officer and need your assistance to get to the nearest Political Adviser or Government Representative. For this good deed the British Government will reward you well. This paper is a safe conduct and guarantees that you may return to your people unmolested by the Government.

'Goolie' Chit. Carried by all Hunter pilots in Aden, in the hope that reward would persuade the indigenous people of the Aden Protectorates to help any airmen to survive should they have the misfortune to come down in the desert. *Peter Taylor*

T7s. The Hunter element of Tactical Wing now comprised the FR10s of 1417 Flight and the FGA9s of Nos 8 and 208 Squadrons (which had been rotating to Bahrain on a two monthly basis since the Kuwait crisis of 1961), together with those of No. 43 Squadron which had arrived in Aden from Cyprus in March 1963. This formidable, well-rehearsed force of Hunters was now well placed to provide immediate tac recce and offensive support.

Flight Lieutenant Peter Lewis, originally assigned to 8 Squadron, was chosen to command the new FR flight by Wing Commander John Jennings, who had recently taken over from Wing Commander Chris Neville as OC Tactical Wing. The new unit was accommodated in what had been a drop-tank store, suitably modified into offices and crewrooms with help from the station 'works and bricks' department and a great deal of DIY. By popular consensus, an office was partitioned off for the boss, Peter Lewis having quickly earned the name 'Prussian Pete': 'the man who says and does the nastiest things in the nicest way'. Peter was, however, fulsome in his praise of those who helped meld the flight into a fully operational unit so quickly. His worldly wise warrant officer knew how to get the best out of the Hunter engineering expertise he had available and the 'thoroughbred' FR10s which had yet to be used to best effect in their primary role. The F95

cameras and their protective eyelids, often engrained with sand, needed a great deal of attention; the radio compasses were at best temperamental; the gauging of the 230 gall drop tanks was troublesome and the guns needed harmonising. All this, in addition to some

VIP Visit. Lieutenant General Sir Charles Harington, C-in-C Middle East Command, escorted by OC Tactical Wing, Wing Commander John Jennings and hosted by flight commander Peter Lewis at 1417 Flight. *Peter Lewis*

construction work on their facilities, the warrant officer and his men achieved in no more than a couple of weeks. SAC Ray Deacon, a wireless mechanic on 8 Squadron (who has become a well respected aviation archivist), remembers that 'a strong and productive bond developed between the squadron and the FR flight'.

The officers posted to 1417 Flight, all flight lieutenants at least 30 years old, married, over six feet in height and on their second or third fast-jet tours, did their bit. While Prussian Pete, as QFI and IRE, flew the mandatory dual checks, Geoff Timms provided the link with engineering support. Jim Dymond, a PAI and avid photographer, concentrated on the guns and cameras (it was he who was said to have had the idea of storing the F95s in plastic bags in the fridge for 'dust free environmental control').

Serious role training was already on the agenda, led by Johnny Morris (who knew a thing or two about FR and FGA operations from his time on Mustangs with the South African Air Force in Korea) and Tony Rimmer, an ex-Meteor FR pilot from the APRF. Johnny was a hard master. Typically, in order to demonstrate visual recce techniques and the difference between looking and seeing, he introduced a masochistic variation of 'Kim's Game'. For this, each pilot was required to stand on a chair while he sprinkled mapping pins on the floor behind them, then turn round for 15 seconds to memorise the number of pins and the pattern they had formed. Much emphasis was given to planning the use of terrain masking to achieve surprise and escape from the target unscathed, with the careful selection of IPs for the best photo runs. In prudent anticipation of long range sorties and joint operations with the FGA Hunters, cardboard 'prayer wheels' were constructed for quick and easy guidance in the air on the optimum use of speed, height and fuel management to achieve required ranges and precise timings. The flight was up and running.

A resourceful Peter Lewis also persuaded a specialist in Arab ways to give an insight into local cultures, an education which might stand the pilots in good stead should they have to eject 'up-country' and fall into dissident hands. This expert suggested that neither 'goolie chits' nor bribery with the gold coins carried by the pilots was likely to ensure their survival (and could indeed have fatal consequences), whereas a show of friendship with offerings of precious food or water might.

Everyone on the flight was invited to have a say in designing the insignia to adorn its FR10s, to signal their independence on the station. The outcome was a station crest enclosed in a black, green and yellow arrowhead (the colours of the Aden Protectorates), each aircraft also carrying the initials of one of the flight's pilots on its fin and nosewheel door. With all hands to the pump to achieve maximum impact, the whole job was completed in one night and, by the end of April 1963, Peter Lewis was able to tell John Jennings that 1417 Flight was officially ready for operations.

In June and July the FR10s joined the FGA9s in 'flag waving' sorties and recce missions before and after airborne resupply of troops in contact with hostile forces around Hilyan, and in support of ground operations generally in the Beihan area. Earlier, some supplies were seen to fall into the hands of hostile forces, but accurate photographs of the drop zones now helped to minimise this wasted effort. The FR10s also remained at various states of readiness, on and off for the next four months, to cover road convoys from Aden to Dhala, Lawdar and Ataq, and to carry out specific tasks, visual and photo, in the Mazut and Thoumar region.

Johnny Morris was as demanding in the air as he was on the ground, tasking the FR pilots with the most difficult of targets, from small caves hidden in steep-sided wadis to single, well-camouflaged military vehicles, and he would often lurk in target areas hoping to catch pilots unawares and prove as much with embarrassing gunsight film. He himself would fly as low as possible, making good use of terrain masking. As for the use of the FR10's four cannons, the overriding priority for the recce pilot was to survive and return with information, so hostile action would normally be avoided; however, knowing that air-to-air engagements were possible at any time the recce pilots were well versed in defensive combat and could use their guns to that end. There would also be times when braving ground fire was justified, and the FR10 pilots were ready to use the Hunter's guns to keep heads down, attack lucrative or fleeting targets on the ground or mark them for a strike force. Even then exposure would be kept to a minimum; whenever possible, strafing was carried out from the lowest practicable height on

Tank Troubles. FR10 XE589 ('RC') seen carrying four 100 gall drop tanks, perhaps as a temporary expedient while the inadvertent detachment of a 230 gall tank was investigated and remedial action taken. The tank had not taken kindly to its treatment on FR10 XF436 and tore away from its pylon, damaging the aircraft's wingtip as it made its way harmlessly to the ground – never to fly again. *Ray Deacon*

single passes and at precise timings, and this was practised regularly on the weapons ranges. Gunnery training also included the use of the fixed cross as an aiming alternative to the gyro gunsight pipper during severe turbulence. With meticulous attention to their weapons systems and continuity of training, the very experienced

Fighter Reconnaissance Pilot. Flight Lieutenant Roger Pyrah took command of 1417 Flight from Peter Lewis in 1964. *Roger Pyrah*

pilots of 1417 Flight soon proved themselves more than a match for those on the FGA9 squadrons. It seems likely that gunnery led to the loss of an FR10's 230 gall drop tank over the desert, fortunately causing little damage to the aircraft but requiring modifications to all the pylon mountings before the Hunters were authorised to fly again with the original clearances.

With a little help from one of Khormaksar's 37 Squadron Shackletons, Peter Lewis found a Russian submarine chaser some 180 nm out in the Indian Ocean after it had refuelled off the coast of Ethiopia. The photographs he took with his starboard-facing camera in a single pass showed that every gun on the warship that had him in its field of fire was tracking him; the Russians were clearly ready for anything. He was not so lucky when, on a similar search mission, he found a harmless cargo ship rather than a Soviet vessel and became trapped below a towering and very forbidding cumulus nimbus cloud - with no way out but up. The first 5,000 ft were bumpy but then everything went mad. Flashing blue and yellow lights accompanied uncontrollable pitching and rolling as he reduced to the recommended speed for the circumstances, clamping the rudder pedals with his feet and the stick with both hands and knees. The accelerometer hit the stops in both directions, the artificial horizon toppled, the G4F compass rotated 'like a roulette wheel', the airspeed indicator fluctuated wildly and the vertical speed indicator seemed stuck on 'up'. Still he went up at an alarming rate until he topped out, thankfully in clear blue sky, at 56,000 ft. The instruments began to recover during a prudently subdued descent, recovery and landing, after which the aircraft went straight into the hangar for a stress test and Peter headed for the bar to reflect on this interesting experience.

The intelligence staff in Aden and London were now most anxious to know what was going on at the Yemeni port of Hodeida, but this was a 'no-go' area for the recce aircraft and no such flight could be authorised. However, Peter Lewis had a plan. Ostensibly on an 'air test', he just happened to find himself within camera range of Hodeida and seized the opportunity to take some oblique shots, standing off at 10,000 ft. Pushing his luck, he then swooped down to 500 ft for one run with his port camera aimed at Hodeida, during which he caught sight of a couple of MiG fighters taking off from an airfield of which he was unaware. Deciding that caution was the better part of valour he made off with all possible speed at sea level hoping to obscure his presence against the waves breaking over the shore. In fact, it seems that the MiGs had not noticed him and he escaped. The films from this mission were processed secretly and successfully, but Peter would never see the results of the mission that never was.

The author's old friend, Flight Lieutenant Roger Pyrah, was posted to 43 Squadron in Aden in the summer of 1963, but as an accomplished FR pilot from his days with No. 79 (Swift FR5) Squadron he was quickly reassigned to 1417 Flight. He had hardly settled in than he was 'volunteered' to do a spell as the RAF Air Liaison Officer and FAC with the British commander and 600 local Arab soldiers of the Hadramaut Bedouin Legion (HBL). Their task was to establish some form of administration among the Mahra people in the area of Al Ghaidha some 500 nm north-east of Aden. The party set out in October for a very uncomfortable but interesting and demanding three weeks 'up-country', living with the natives in their very frugal and rather unhygienic conditions in the field. Fortunately, Roger had heeded advice and carried with him copious quantities of whisky, which may have helped to keep any desert malady at bay. On the plus side he learned how the soldiers operated in the desert and how best the FR flight could help them, of the practical problems of employing Aden's tactical air support in all its forms, and even how to build an airstrip.

No sooner was he back in Aden than he was recalled to Al Ghaidha, where his friends in the HBL had suffered some fatalities when attacked by the neighbouring Kidda Tribe. A retaliatory strike by the Hunters had been authorised and it was up to Roger to make the necessary arrangements and manage the operation on the spot. Kiddas in a local village were warned that a particular house would be targeted at a time given, and they very wisely witnessed its destruction from a safe distance. This was enough to convince them that further hostile action against the HBL was imprudent, the guilty who had 'lost face' having fled to the hills in shame to lick their wounds. A relative calm descended on the area but Roger was required to remain in situ for three weeks – just in case.

Exercise Biltong took Peter Lewis and Johnny Morris to RAF Muharraq in Bahrain for a week in October 1963, officially for a 'communications exercise' but in reality for a thorough recce of an area east of a line from Abu Dhabi to RAF Masirah, looking for illicit oil prospecting. With no detailed maps of the area this called for sightings to be plotted and double-checked with a bearing and distance from known features. Peter remembers one such trip in which he verified Johnny's report of 'an unusual encampment' as the sun was setting but with just enough light for what turned out to be useful photographic cover. With fuel getting low, he then climbed for home into the setting sun, levelling in the near silence at 40,000 ft as the stars began to glitter in the now purple sky above a desert wilderness scattered with the pinprick lights of the Bedouin fires. Peter was equally lyrical about those sorties flown in the growing light of dawn, quoting as he was wont from the Rubaiyat (The Rubaiyat of Omar Khayyam, a Persian Poet of the Middle Ages, translated by Fitzgerald):

Awake, for morning in the bowl of night
Has flung the Stone that puts the Stars to
    Flight
And lo! The Hunter of the East has caught
The Sultan's Turret in a Noose of Light.

Dawn Sortie. Peter Lewis sees the sun come up as he searches for illegal shipping off Aden. *Peter Lewis*

His wingman having gone unserviceable after take-off and aborted, Peter's return trip to Aden was equally long and lonely, but having used the cruise climb technique to 50,000 ft he landed with plenty of fuel at Khormaksar after a trip of 2 hours and 35 minutes. This may have been the first solo crossing of Rub al Khali, the 'Empty Quarter' (a sand sea in the south of Saudi Arabia) by a single engine jet. It was on sorties such as these that he sensed 'that nearness to God' which can be felt at such magical times by those with the good fortune to fly.

While his old friend was up country, the author was appointed to the air offensive staff in HQ MEC at Steamer Point, where the famous WW2 ace, AVM 'Johnnie' Johnson had just taken over as AOC. He would work in his office from 0700 to 1300 hours, normally the end of the working day, and then go to Khormaksar to talk to, or fly with, any of the four Hunter units, thereby acquainting himself with their operations and operating area. He recalls only too well a flurry of activity in the HQ when a Russian-built 'Crate' transport aircraft infringed WAP airspace and the pair of Hunters on patrol for just such an exigency requested authority to fire warning shots in an attempt to persuade the pilot to land. Unfortunately, the only officers able to give this permission were not immediately available before the intruder retreated across the border, followed by the Hunters - and an international incident was only narrowly averted. In a similar incident on 2 December 1963, a Crate landed on the Allied airstrip at Lawdar, perhaps in error, and was prevented from taking off again by a British officer who, with great presence of mind, parked his Landrover immediately in front of the taxiing aircraft. The errant Crate was quickly flown back to Khormaksar by an RAF crew, escorted by FR10s.

Matters took a nasty turn on 10 December when a grenade was thrown at the High Commissioner as he and his entourage were walking across the pan on the civilian part of Khormaksar. His aide, George Henderson, promptly flung himself on to the grenade to take the full force of its detonation, an heroic act rewarded by a posthumous George Cross. This prompted increased vigilance and security measures; wire guards appeared on the windows of buses, military lorries and vulnerable buildings, the huge airbase thereafter patrolled by three RAF Regiment squadrons. The Officers' Mess was among the attractive targets, and indeed in the final years a bomb was hidden below the floorboards of the dining room, set to detonate at breakfast time; fortunately it exploded without causing injury during the night. With such threats, one officer slept with a sidearm under his pillow, firing it at a nocturnal intruder before recognising him as an RAF policeman searching for a villain. This excessive prudence earned him a court martial.

The tranquil days of relative calm in Aden may now have been over but after acclimatising to the unfamiliar environment life was still good. With heat hovering consistently between 90-100 deg F and humidity at 80 per cent by day and night for much of the summer season, air conditioning was highly desirable (but rarely provided) in working and living accommodation (the author had only a fan in his bedroom). Much of the married accommodation was new, particularly the flats on the Ma'alla Strip, and officers' wives had the help of Ayahs, often young Somali girls, who were given basic living quarters nearby. They would look after the domestic chores and any young children, allowing the British to take every advantage of the excellent sporting and social facilities in Aden. Many of the British servicemen (but not all) worked only in the mornings, spending the rest of the day on one of the beaches set aside for them, with every refreshment available and served at their whim.

The author's log book shows that he flew on Christmas Day 1963 as No. 2 on the standby pair, with 43 Squadron flight commander Anthony Mumford in the lead. It was an uneventful trip but Anthony made sure that his wingman was properly debriefed on shortcomings in his performance before they joined the festivities – Aden fashion.

1964: The Radfan Campaign

Then it began in earnest. An 'O Group' on New Year's Day 1964 heralded a major offensive in the Radfan area, some 35 nm north of Aden, an

Strike! A British soldier looks on a Hunter pulls up having struck its target, top left. *Roy Bowie*

inhospitable, mountainous region, with peaks and plateaus towering to 7,000 ft traversed by deep wadis. It was home to a multitude of hostile tribes and ideal terrain for their hit and run tactics, the rebels hiding in numerous caves by day and striking by night over ground well known to them. For some time Yemeni propaganda had been fermenting unrest among the local tribes and tension mounted when Egyptian-backed Yemeni intruders infiltrated across the nearby border. A counter-offensive was launched by the British-led but untried Federal Regular Army (FRA), the local Arab force which had replaced the Aden Protectorate Levies, but it had very limited success. The road from Aden to Dhala, close to the Yemen, then became all but unusable through mining and ambushes and at this point it was decided to commit British forces. The author went to the O Group to ensure that the potential of Aden's Hunter force in this context was fully understood, and that it would be employed productively. Events were to prove its contribution invaluable, a commitment shared between 8, 208 and 43 Squadrons and 1417 Flight, until 208 Squadron moved to Bahrain permanently, to bring to an end the turbulence of rotational detachments to the Gulf.

A brigade headquarters was set up at Thumair on the south-western edge of the Radfan to run Radforce (a combined FRA and British force), tasked with reopening the Dhala Road and securing the Radfan (much easier said than done); a small BASOC was included in the HQ to coordinate all offensive and air transport support. The strike force consisted of the FGA9s and FR10s (which also fulfilled all their recce responsibilities), and Shackletons which maintained a continuous presence with flares to illuminate targets during the hours of darkness. HQ MEC issued pre-planned tasks but the BASOC could call for immediate assistance, moving their FACs forward to direct fire and safeguard their own troops from the air strikes. The FACs were trained by British Army GLOs attached to Tactical Wing, and practised with the Hunter pilots they would control in earnest.

It was no surprise when Johnnie Johnson declared that he wanted to see action in the Radfan first hand. The author recalls: 'I went too, sitting in the doorway of a Belvedere helicopter with an automatic rifle on my lap to witness the effect of the Hunter's 3-inch rockets and cannon

Forward Air Control Training. Ken Simpson demonstrates low flying and the excellence of the aircraft's F95 cameras over FAC staff and students. *Ken Simpson*

Riding Shotgun. The author, Stirling automatic to hand, legs protruding from the doorway of a Belvedere helicopter of No 26 Squadron, flies shotgun with the AOC in a mission over the Radfan. *Author*

against rebel positions and supply dumps discovered by FR10s in well-concealed caves. As soon as the smoke had cleared, the FR10s were there again to take post-strike photography. It was an awesome demonstration of the Hunters' capabilities and only the braver dissidents risked giving away their precise positions by retaliating with largely ineffective small arms fire. That said, one bullet did find its mark in the backside of one of the helicopter pilots – without doing much harm.

Three particular actions in the Radfan illustrated the effectiveness of these joint operations involving the FR10s. When an SAS patrol was ambushed and surrounded on 30 April 1964, Hunters carried out continuous recce and repeated attacks with rockets and cannon until nightfall, when the patrol was able to break out, albeit with the sad loss of two men. The Hunters were similarly helpful when a combined force of Royal Marine Commandos and Paras were tasked to seize 'Cap Peak', a high point which dominated the Wadi Taym and Danaba Basin. During the action some of the Paras became separated but with immediate assistance from the Hunters they regrouped and the objective was taken. In a third emergency, soldiers sent to assist the crew of an Army Air Corps (AAC) helicopter which had been shot down on the slopes of the Bakri Ridge, came under heavy fire and the Hunters again saved the day.

As in most of such actions in the region, operations were carried out in searing heat, immense convective clouds developing to cover high ground and blinding sand storms sometimes reducing visibility to almost nothing. Aircraft canopies became sand-blasted, seriously affecting the pilot's vision and sand found its way into the Hunters' systems. All this made flying very difficult, added to the groundcrews' problems and made life on the ground generally most uncomfortable for all.

Coincidentally, trouble was brewing in East Africa. It was in the quiet hours of the New Year stand-down that the duty staff officer received a signal which he could not leave until morning, to the effect that British residents were being pulled from their houses in Nairobi and shot. This turned out to be a gross exaggeration, although one man did suffer a bullet wound in his foot. However, the signal was quite enough to galvanise the Paras in Aden, who were always spoiling for a fight; they were ready, willing and able to go to Kenya post-haste by Argosy and Beverley to deal with the problem, whatever it was, in their own inimitable way. As the confusion subsided and the situation was found to be less urgent they were stood down, but HMS *Centaur* embarked troops and Belvedere helicopters of No.26 Squadron and sailed for Dar Es Salaam on 20 January 1964. As back up, five FGA9s and two FR10s were brought to a high state of readiness to fly to Eastleigh in Kenya if required; they were not deployed but the crews were kept incommunicado on the airfield, much to the irritation of their wives.

With maps of the Radfan area so poor, 1417 Flight was often called on to find a target specified by soldiers in the field by name but without a precise grid reference, and then to produce nose oblique photographs of the attack direction to be used by the FGA9 pilots. FR10s were also on standby to update enemy movements and to give immediate support to ground forces in difficulty; this generated increasing confidence among Allied ground troops in the service provided by the flight and thus the number of demands made on it. Some of their requests were theoretically or practically beyond the FR10's capability. Peter Lewis remembers that the army called on him for complete cover, with all three cameras, of a nine nm wadi at 200 ft, which would have required more than the total film carried by the Hunters and involve some risky flying. Undaunted, Peter calculated that much of the cover could be obtained from the alternative of a very fast run using the nose facing camera with its 12-inch lens. He flew the sortie between 1300-1400 hours to keep the shadows to a minimum, coping with the severe turbulence along the valley bottom with its steep sides towering 1,000 ft above, his thoroughbred Hunter surviving the high 'G' forces and a rifle shot through its fin. There were limits to what 1417 Flight could do, but they always did their utmost to satisfy.

On another exciting trip the fire warning light came on in Peter's Hunter after he had returned fire with all four guns at a group of tribesmen, leaving him with an agonising choice of ejecting over hostile territory or hoping that the warning was spurious. With no other signs of fire he chose the latter, only to find that the aircraft's desert survival pack had come loose and triggered the fire warning light test switch. It had indeed been a false alarm!

The Hunters were often involved in clandestine surveillance operations mounted by the SAS, and were once called to verify the

Fair Play. Camels were often known to carry the rebel arms and ammunition and were, therefore, legitimate targets. *Roy Bowie*

position of a camel train thought to be resting on the border with the Yemen. Although certain that he was in the right place, Peter Lewis could not see his quarry, but then he heard an unannounced voice on a pre-arranged frequency say "They're there", and a closer look revealed tell-tale signs in the sand which led to the camels. These poor beasts of burden, with their cargos of what turned out to be explosives, were then dispatched to their maker with a two-second burst from the FR10's cannon. Years later, in a most unexpected sequel to this story, Peter was recognised by the local postman in The Sailor's Safety public house, West Wales, who told him that he was the man on the ground who had passed that curt message "They're there"

The author returned to the UK in February 1964 to take command of a squadron on the OCU at Chivenor, now better able to understand the requirements of the Hunter FGA and FR units in the Middle East. His post in HQ MEC having been upgraded, he was replaced by Wing Commander H S 'Tony' Carver. Squadron Leader Roy Bowie, another accomplished fast-jet

Attack Harib. The 'brown map' used to plot the attack on the Yemeni Fort Harib. *Roger Pyrah*

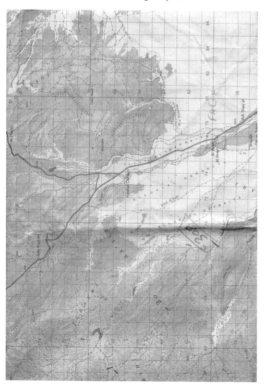

pilot, also arrived, to take over from Squadron Leader Jack Dymond as deputy OC Tactical Wing at Khormaksar. Roy's credentials were ideal; he had previous experience in theatre and was well versed in the fighter, ground attack and fighter reconnaissance roles, knowledge which he would now put to good use.

It was Roy who, after ringing the doorbell for some 15 minutes, eventually woke Peter Lewis from a deep slumber at 0400 hours one morning at the start of what turned out to be a classic joint mission with the FGA9s. The operation was mounted against the Fort at Harib, just across the border in the Yemen, in retaliation for attacks on Allied forces within the WAP. Peter's job was three-fold; firstly he would drop leaflets on the fort, then stand off at height to watch for any opposition while the follow-up strike force of eight FGA9s led by John Jennings did their business, before finally taking post-strike photographs. On 28 March 1964, the leader's salvo hit the mark, probably a munitions store, causing a massive explosion and a 'mushroom of dirty brown and black smoke' which obscured the target and delayed Pete's post-strike photo run. In the end, everything went well with excellent photographs revealing hitherto unknown AAA defences, severe damage to the target and several rebels dead or injured. All this led to Johnnie Johnson's signal to 'the largest and most complex station in the RAF' congratulating all concerned.

In what Peter Lewis claimed had 'strengthened the links between his flight and the FGA9 squadrons considerably' (and Roger Pyrah's log book shows), FR10 support for operation Radfan increased markedly in April 1964 to peak two months later and continue sporadically into the autumn. However the FR10s also had other commitments. They were now involved continuously in maritime operations, one chance sighting of the Russian ship *Nicolai Pirogrov* in April prompting a shadowing operation by the Aden-based Shackletons.

Over land, at the behest of the Federal Government, a number of FR10s and FGA9s were held at high states of readiness to meet urgent needs in the forward areas, while the remaining FR10s searched for widespread enemy observation posts and defensive positions believed to be occupied by dissident leaders. The FR10s also took part in further pre-planned offensive operations, again forewarning local residents by leaflet drops, specifically around Bakri and Da'Iri Harath.

Target Harib. Peter Lewis carried out the pre- and post-strike recce of the Yemeni fort at Harib, attacked by Hunter FGA9s on 28 March 1964. *Peter Lewis*

More often than not the FR10 pilots were required to fly or stand-by to do so while others besported themselves on the officers beach at Tarshyne. It is unlikely that there were any complaints from them on lack of social opportunity, but Roy Bowie remembers the story of an amorous school teacher in Aden who became less than enamoured with the Hunter breed (perhaps because her man of the moment was not as readily available as others). She is said to have found that Shackleton crews withdrew from a romance when it ripened and 'turned to booze'; the Beverley boys were apparently 'super' and those on the Argosy 'nice too', because they were generally much older and married, while Hunter pilots were 'terrible,

irresponsible, hard living and hard drinking, always blaming their behaviour on the dangers they faced'. She probably married a Hunter pilot.

Roy himself flew on many Hunter operations and had his share of incidents. Once, while on an FR sortie in the Radfan, the engine of his FR10 shed turbine blades and he barely cleared the mountains at 180 kts as he pulled out of the Wadi Dubsan. Having been strafing rebels in the same area the day before, he had an anxious few minutes searching frantically for his 'goolie chit' as he coaxed the Hunter back to Khormaksar at 7,000 rpm and 180 kts, finally landing safely.

Soldier Airborne. Squadron Leader Roy Bowie (right), Deputy OC Strike Wing, gives Brigadier Bremner, Brigadier General Staff, HQ MEC, an airman's perspective of the battleground. BASO, Squadron Leader Peter Biddiscombe (left), and Wing Commander Martin Chandler, OC Strike Wing, welcome them back. *Roy Bowie*

Siesta. Theoretically, the working day in Aden ended at 1300 hours, after which many of the more fortunate officers found their way to Tarshyne Beach. *Ken Simpson*

In June, the Hunters of Tactical Wing were scrambled frequently to assist the East Anglians and FRA who were meeting heavy resistance in the Wadis Misra, Dubsan and Durra. During this action the FR10s flew sixty three missions, firing their guns and taking hundreds of photographs, while the FGA9s completed 250 operational sorties, firing 1,242 rockets and 84,300 rounds of ammunition, until the Anglians took vital ground, 6,000 ft above sea level.

Peter Lewis handed over command of 1417 Flight to Roger Pyrah in that June. For a successful command, and the 112 operational missions he had flown in Aden, he was awarded an AFC. In later life Prussian Pete became a magistrate on the County Bench, earning much the same reputation as he had in Aden.

The always controversial 'centralised servicing' system was introduced in June for all the Hunter units at Khormaksar, for what was claimed to be a trial period. This deprived the squadron commanders and flight commander of 1417 Flight their traditional and much cherished discretion over engineering priorities, but powerful voices lobbied for the pooling of all engineering resources in search of efficiency and economies. It is believed to have been Roy Bowie (no advocate of centralisation himself) who suggested a compromise. With centralisation at the core, the two FGA9 squadrons initiated a 24-hours 'on', 24-hours 'off' system, each with a dedicated servicing flight, while 1417 Flight worked a flexible, 'as required' schedule using this ever-present engineering support. Opponents of centralised servicing were quick to point to troughs of unserviceability which followed, but it is fair to point out that many of the problems which prevailed at the time were due to a shortage of spares, probably exacerbated by conflicting priorities for air transport from the UK. On the FR Flight, Roger Pyrah made his first-line crews as comfortable as was possible by designing and having built white canvas covers which protected those working on the aircraft when they were on the flight line, an initiative which was envied by those exposed to the brutal sunshine of the hot season.

Throughout July and August 1417 Flight was busy again, exercising their particular talents for spotting largely covert troop movements and supply dumps, if only by tracks and other tell-tale signs, along the wadi routes in the Radfan

Leading From the Front. OC 1417 Flight, Roger Pyrah, and OC Tactical Wing, Wing Commander John Jennings, were greeted with gunfire as they took a look at Qataba Barracks and Fort just across the border in Yemen. *Roger Pyrah*

and the border with the Yemen. It was on one such border patrol that John Jennings and Roger Pyrah attracted ineffective gunfire from Qataba Fort just inside the Yemen. The recce men were also perfecting techniques for looking into and photographing the many caves used by the rebels and for spotting targets despite camouflage and other methods of concealment. Group Captain A.C. Blythe, who had been

'Wadi Bashing'. Two FGA9s in arrowhead formation near Beihan, caught on the nose-facing oblique of an FR 10 astern. *Peter Taylor*

Recce/Attack Interface. Caves storing ammunition and supplies and protecting guns, found by Roger Pyrah, who returned to mark them for a strike led by OC 43 Squadron, Squadron Leader Phil Champniss. *Roger Pyrah*

Photo Call. 1417 Flight could deliver urgently needed F95 prints from the Hunter's airbrake. *Derek Whitman*

commanding Khormaksar, now handed over to Group Captain M.J. Beetham.

From his experience up-country with local ground forces, and well aware how much the soldiers wanted photographs taken by the FR10s, Roger Pyrah developed the means of delivering selected prints to them as soon as possible. An FR pilot would land without delay after completing his recce tasks and have the film off-loaded and processed without leaving the cockpit or stopping the engine. A second pilot, properly briefed, then chose the best prints for the purpose and packed them securely in a bag (which also contained Roger's 'secret weapon' – four ice-cold beers); the bag was attached to a redundant drogue parachute and lodged in the airbrake of the waiting Hunter. The first pilot then took off again and returned to drop the precious cargo to the troops who had requested them. Flying low and slow, the bundle of photographs could be dropped within 20 yards of their intended recipients.

Roger's secret weapon encouraged troops on the ground to keep the recce tasks coming, as a result of which 1417 Flight always had an abundance of interesting and legitimate

operational tasks and was authorised to exceed its official allocation of flying hours. Although this splendid initiative, banned in Germany allegedly because the aircraft had not been cleared for the purpose in its Release to Service, usually worked faultlessly, this was not always the case. On one occasion 300 prints decorated Habilayn, site of HQ Area West, confetti fashion, the bag having burst open in mid-air; fortunately, each print had been carefully annotated and 'the situation was retrieved with no great difficulty'.

In December 1964 the offensive element of Tactical Wing, primarily the Hunter force, came under the new umbrella title of Strike Wing (the name conflicting with NATO terminology, in which 'strike' refers to nuclear forces).

1965: MiGs, Thesiger and Ranji

The change of name made no difference to the FR10s, their first major joint operation in the new year being against dissident convoys and a supply storage in the Wadi Jahra on 16 January. They were very active again in February, providing close support for Royal Marine Commandos around Dhala, with 'flag waving' sorties in the Jebel Khuder and Awabil areas and

Mission Accomplished. Roger Pyrah confirms the success of a strike sortie with 'before and after' F95 photographs of a target in the Wadi Tayme. *Roger Pyrah*

leaflet drops around Ruseis. For a little light relief in February, fifteen Hunters from Strike Wing flew in a numerical '78' formation for the presentation of a Standard to No. 78 Squadron.

MiG fighters strayed once more into WAP airspace in March and April, and again the Hunters (including FR10s) were scrambled too late to intercept them. Expensive CAPs were set up but fared little better, the intruders perhaps forewarned by Yemeni radars. Roger Pyrah's

FR10s tried hard to surprise them by approaching the area at very low level, using terrain screening before pulling up in the hope of an interception, but by then the MiGs had become more cautious and there was no visual contact. Many years later, when looking for a first officer to fly with him on an executive jet in the Middle East, Roger interviewed an Egyptian pilot who admitted that he had been flying MiGs over the border country at that time. Had they met before?

Before and After. Courtesy 1417 Flight, note the building marked 'X' and the effects of 3-inch RP and 30-mm cannon fire after a strike by FGA9 Hunters. *Roger Pyrah*

Eagle Eyes. Roger Pyrah spots rebel positions deep in the mountains around Khundara. *Roger Pyrah*

Wing Leader. Wing Commander Martin Chandler took over from John Jennings, as OC Strike Wing, in 1965. *Ken Simpson*

To cater for the elusive in difficult terrain, a procedure had now been perfected within the Wing to overcome any delays while a strike force leader tried to locate his target, perhaps allowing the rebels to take cover or escape. Again making use of their special expertise and any prior knowledge, the FR pilots would seek to identify the required aiming points (with any gun defences a priority) marking them with their cannons at an agreed time (say 45 seconds) before the strike force tipped in for the attack. Often from tell-tale signs rather than firm evidence, the FR10 pilots seemed to develop a sixth sense about which caves were being used by the rebels and would direct fire into their entrances. This was the pattern developed jointly by Roger Pyrah and Squadron Leader Phil Champniss, OC 43 Squadron, which led to successful strikes, sometimes with the added bonus for those involved when huge explosions confirmed the recce pilots' initial suspicions. The classic recce/attack interface worked.

In a personal tribute to John Jennings as he departed from Aden, and a welcome to the new OC Strike Wing, Wing Commander Martin Chandler, Roger Pyrah made the best of a chance find while he was flying down the Wadi Bana on 29 April. At first he was attracted to and fascinated by a blue haze rising from the small

Wadi Khundara, until he realised that this was gunfire directed at him: 'I cleared off for a while and returned at very high speed before closing the throttle to approach very low at about 140 kts to achieve surprise and managed to get some excellent photos of rebels at a supply dump'. A strike was mounted by FGA9s, with great success, underlining the value of the carefully planned and executed recce/attack interface. This was a hallmark of John Jennings' time in Aden, at the end of which he was awarded a DFC. Martin Chandler was taking over a going concern.

Alan Pollock, then an FGA pilot on 43 Squadron at Khormaksar, enthused over the contribution made by collocated FR10s to the collective effort: 'Every Hunter FGA9 pilot would pay handsome tribute to those superb F95 pre-sortie briefing and post-strike photographs which we quickly took for granted. It was often the target photographs which gave that 'fixed ring of confidence' as one acquired the target on pull up and began tracking ahead of release. FR photographs at briefings were an essential force multiplier for concentration of force and accuracy in our weapons deliveries'. Alan had taken the trouble to find out about FR first hand in Germany, persuading 79 Squadron to let him fly the Swift FR5 and later IV Squadron the Hunter FR10 on typical operational recce sorties. On arrival in Aden he used similar persuasion to get airborne with 1417 Flight, and in all cases he has photographs to show that he took the privilege seriously.

Apart from the excitement of another border violation by MiGs in May, the spring and early summer of 1965 were relatively quiet periods for the FR pilots in Aden. Only eight operational missions were flown in May, with a total of fifteen in June and July, in most cases escorting convoys on the Dhala Road. In August there were eleven sorties into the Wadis Kurdara, Yahar and Mayfa'ah, while a firepower demonstration took place at Jebel Hanak. Eight sorties were also flown into the EAP from RAF Salalah, an airstrip with a sand runway which required take-offs to be staggered, no air traffic control and no diversion closer than 400 nm away at RAF Masirah.

It was fitting that, on 27 August 1965, Roger Pyrah completed his final operational sortie against a dissident base in Wadi Yahar, before handing over command of 1417 Flight to Flight Lieutenant Ralph Chambers. He had flown a total of 362 hours, many on operations, during his two year tour.

Ready to Go. Ralph Chambers flew a successful acceptance test flight in 'his' FR10 before the crest had been included in the 1417 pennant, and pronounced it 'ready to go'. *Ralph Chambers via Ray Deacon.*

In September, a pair of FR10s was detached to Salalah for Operation Thesiger. Highly classified at the time, these long range missions penetrated deep into the Empty Quarter looking for convoys bringing arms and supplies to dissident tribesmen in the EAP and Oman. Again with few if any features by which to navigate, the FR pilots stuck rigidly to the very basics of heading and timing, typically starting the stopwatch from directly overhead Salalah on a set heading and at a constant speed, not deviating for perhaps a hour, as they plotted on their maps any targets they encountered, together with features which might ease navigation on future sorties.

Back in Aden there were post-strike recces to be flown in the Wadi Maraban and Operation

Flight Lieutenant Ralph Chambers, who took command of 1417 Flight in 1965, flew his personal FR10 (XE589-'RC') back to Aden from a major servicing in the UK. *Ralph Chambers*

Operation Thesiger. Dick Johns (third left) and Ken Simpson (first right). *Dick Johns*

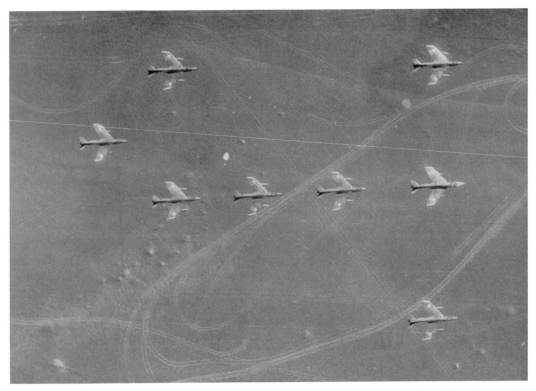

Symbolic 'J'. A flypast of 8 Squadron Hunters, this 'J' formation perhaps an appropriate farewell to the outgoing AOC, AVM Johnnie Johnson on 14 December 1965? *Roy Bowie*

Ranji called for surveillance of the coastline and waters out to 3 nm in search of gun-runners; forty three operational sorties were flown by the FR10s in that month. Ranji predominated in October, its scope being extended by the end of 1965 to cover the coastal waters off Ras Fartak. Elements of 1417 Flight also accompanied 8 and 43 Squadrons to Masirah for tactical training, and while there the FR10s were given the difficult task of finding suitable sites for airfields in the Oman. On 14 December a flypast of eight Hunters marked the departure of Johnnie Johnson, he being succeeded as AOC by AVM Andrew Humphrey. So ended another busy year.

1966: Escalation – As the End is Signalled

Poor serviceability and a petroleum workers' strike in Aden during 1966 reduced the number of FR10s on the line to two/day. However, 69 hours were flown in January and Martin Chandler was able to fly the C-in-C, Admiral Sir Michael LeFanu, around the Protectorates in the T7, with Ralph Chambers accompanying them as top cover and photographer. The Admiral was a popular master, 1417 Flight's Dick Johns recalling that he often included young officers participating in the current operations at his dinner parties, thus allowing his guests to hear first hand how it was all done at 'the sharp end'.

The 1966 Defence White Paper forewarned the end of a British presence in Aden, which was to become independent in 1968, but with no let-up in military operations as anti-British feeling and activity increased, the final day for the evacuation was brought forward to 29 November 1967. During the run-down Khormaksar became very busy, handling strategic transport aircraft and every form of tactical air power while 1417 Flight watched over the huge area of responsibility. The fuel workers went back to work in February which, together with a lull in terrorist activities, allowed 106 hours to be flown in a well-balanced operational and training programme.

On 14 February Dick Johns took the pre- and post-strike photos of a fort in the Wadi Yahar, after which he and Ken Simpson went to Masirah to resume Operation Thesiger. When

Fort at Wadi Yahar. Pre-Strike Recce and Bomb Damage Assessment (BDA). *Dick Johns*

AOC's Inspection. Two FR10s flank a T7 trainer with the officers and men of 1417 Flight on parade. *Ken Simpson*

flying on these operations from Masirah single FR10s were often escorted by pairs of 208 Squadron FGA9s, high level to Midway (now Thumrait), some 60 nm north of Salalah, before descending to continue over the desert at low level.

The fifth FR10, the frequently used 'reserve', now returned to the UK but the two aircraft at Masirah remained serviceable and the monthly target of 120 hours (79 on operations) was achieved with ease.

Back in Aden the AOC's Inspection went well on 15 March 1966, as the Flight prepared for a visit by the CFS agents, moving the new scribe of the ORB, Dick Johns, to observe that: 'as the slap of paint brushes died, the buzz of study rose to a new crescendo'.

While all this was going on, Dick was among those who searched in vain for vehicles of the Royal Engineers which had been reported missing between Abyan and Shuqra, but which turned out to be at home all the time in Normandy Lines. Ken Simpson and Ralph Chambers also failed to find an errant Ferret scout car belonging to the HBL but its commander was spotted elsewhere by others, literally with his trousers down *'in flagrante delicto'* dealing with a local girl, while his driver awaited his turn nearby. The finders were pleased to note that the HBL observed the niceties of rank!

The flight's photo album for March contained two nautical photographs of interest: a Russian floating dock which had weighed anchor in Aden Harbour and the SS *Verona,* a three-masted schooner on which the High Commissioner was relaxing at sea. He expressed suitable surprise and delight when presented with the resulting print on landing back in Aden, especially since the Hunter pilots should have been on stand-down on that Saturday afternoon.

The Hunters were now rotating through RAF St Athan for major servicing, and as soon as Derek Whitman joined the flight in February 1966 he was sent back to the UK with Ken Simpson and a pilot from 43 Squadron to ferry three FGA9s from Kemble to Khormaksar. On what was known as the northern route, via Istres (France), Luqa (Malta), El Adem (Libya), Akrotiri (Cyprus), Diyarbakir (Turkey) Tehran (Iran), Muharraq (Bahrain) and Masirah (Oman); this trip took five days and was without incident but others were very different. Dick Johns flew an FR10 back from the UK on the wing of a T7 flown by an 8 Squadron flight commander Flight Lieutenant Graham Williams, who was determined to beat the record time for completing the northern route. All went well until they departed from Diyarbakir, when Dick became concerned first at his leader's lengthy pre-flight checks and then with the T7's excessively long take-off run which forced him to overtake his leader on the runway. With no comment from Graham, he dutifully regained his position in formation and they proceeded without explanation to Tehran, where again Dick

Arab Fashion. 1417 Flight pilots (L–R) Ken Simpson, Derek Whitman, Ralph Chambers, Dick Johns, Frank Grimshaw and Roger Neil squat, Arab fashion) with their Somali cleaner. *Ken Simpson*

Rest and Recuperation. Flight Lieutenant Dick Johns, 1417 Flight, takes time out to improve his mind - before the bar opens. *Ken Simpson*

Hors de Combat. An 'occupational hazard' caused Ken Simpson to suffer this debilitating injury in the bar at Khormaksar. *Ken Simpson*

was nearly caught short by his leader's untypical lazy break to land. It transpired that Graham had been unable to select power controls at Diyarbakir and decided to fly the remainder of the trip in manual rather than incur a huge logistic problem and endure a prolonged stop in less than agreeable conditions there. So the trip was completed in manual, with Graham perhaps reporting that the fault had occurred on the last leg. No. 1417 Flight now comprised Ralph Chambers, Derek Whitman, Roger 'Phred' Neal, Ken Simpson and Dick Johns.

In April, 1417 Flight provided more pre- and post-strike photographs in the Yaffa region, an area in which recce tasks could be particularly demanding and where the threat of small-arms fire justified top cover from another Hunter. Dick Johns was once required to find and photograph the main gate into the village of Al Qura, a settlement about which little was known, that was situated on a terraced plateau in a steep-sided wadi. The village was thought to have been visited by only one white man (or from which only one white man had ever returned), wherein an extreme Moslem sect paid homage to a spirit purported to live in a big drum (which was also

Al Qura (W'ilen). The forbidding town of Al Qura, to which Dick Johns was sent to find the way in. *Derek Whitman*

used to summon support against any threat). There was certainly no doubt as to the hostility of the local tribesmen, who welcomed Dick with a fusillade of shots as he sought the elusive gate. The Hunter pilots were often cleared to fire at ground targets in the Yaffa, at their discretion without further authority, and it was on one such occasion that two recce men took out their boredom on 'a fast-moving camel'. This was not the sort of target the commanders and staff had in mind when they delegated this authority and indeed they remonstrated with the pilots on their return – not only for wasting ammunition but also for failing to hit this very mobile target.

In a less exacting role, the four FR10s got airborne as spares for a sixteen ship Hunter FGA9 flypast to celebrate 43 Squadron's 50th birthday in June and when not needed joined the formation as numbers 17-20 for the final run-in and break, earning a place in the inevitable celebrations which followed.

Squadron Leader Fred Trowern returned to Aden in May 1966 after a ground-breaking tour on the Kestrel Tripartite Squadron and instructional duties with the FR training cell of 229 OCU at Chivenor, to replace Roy Bowie as the Deputy OC Strike Wing. Current on the Hunter, Fred was quick to get back into the air in the FGA9 and the FR10 although there was little spare flying for him on the FR flight, its strength having been reduced to three aircraft on 9 May when Ken Simpson in XE589 collided with a Griffin Vulture. The big bird entered the starboard intake and although much of it was blown out through the upper skin of the wing, sufficient went into the engine to cause it to surge. Fortunately the rpm stabilised in mid-range where Ken sensibly left the throttle and, by dropping his external tanks, he managed to nurse the aircraft up to 10,000 ft on a heading for Aden where he carried out an immaculate emergency landing.

Birdstrike. Ken Simpson recovered this FR10 to Khormaksar after an unpleasant meeting with a Vulture Eagle.
Ken Simpson

Notwithstanding the three aircraft complement, a pair of aircraft remained available for much of May and June, enabling Frank Grimshaw to contribute pre- and post-strike recce to a Wing strike on Qaraba and Ralph Chambers to support a strike by 43 Squadron against a clump of trees believed to hide dissident arms. The flying task was reduced to 75 hours in June, FR pilot proficiency being maintained by allocating hours on FGA9s.

Back in Aden the security situation had worsened, two 1417 Flight airmen were injured slightly by grenade splinters when walking in Tawahi and attacks on the Aden Supply Depot became nightly events. Derek Whitman recalls that this type of incident led periodically to higher states of alert and various restrictions, including the temporary closure of the highly popular officers' beach at Tarshyne, together with advice on places to avoid, such as the town of Crater. Certain activities, typically the tourist flights to the impressive city of Tarim in the Wadi Hadraumat, came to an end when one of the Aden Airways aircraft was blown up by terrorists. Aden was then declared an 'Active

Service' area and constant vigilance was the name of the game, but personal security was generally left to common sense.

In July 1966, Ralph Chambers handed over command of 1417 Flight to Derek Whitman, who was now 'operational'. Ralph too would be rewarded with an AFC for his very successful year in command and for his particular skills on operational missions.

With trouble also increasing up-country and sporadic Egyptian air attacks in the Nuqb border area, it was decided that a pair of Hunters should be positioned throughout daylight hours at the makeshift airstrip of Beihan (some 200 nm north-east of Aden). The AOC had already taken a look for himself in an Andover, with Dick Johns providing top cover, but Martin Chandler was the first to land there in an FGA9 on 5 August, Ken Simpson going with him in an FR10 as escort and photographer. Wing Commander John Severne, who had taken over from Tony Carver as Ops 2 in MEC, was there to witness the event from the ground. Martin found the short, narrow and largely sandy strip high on a plateau far from ideal for Hunter operations but

Beihan. Dick Johns escorted the AOC MEC, AVM Johnnie Johnson, to the airstrip at Beihan. *Dick Johns*

authorised selected pilots to take pairs of Hunters there at dawn and recover to Aden at dusk, ready for any eventuality. There is no record of them being scrambled, which is just as well because take-offs from there in the heat of the day might have been somewhat of a gamble.

On 3 September Ken Simpson was tasked with a recce mission to Perim Island, some 95 nm west of Aden, followed by a 'photo-drop' to the troops deployed there. In line with a now common practice, Ken had enough fuel after the recce for a rapid turn-round with the engine running, his film to be processed, selected prints bagged and installed in his airbrake, to fly back to Perim Island for the drop. Sadly, it was not to be. On his initial landing the aircraft overshot the runway, the starboard undercarriage all but shearing off when it hit a hidden object in the overrun and the aircraft suffering Cat 4 damage. It transpired that the brake pads, which should have sufficed in normal circumstances, were not up to the job for this heavyweight landing.

With FR10 availability in October now very poor, this was not the best time for Flight Lieutenant Horace Farquhar-Smith to arrive on the flight. Despite the two remaining FR10s generating a commendable 74 hours, this was not enough when so much was being asked of the flight to support operations in the Jebal Mishwara, Wadi Milah, Jabal Radfan, Dhala areas and tasks further afield.

That autumn, dissident ringleaders were thought to be assembling in the coastal village of Hauf, on the border between the WAP and EAP, and an amphibious landing was planned to apprehend them. To that end Derek Whitman and Dick Johns were dispatched to take low-level oblique photos of the coastline nearby, to pinpoint possible sites for the landing; they would then refuel at Masirah and repeat the job on the return trip to Khormaksar. On this first operation for the assault ship HMS *Fearless*, a company of the Irish Guards was to disembark to capture the village already picketed by the SAS under cover of darkness. However, their kilted piper is said to have stepped off the first landing craft into water deeper than expected, his pipes gurgling into silence as he and the leading guardsmen disappeared below the waves, their craft having beached prematurely

Overshoot. Ken Simpson, 1417 Flight, overshooting at Khormaksar. *Ken Simpson*

Beihan Alert.

Ken Simpson escorts Wing Commander Martin Chandler, OC Strike Wing, to Beihan.

Martin Chandler lands at Beihan, in what was thought to be the first Hunter to use this short, narrow and largely sandy airstrip. *Ken Simpson*

Martin discusses Hunter operations with Peter Taylor, 8 Squadron flight commander. *Ken Simpson*

Martin Chandler and Peter Taylor on stand-by at Beihan. *Peter Taylor*

The pilots selected for this operation had to get their landing speeds right, pairs or stream landings out of the question. *Peter Taylor*

A launch from Beihan in the midday sun would use all the runway. *Peter Taylor*

on a hidden sandbank. Awakened by this extraordinary noise those dissidents who had evaded capture by the SAS high-tailed it into the desert. *Fearless* was on her inaugural tour and it was a better story for a lucky few, selected from all ranks serving in Aden, who enjoyed her lavish hospitality as they joined the ship on a two-week recreational cruise to Mombasa, Kenya. Derek Whitman headed the RAF contingent and was honoured with the helm of the ship as it rounded the Horn of Africa inbound to Aden.

No. 1417 Flight also had better fortune temporarily in October, when four aircraft became available, but it was short lived as poor serviceability struck again, allowing only 90

hours flying in that month. Derek Whitman flew the only truly operational sortie against a target for the FGA9s in the Wadi Bana, believed to be a store for arms and ammunition. Accompanying the strike force of four FGA9s, each armed with eight rockets, he took pre-strike pictures and marked the target with cannon fire, then stood off until able to take post-strike photographs. Unfortunately, at no time did anyone see the tell-tale explosions which would have confirmed the presence of ammunition. The building, which had been flattened, was totally rebuilt within days.

Meanwhile, Dick Johns had been sent to Mukulla, on the coast near RAF Riyan, to carry out an initial recce and then co-ordinate a flypast for the coronation of the new Sultan of Qaiti, a young Oxford graduate. There he was puzzled by all the wailing from what he described as a 'hen coop' above the Royal Palace, until told by the British Resident that the ladies of the Royal harem were celebrating the arrival of a younger master. Dick travelled there and back in an RAF Dakota which, on its arrival to take him home from the recce, disgorged a cargo of heavily manacled tribesmen who had been 'persuaded' to swear allegiance to their new Sultan. While fulfilling his task, Dick was accommodated at Riyan, a small RAF airstrip run by two officers (an air traffic controller and an administrator), his presence allowing them to hold an Extraordinary Mess Meeting while he tended to

Staff Support. Experienced Hunter pilot Wing Commander John Severne took over from Tony Carver as Ops 2 in HQ MEC in 1966. *John Severne.*

their needs from the bar. The subject was the Summer Ball, with the president and the sole member covering its every aspect from invitation list to gramophone music, until Dick's ample re-supply got the better of them and they brought the meeting to a close.

The overall situation improved in December, with less terrorist activity and four FR10s again available for the increasingly diverse joint operations required by the security forces. Close to home, Roger Neal photographed 'shacks' just north of Khormaksar, believed to have been made ready for mortar attacks on the airfield, while Dick Johns carried out extensive oblique photography in preparations for further ground operations on the northern slopes of the Jebel Radfan.

The ORB also reported the great precision needed for special missions flown in support of the SAS and Derek Whitman believes these involved camouflage and concealment trials. Interestingly, pale pink netting was found to be preferable to a natural sandy colour but it was movement, however small, that really attracted attention from the air. Derek claimed that in normal visibilities (10-20 nm) a single man moving slowly in the desert could be seen when flying between 250-500 ft at a distance of 6-8 nm. Conversely, if the same target was static it would be very difficult to see against the desert background at any range. Dick Johns recalls other, less official tasks with the SAS, typically helping them prepare for forthcoming operations in particularly difficult wadis. In such terrain, the FR10s would fly as low as possible down the valleys taking 'nose facers' along the route to be taken later by the troops on the ground, and then in the opposite direction to identify the most likely ambush points. In all such operations in-flight reporting was exploited to the full, more so in the Middle East than in Germany, although to an extent this was understandable because of the very different operating environments. Whenever operations were scheduled in the Federation of South Arabia, well-rehearsed in-flight reporting cells in HQ MEC and with army units deployed in the desert, were ready to take messages from the Hunter pilots and react to them without delay. This was particularly useful in actions against infiltrators seen crossing into the Federation from the Yemen.

John Severne contrived to see some of the operations for which he was involved as a staff officer, once viewing a highly successful strike by Hunters from a T7 flown by Fred Trowern, who commented: 'And to think we actually get paid for this' He saw an equally effective strike from a Beverley orbiting at low level, controlled by an army officer trained as an airborne FAC by the RAF in Aden. Good staff support, sensible tasking and joint training, with careful mission preparation, planning, co-ordination and execution all paid off, optimising the employment of the flexible FR10s.

1967: The End of an Era
Squadron Leader Dickie Barraclough took command of 1417 Flight on 28 December 1966, as offensive air operations were on the increase

and internal security was being tightened following the murder of British dependants, including a five year old child. More specifically, the ORB recorded operations in the Wadi Bana and in the Shabwash region, some 200 nm north east of Aden, which were enough to justify a significant increase in the authorised flying task for January.

In February, a general strike was called by the NLF, now the dominant opposition group, and there was further civil unrest in protest against the security restrictions, all of which led to a curfew on the civilian population. No. 1417 Flight had its share of drama when Derek Whitman, searching for a stolen Landrover between Little Aden and the border with the Yemen, noticed 'a spume of vaporising fuel' coming from the starboard wing of his FR10. A hurried discussion ensued between Derek and Dickie Barraclough in the tower, the upshot of which was an airborne inspection, the jettisoning of external tanks into the sea (photographed by Dick Johns in another FR10) and a cautious landing without further incident. It transpired that Derek had been the recipient of a lucky shot from an over-zealous Yemeni sergeant at a customs post on the border at Al Ghurayq. Diplomatic notes were exchanged and the miscreant was said to have had his rifle confiscated for two weeks. Only one aircraft was now fit for flight, and indeed for a five day period in March there were no FR10s on the line. Then came another strike by fuel workers which limited 1417 Flight to one sortie a day, but Horace Farquhar-Smith was now 'operational' and put to good use at once in the sole aircraft available, photographing the friendly village of Hilyan which had been attacked and badly damaged by unidentified hostile forces.

One sortie a day remained the norm for much of April 1967, the month in which an unprecedented cloudburst flooded the airfield, put electrical services out of action and gave rise to many tales of domestic woe. This, combined with 376 security incidents and another general strike, curtailed many of the normal activities on and off duty. Later in the month, as the airfield recovered from the rains, flying increased to enable much needed support for the Irish Guards around Habilayn, but the month ended with only 70 hours flown of the 90 hours allocated, a high price for a bird strike on one FR10 and a bullet hole in another. Helped by the experience he had gained on previous Hunter tours, Dickie Barraclough achieved operational status at the end of April.

All Together Now. The Officers and men of 1417 Flight, 1967. *Dick Johns*

Follow Me. Squadron Leader Dick Barraclough leads Derek Whitman, Horace Farquhar-Smith, Roger Neal, Ken Simpson, Dick Johns and Frank Grimshaw into 1967 – the last year for 1417 Flight. *Dickie Barraclough*

As the British troops withdrew into Aden itself, priorities began to change. No. 1417 Flight was now required to monitor the FRA's movements as it took over tasks up-country, and in covert missions at high level to keep an eye on a police convoy touring out-lying posts in an attempt to assess support for the NLF. There was also a new emphasis on shipping surveillance as work with the RN and Naval Intelligence increased – *Janes* and the Lloyds shipping registers now much in use in 1417's crewroom.

From April 1967, one FR10 was held on standby throughout those afternoons when the flight was otherwise on stand down, to be launched and recovered when necessary by groundcrew working shifts with the FGA9 squadrons and, as always, some tasks were out of the ordinary. Dickie Barraclough remembered one in which he followed up an Argosy pilot's sighting of an airfield 100 nm up the coast east of Aden, hitherto unknown to the British, which seemed to be operating at night. He found nothing during a daylight sortie, or indeed on one at night, except numerous Bedouin campfires at the position given. Dickie also remembers seeing nothing but a burning fort when sent to verify a report of 'large forces crossing the border'. There were several false trails of this sort at the time but all had to be looked into.

May was a time for aircraft in Aden to carry out courtesy flypasts, farewells and 'flag waves'. On 1 May, Ken Simpson photographed a diamond nine of 8 Squadron Hunters bidding farewell to the General Officer Commanding, MEC, and on 12 May a mixed RN/RAF formation of eight Sea Vixens, six Buccaneers and twelve Hunters. Then on 19 May Derek Whitman recorded a flypast of sixteen Hunters paying tribute to the High Commissioner, His Excellency Sir Richard Turnbull, and on 17 May fifty-five Sea Vixens, Buccaneers and Hunters overflying Aden in a show of strength.

Meanwhile, there was more serious work for the FR10s with the Irish Guards, SAS and 45

It never rains but......! On I April 1967, the normally arid Aden suffered heavier rain and flooding than any of the airmen there could remember – rendering many of the airfield's facilities unserviceable and the need for Peter Taylor to rescue Flight Lieutenant John Hill's transport on his wedding day. *Ken Simpson and Peter Taylor*

Marine Commando around Habilayn, and in support of Operation Knit in Wadi Bana. At this highpoint in air activity the Arab/Israeli War, which began in June 1967, stopped normal fuel

Show of Force. Fifty five Sea Vixen, Buccaneer and Hunter aircraft in a show of force on 17 May 1967. *Ken Simpson Collection*

supplies to Khormaksar, and consequently all but essential flying operations and air tests, to result in a monthly total of only 30 hours FR10 flying against a target of 120 hours. This did not affect Frank Grimshaw, Dick Johns and Roger Neal who left the flight, but it did not bode well for new arrival Flight Lieutenant Dave Bagshaw. Gradually flying resumed, demanded by a rise in terrorism which culminated on 20 June with a mutiny among the armed police in Crater and factions of the newly formed South Arabian Army in the local barracks. Gunfire and the occasional crump of a grenade or mortar could now be heard in and around Khormaksar but this caused little more than curiosity among those going about their business on the Hunter flight line, until they became aware of 'little zippy noises and metallic pings' from the upper part of the hangar behind them. It was then that prudence overcame valour and they 'legged it smartly indoors'. Then, on 30 June, an aircraft belonging to Aden Airways was destroyed on the ground by a bomb, all of which resulted in a flurry of staff activity, including a major conference at HQ MEC, as everyone began to take security more seriously. No. 1417 Flight was much in demand as the primary source of immediate,

The Navy Game.

RAF Welcomes FAA. Strike Wing Hunters overflying HMS Hermes. *Dave Bagshaw*

Air defence Sea Vixens flew ground attack missions *Derek Whitman*

RN ships re-supplied underway. *Ken Simpson*

HMS Hermes. *Ken Simpson*

local intelligence, its T7s now being used continuously to give commanders a bird's eye view of the operating area and up-country operations.

The plan was to complete the final evacuation of Aden by sea, it being considered unwise to expose transport aircraft to dissident mortars from Sheikh Othman and other unforeseen threats. To this end much of the Far East Fleet mustered off Aden, and John Severne was allocated a control cell on HMS *Fearless* from which he could continue to conduct offensive

operations. The evacuees would be taken by sea to Masirah, where they would board aircraft for the UK. With 1417 Flight to become part of 8 Squadron again when the Hunters moved to Bahrain, the Strike Wing photo processing caravans were now made ready to move to RAF Muharraq; any residual photo processing for the FR10s to be carried out thereafter by the AFME Photo Centre.

Terrorist activity was now getting steadily worse and by July 1967 most of the squadron wives and children had returned to the UK in an

Commanders and Staff. A joint conference in Aden, chaired by the AOC, AVM Andrew Humphrey in the summer of 1967, charted the way ahead for the land/air campaign. *Peter Taylor*

Grand Tour. Derek Whitman, in an FR10, escorts Wing Commander 'Pancho' Ramirez as he flies the Deputy High Commissioner over the Aden Protectorates in a Hunter T7 of 1417 Flight. *Derek Whitman*

The Fleet's In. The composite evacuation fleet stands off Aden. *Dave Bagshaw*

evacuation noted for its efficiency; the quarters 'within the wire' thereby vacated were then taken over by those who were to remain in Aden. A pair of FR10s was now on constant standby and sufficient fuel was made available in July for two FR10 training sorties/day, allowing 66 hours to be flown by the recce pilots that month, albeit none on operational missions. Although rather late in the life of the FR10 in Aden the F95 cameras were now being fitted with an automatic iris.

On 9 August, with Fred Trowern now in command, 8 Squadron departed Khormaksar for good, going first to Masirah to be close enough to Aden to return if the situation required and to avoid congestion at Muharraq (which was being used extensively in the evacuation), before taking up residence in Bahrain. With centralised servicing now in the past for the squadron, the joint 8 Squadron/43 Squadron markings were removed in favour of the squadron's yellow, blue and red stripes, dayglow Gambias (the Squadron Crest) once more adorning the nosewheel doors of their Hunters. The squadron celebrated Fred Trowern's 35th birthday in the time-honoured manner, if to the dismay of the very co-operative

station commander at Masirah, Wing Commander 'Reggie' Spiers, when the officers drank his whole year's allocation of champagne! Horace Farquhar-Smith and Ken Simpson accompanied 8 Squadron with two FR10s, presaging the flight's reintegration with the squadron, while Dickie Barraclough, Derek Whitman and Dave Bagshaw remained at Khormaksar with two FR10s for the many residual tasks ahead.

When Foreign Secretary George Brown announced unexpectedly in the House of Commons that Independence Day in Aden would be in ten days' time, the shooting stopped; the rebels had got their wish and it was now considered safe to use transport aircraft for the final departure. 1417 Flight left the building which had been its home for the last four and a half years, moving into Wing Headquarters, and Dickie Barraclough became deputy to OC Strike Wing, Wing Commander 'Pancho' Ramirez, who had taken over from Martin Chandler. Despite this turbulence, the FR pilots flew 96 of the 120 hours allocated in August, many in joint patrols with the FGA9s along known dissident routes from the Yemen. When the NLF flag was found to be flying over the fort at Shurjan, a strike was mounted by FGA9s and Dickie Barraclough took post-strike photographs, but this was all but their last gasp. Within days, the NLF flag was also flying over the Aden Airways building, only a few hundred yards from Strike Wing HQ. The end was clearly nigh.

September 1967 was the last month in the life of 1417 Flight, but its work was not yet done. In the first week of September the FR10s were airborne searching for an AAC Scout helicopter, believed to have been shot down and the crew killed between Ataq and Mayfr'ah, and indeed Derek Whitman and Dickie Barraclough found a large burnt area which seemed to confirm this. The flight also had an interesting diversion tracking an Air Djibouti Dakota which was supposed to be carrying the payroll for the HBL to Riyan, but was suspected of gun-running.

Then came the end. With a memorable airmens' party in the RAF Police Club,'The Hair of the Dog', and a formal lunch for the officers, 1417 Flight disbanded once more on 8 September 1967. To mark the event, the Senior Air Staff Officer, Air Commodore Freddie Sowrey sent the following signal: 'Thank you, on behalf of the Air Officer Commanding, for the excellent work done by your pilots and groundcrew during your time in AFME. Your skill and knowledge remain within the theatre. Good luck for the future'. The FR10s now lost their separate identity and insignia, adopting the 8 Squadron logo with the tail letters W, X, Y and Z. Derek Whitman became OC B Flight, No. 8 Squadron, and thereafter he and Dave Bagshaw, with their two FR10s, became the 8 Squadron detachment in Aden.

No. 1417 Flight had the distinction of being the only independent Hunter FR10 unit committed operationally during the aircraft's lifetime, and it had done well. In his comprehensive summary of the flight's contribution to air and ground operations in South Arabia during its eventful four years and five months in Aden, Dave Bagshaw recorded the following facts: Nineteen pilots flew 765 operational sorties in the Middle East theatre, including South Arabia, Oman, the Trucial States and the Persian Gulf. Operational activity peaked in mid-1964 when 205 sorties were flown during the Radfan campaign, sixty three of these in June alone. In Operation Ranji, the

flight kept a careful watch off the coast and over the immediate hinterland for illegal movement of guns, ammunition and supplies to dissident tribesmen, doing likewise on behalf of the Sultan of Oman over the wastes of the Empty Quarter while flying out of RAF Masirah and RAF Salalah in 1965 and 1966 on Operation Thesiger. These operations should not overshadow the important but more routine and local recce tasks, which ranged from the pin-point targets such as forts, shacks and caves, to line searches and the production of line overlap photographs covering several miles. The FR10's versatility was used to the full, with pilots always ready and able to use the Hunter's 30-mm cannons very effectively, either to mark or destroy targets, and they kept their air combat skills well honed. With in-flight reports they were able to offer immediate, visual information on friendly and hostile movements and follow this up most expeditiously with offensive action and photographic evidence for joint air/ground operations. The latter often involved rapid turn-rounds, photo processing and air drops of prints to forward troops.

All this was not achieved easily, but these FR pilots were chosen men, most with a wealth of fast-jet experience but also with a sprinkling of very capable 'creamed off' ex-instructors who added QFI and IRE expertise in support of the wing as a whole. Whatever their background they all underwent rigorous training in theatre before being committed in earnest. Not all their flying was 'operational'; as with every Hunter pilot in Aden they took their turn in firepower and 'flag waving' demonstrations, flypasts and carrying VIPs in the Hunter T7, and they did their fair share of ground duties.

Dave Bagshaw summed it up well: 'To have served with No 1417 (FR) Flight was the good fortune of very few pilots but an achievement coveted by many. The role of tactical reconnaissance in South Arabia was extremely demanding of a pilot's professional knowledge and ability on any sortie, be it operational or training – and success was always hard-won. The rugged and varied terrain never failed to impress, no matter how hardened one might have professed to have been; the 'world's best low flying area' was no misnomer when applied to South Arabia. A tour in an operational theatre devoted to very useful, always interesting and

Hunter Down! Ralph Chambers, in an FR10, was quickly on the scene when multiple technical problems caused the pilot of this FGA9 to eject – which he did successfully. *Ralph Chambers via Roger Pyrah*

Lost at Sea. FR10s could provide useful information for boards of inquiry but this RAF Britannia, which ran off the end of the runway at Khormaksar was lost forever to the sea. *Dave Bagshaw*

rewarding flying, was the hallmark of any pilot's career, and it was not without justification that the nineteen fortunate officers remain unanimous that in serving with 1417 Flight they had had 'the best flying job in the Royal Air Force'.

The FR10s also contributed to search and rescue operations and aircraft accident investigations by photographing crash sites. So it was in the case of an FGA9 which had caught fire after multiple failures (the pilot ejecting successfully to tell the tale) and when a Transport Command Britannia had failed to come to a stop on the runway at Khormaksar, at night in the rain, and ended up in the water. Photographs may have done nothing to explain why a resident Argosy came to grief in the water short of the runway at Khormaksar, but fortunately there were those on board who could. It seems that a 'trapper' (flight examiner) testing the crew's reaction to an engine failure on the final approach stop-cocked one engine while the crew, believing they were required to do so, did the same to another and the aircraft refused to continue flying on two. None of this seemed to deter the more dynamic transport pilots from trying to behave like their Hunter brethren.

No. 8 Squadron moved from Masirah to RAF Muharraq on 8 September 1967, arriving in a mixed formation of twelve FGA9, FR10 and T7 Hunters, to be greeted in the traditional manner by Squadron Leader Tony Chaplin, OC the resident 208 Squadron – also flying Hunter FGA9s.

Copy-Cat. A Khormaksar Beverley behaving like a Hunter as it breaks over FR10 XF441. *Ray Deacon*

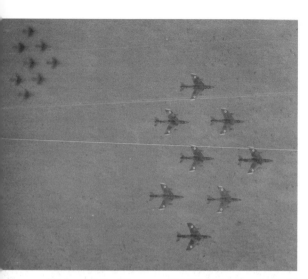

Welcome! Fred Trowern, OC 8 Squadron, arrived with his squadron to take up residence at RAF Muharraq on 8 September 1967, Squadron leader Tony Chaplin and his 208 (FGA9) Squadron there to welcome the pilots with cold beer. *Fred Trowern*

Back in Aden, Derek Whitman, Dave Bagshaw and Dickie Barraclough continued their surveillance of the coastline in Operation Ranji and became deeply involved in Operation Faldetta. Faldetta took place between 11 September and 27 November with daily sorties over a dozen or so targets and routes to provide updates on hostile activity and the movement of 'friendly' forces, particularly in the border areas around Beihan and Dhala. These missions were invariably flown in pairs at 10,000 ft, in an attempt to obscure their purpose from the ground, the pilots were issued with auto-focusing binoculars to ease identification of vehicles etc. from that height, but trying to fly the aircraft and use them effectively was no easy matter. Where necessary, FGA9s were paired with the FR10s, in which event the leader in an FR10 would concentrate on photography, leaving any visual reporting to his wingman. The Hunter pilots continued to do their own photo interpretation, with the assistance of one of the GLOs remaining on Strike Wing, usually Captain Mike Lees RA, and a qualified PI found in HQ MEC, Flight Lieutenant Les Curtis.

No. 43 Squadron disbanded officially at Khormaksar on 14 October 1967, but some FGA9s and their pilots remained in situ with the two FR10s until the final evacuation at the end of November. With tensions remaining high throughout the area, there were many

tasks to keep the Hunters, and naval aircraft flying from carriers offshore, heavily committed. Derek Whitman and Dave Bagshaw attended the formal disbandment celebrations and festivities which followed, as did Fred Trowern and his A Flight Commander Mike Webb, who had flown back in an FGA9 and an FR10 to see how things were going. Typical missions now comprised an FR10 and two Buccaneers. The Buccaneer had the advantage of two pairs of eyes, the pilot to concentrate on the flying while the observer in the back looked after the visual sightings and reporting. Occasionally the trio would land at Khormaksar, but living conditions were becoming increasingly difficult there and the RAF pilots welcomed invitations to go aboard HMS *Eagle* (by liberty boat) to sample some of the Navy's legendary hospitality.

The FR10s flew 84 hours during their last month in Aden, keeping an eye on the movements of friend and foe in the Kirsah, Mukeras, Beihan, Ataq and Dhala areas, while providing air defence cover for the final withdrawal of British forces. Dickie Barraclough completed sixty two sorties from 1 September until his last flight on 27 November and, in the 77 days which spanned Operation Faldetta, Derek Whitman logged 127 flying hours in seventy-eight sorties, of which seventy were 'operational' and fifty-seven were devoted to Faldetta; Dave Bagshaw also flew a

Fly Navy. As tensions in the Aden Protectorates increased, so did the air power of the RN and RAF combine to support the ground troops. For professional reasons (and perhaps a little socialising) Ken Simpson was one of the first to visit HMS Eagle – and witness the unique activity of carrier life. *Photos via Ken Simpson*

HMS Eagle via 'Tilly'

Scimitar reconnaissance and ground attack.

Sea Vixen air defence and ground attack.

Buccaneer strike, reconnaissance and ground attack.

similar number. Dickie was in the control tower when all Hunter flying was brought to a close on 28 November 1967 with a fly-by of eight FGA9s and the two FR10s. These aircraft were then to fly on to their new homes, with any left unserviceable pushed into the sea. This nearly happened to an FGA9 which had an undercarriage problem and had to land back at Khormaksar but its life was saved by a judicious swipe in the right place by an all-knowing airframe rigger with his faithful hide-head hammer.

One of the last Hercules to leave carried Dickie Barraclough and John Severne. In his last months in Aden, John had been given the additional task of Air Adviser to the South Arabian Government

at the new capital Al Ittihad. In that role he was charged with forming an all-purpose (transport, helicopter and strike) South Arabian Air Force by Independence Day, but with a budget of only £2M. With great enterprise, he acquired four Dakota transports, four Beaver communication aircraft, four Jet Provosts (modified by British Aerospace to carry the very accurate and effective SURA rockets) and some Sioux helicopters. He even designed the pilots' wings and aircraft markings, leaving this legacy to roam the skies where the RAF had been so prominent.

The AAC also left their own legacy, their 'run-about' Auto Union car, suitably adorned, lifted by its helicopters close to the summit of Shamsang mountain in Aden.

VIP Farewell. Derek Whitman photographs the Britannia carrying the High Commissioner, Sir Humphrey Trevelyan, from Aden on 28 Nov 1967, with Dave Bagshaw flying the second FR10 on its port side. *Derek Whitman*

After the final flypast on 28 November, Derek Whitman and Dave Bagshaw escorted the Britannia carrying the departing High Commissioner, Sir Humphrey Trevelyan, out of the area, then flew on to join 8 Squadron on APC at Sharjah. They went via Salalah to refuel and continued across the Empty Quarter (which they found to be far from 'empty') at low level initially, an experience few of their peers would have had, before climbing to height. All went well until Dave Bagshaw reported an unsafe indication on selecting his undercarriage down for landing. This in itself might not have been too worrying but he had aboard what remained worth drinking from the Officers' Mess bar at Khormaksar. Aware of this, Fred Trowern rushed to the tower, perhaps already preparing a form of words to explain

In Memoriam. An AAC helicopter left this Auto Union 'run-about' just below the summit of Shamsang, for Aden to remember them. *Dave Bagshaw*

what might be a messy arrival. Fortunately it was not, the fault being in the undercarriage warning circuit.

So ended the only fully operational commitment of the RAF's Hunter FR10s. The pilots and aircraft had done more than was asked of them but, after the British departed and the federal government collapsed, Aden and its former protectorates fell to the nationalists to become part of the independent state of South Yemen.

Chapter 10
Gulf Watchdogs

RAF Muharraq was linked by causeway to the main island of Bahrain, the capital Manama and Joint Headquarters British Forces Gulf (land, sea and air), at Jufair (hitherto HMS *Jufair*). The JHQ was commanded by a two-star officer, the post rotating between the three services, while one-star officers were responsible for their respective land, sea and air forces. At the height of the FR10 era in the Gulf, Air Commodore John Ellacombe was air commander, Group Captain John Jennings (of Aden fame) the Senior Air Staff Officer and Squadron Leader 'Tinkle' Bell the Hunter staff officer. The British were there at the discretion of the ruler of Bahrain and exercised widespread responsibilities throughout the region.

In December 1967, their first full month at Muharraq, the FR10s of Derek Whitman's B Flight, No. 8 Squadron, flew a commendable 134 hours on theatre orientation and training sorties, the flight starting as it would go on, fully involved with the FGA9s of A Flight as indeed in all squadron activities. To maximise this 'togetherness', capitalise on the specialist expertise available and enhance flexibility in the squadron as a whole, flying programmes were henceforth planned and executed jointly to the

benefit of all. Every pilot would be familiarised with both aircraft and given a taste of both roles without prejudice to their specialisations. So it was that the FR10 pilots had a chance to learn about (or re-familiarise themselves with) the delivery of rockets (still 3-inch 'drains' at this time), for which their aircraft was not equipped, and to pit their skills against the ground attack pilots in gunnery (soon justifying their above average ratings). Air-to-ground training was carried out during regular APCs at Sharjah using Rashid Range, an academic 'scored' facility just south of the airfield, and Jebajib Range, set on a nearby rocky promontory with vehicle hulks as targets for HE ammunition only (to minimise the risk of ricochets). For their part, many FGA pilots found that taking photographs with the F95 was not the 'black art' they might have been led to believe. This seamless rejoin promised well for constructive, harmonious relationships.

The two Hunter squadrons at Muharraq, 8 Squadron (commanded by Fred Trowern) and 208 Squadron (commanded by Tony Chaplin) shared a hangar overlooking the flight line but had separate offices and accommodation blocks; both would use the station's photographic facilities. They were fully autonomous units, allocating priorities within their own organic resources rather than having to vie with each other for all their needs from the centralised servicing practised in Aden. True, B Flight had to compete with A Flight for squadron resources but this was made to work. On its arrival B Flight comprised Derek Whitman, Horace Farquhar-Smith, Ken Simpson, Dave Bagshaw and Derek Bridge; all were 'second tourists', whereas most of the FGA9 pilots were on their first tour. Only the squadron executives and weapons specialists were accompanied by their wives in Bahrain, the remainder of the pilots serving on thirteen month unaccompanied tours.

It was a bright start for the squadron in 1968, as the FR experts honed their basic skills with their new FGA9 colleagues in battle formation, cine weave and air

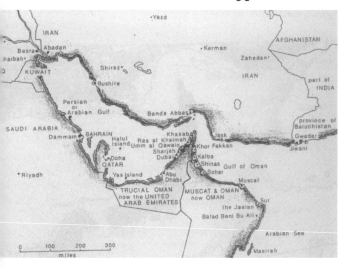

Persian Gulf and Gulf of Oman – hunting ground for FR10s.

Flight Line Maharraq. FR10 finds VC10, Andover, Argosies and Pembroke aircraft on the pan at Maharraq. Fred Trowern & Tim Thorn

combat, while many of the latter learned the rudiments of visual and photographic reconnaissance. With double the number of Hunter pilots now on the station, most of them unaccompanied, high spirits were rampant on and off duty and pyromania was in vogue. Perhaps conscious that the then station commander, Group Captain 'Twinkle' Storey, was no newcomer to the science himself, the young gentlemen of the Hunter breed, reputedly led by Dai Heather-Hayes of 8 Squadron (Al Mathie claims unconvincingly to have been an 'incompetent bystander'), announced their arrival at their first dining-in night with a huge bang followed by a cloud of fluorescent sea dye

And So to Bed. Muharraq flight line at dusk. *Tim Thorn*

marker billowing out from the air conditioning system overhead. This noxious cloud was supposed to envelop the rival 208 Squadron but drifted quickly out of control to do exactly that over the station commander and his entourage. Twinkle was not amused as his once immaculate tropical mess kit changed colour rapidly, and he invited 8 Squadron to step outside with him to discuss the matter. There, he delivered what Fred Trowern called 'an enormous roasting' before getting his own back by tossing a thunder flash amongst them as he beat a hasty retreat. Legend has it that this was not the only guest night entertainment laid on by the Hunter pyromaniacs of Muharraq; there are many versions of a story featuring T7 starter cartridges and 3-inch rocket initiators, placed in flower vases on formal dinner tables and connected by wires hidden beneath carpets to enable simultaneous explosions either on the flick of a switch – or a timer to give the main perpetrator an alibi. The author cannot confirm whose finger might have been on the trigger (although the name Dai Heather-Hayes kept cropping up); suffice it to say that everything worked much as planned to leave hosts and guests (including prominent local sheiks) covered with white flour. Again, traditional RAF ways of dealing with such incidents, vanishing fast elsewhere, could still be found in some far flung outposts of the one time Empire.

As in Aden, there were living and operating problems during summer temperatures of 100 deg and humidities of 90 per cent. Air

No. 8 Squadron – 1968. Fred Trowern, flanked by his flight commanders Derek Whitman and George Aylett, looking their best. *Fred Trowern*

conditioning was even more essential and the Hunter pilots were (in theory) allowed to remain in their cockpits on the ground for a maximum of 20 minutes, which usually gave them priority take-offs. Sand blowing from Kuwait and the Saudi deserts hampered flying, affected aircraft serviceability and made working conditions for groundcrew on the line very unpleasant.

As in Aden, navigation at low level without adequate maps and with a paucity of natural or man-made features on the ground, and at high level with unpredictable winds, could be very demanding, again calling for more than the usual dependence on the basic techniques of 'heading and time', the stopwatch again being a primary instrument. With very little useful low flying to be had locally (other than over the sea), the FR10s flew long distances south to their main LFAs Alpha, Bravo and Charlie invariably with two 230 gall and two 100 gall tanks, using either high-low-high or high-low profiles landing at Sharjah or Masirah to refuel. Typically, they would fly over Qatar, descending into the United Arab Emirates and over into the largely rugged and barren mountains of Oman, which had only small pockets of habitation in the valleys, but also across the coastal plains which contained a variety of good training targets (forts, aqueducts and other man-made infrastructure). On 19 February 1968, Derek Whitman chased Derek Bridge on his 'op trip' from Masirah, routeing

him for 15 minutes out into the Indian Ocean, then 10 minutes parallel to the coast before having him turn back towards a coastal IP for a target inland 'to see how accurate he could be with his landfall'. Suddenly he noticed that his leader was leaving a strong wake on the water and urged him 'to move up a bit', again underlining the perils of low flying over water. Unperturbed, Derek coasted in over the IP and found his target, helping him earn his squadron tie that day.

A few pilots held that their FR training at Chivenor had not equipped them well enough for these environment difficulties. The author and Fred Trowern dispute this; in their time on 229 OCU they had been at pains to stress throughout the course the importance of heading and timing, just for such exigencies. More specifically, Fred recalls that he and Porky Munro insisted that every student flew at least one sortie at very low level over the sea from Hartland Point to the Seven Stones Lightship close to the Scilly Isles (preferably between 1000 hours and 1200 hours so that the sun was in their eyes) to demonstrate the vital importance of this principle. It cannot be confirmed that this was always included in later courses.

On 20 March 1968, Derek Whitman departed for the UK, tour-expired, having handed over command of B Flight briefly to Flight Lieutenant Alfie Hulse, Alfie passing it on to Horace

Moon Country. Navigation over the desert, in places with very few landmarks (and even less shown on published maps), at the operational speeds and heights considered imperative, imposed unprecedented demands on FR10 and FGA9 pilots. *Mike Barringer*

Farquhar-Smith. The squadron was hard-pressed in March, with both variants of the aircraft heavily committed, dawn to dusk, in 'seek and destroy' training against the ever-elusive SAS in Operation Goldleaf. Then, on 23/24 April, a one-off firepower demonstration was mounted locally for the Ruler of Bahrain, Sheik Isa bin Sulman Al Khalifah. The impressive strike was led by Fred Trowern and followed by an FR10 to take F95 photographs of the distinguished audience from low level. They continued to be impressed when, very shortly thereafter, the resulting 9-inch square prints were dropped to them from the airbrake of a Hunter. However, all this activity took its toll: with the FR10s alone

flying 153 hours in March, servicing requirements had to take primacy in April and May, allowing a total of only 80 hours flying in May. Dave Bagshaw and Ken Simpson had now left B Flight, to be replaced by Flight Lieutenants George Lee and Keith Holland.

Having heard murmurings that some unidentified Hunter pilots were indulging in excessive and sometimes illegal low flying in the Sharjah area, 'beating up' the Range Safety Officer's (RSO's) hut on Rashid Range, Fred Trowern read the riot act before the forthcoming APC at Sharjah in May. Nevertheless, Flight Lieutenant Jim Taylor (A Flight) had to eject after hitting the top 3 ft of a Single Sideband Radio (SSB) aerial on the RSO's Landrover. He was court martialled. A second ejection followed in June when the engine of A Flight's John Pym's Hunter seized off Qatar; he was found quickly by his fellow pilots and picked up by a Wessex from Muharraq's Search and Rescue Flight. John was not to blame and, apart from suffering slight back injuries he was unhurt and returned to flying three weeks later.

As with most squadrons, 8 Squadron had its rogue aircraft, but Wing Commander John Hewitt, an ex-test pilot and now Wing Commander Offensive Support Wing at Muharraq, saw this as a challenge. Because the Hunter's rear fuselage fuel tanks were particularly prone to leaks, were always in short supply and contained relatively little fuel, they were sealed off, but John found that in one aircraft experiencing longitudinal control

Coasting In/Coasting Out. 8 Squadron FR10s in 1969 trained hard over land and sea. *Mike Barringer*

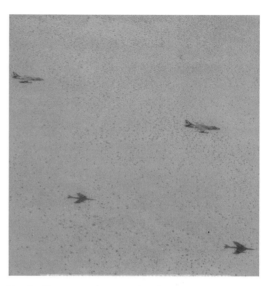

Two's Company. In certain desert areas it was prudent to fly pairs. *Tim Thorn*

sensitivity the tank had been sealed full rather than empty of fuel, thus changing the C of G. The problem was solved by resealing the tank empty of fuel. In another puzzle, one aircraft had been flying straight and level perfectly but with the 'ball' in the turn and slip indicator offset badly to one side. Such a trait was usually cured by re-aligning the drop tanks, but not this time. John Hewitt soon found that the instrument had been mounted incorrectly and the fault was remedied with a simple adjustment. It was useful to have a qualified test pilot on tap.

Chasing Shadows. 8 Squadron FR10 flying at 50 ft over the desert. *Tim Thorn*

John Houghton arrived in May 1968, initially on an unaccompanied tour but later that year taking over the recce flight from Horace Farquhar-Smith. His FR10s went looking for the SAS in the desert again in July and found them, albeit with great difficulty, to provide targets for the FGA9s in a successful joint operation which coincided with Flight Lieutenant Tim Thorn's arrival from the FR Course at Chivenor. Having been a flying instructor on his first tour, Tim was another of the chosen men who quickly dispelled the conventional wisdom that previous experience in low level, fast-jet operations was a prerequisite to success in FR. Tim had completed part of the FGA course in addition to the FR course at Chivenor and lost no time easing himself into both roles at Muharraq, proving to be an exceptional air-to-ground marksman and one of only a few who qualified as a four-ship FGA leader on his first front line tour. 'Tiger Tim' quickly gained the reputation of a 'flying hog' and off duty became a well known figure in the British Olympic Bobsleigh Team, this earning him an invitation to dine with the Queen. Since the invitation did not consider his travel costs from Bahrain and the establishment showed no inclination to fund such a trip, the squadron selected him for a Hunter Simulator and Emergency Course in the UK to coincide with the prestigious event.

Going Nowhere. OC 8 Squadron Fred Trowern makes sure wife Val doesn't go too far in his T7. *Fred Trowern*

'Tiger Tim'. Tim Thorn, qualified in FR and ground attack, on the wing of an FGA armed with 3-inch rockets with concrete heads. *Tim Thorn*

Low flying, equally imperative for tactical surprise in this region, took on a different meaning for a Hunter pilot arriving on 8 Squadron. He would start his visual and photo recce training at 250 ft, with speeds increasing, often chased by an experienced mentor until

Finale. Following a firepower demonstration for VIPs, Tim Thorn took this 'nose facer' as he gave them a farewell flypast, very low at 600 kts, blowing down their enclosure. *Tim Thorn*

considered safe and skilled enough to progress to lower levels. Only the squadron commander and B Flight commander could authorise flying down to 50 ft, and one pilot remembered that the final test included hard breaks at progressively lower levels to check for any inadvertent height loss. Tim Thorn had his check-out with Fred Trowern and is sure that this process was largely responsible for minimising the number of accidents in the theatre due solely to low flying.

Still suffering from a surfeit of flying in the spring, B Flight managed only 65 hours in August 1968, albeit ameliorated by accumulating them from many short duration weapons range sorties, and the situation improved temporarily in September with a total of 120 hours flown.

In October, Squadron Leader 'Jock' McVie replaced the highly respected Fred Trowern, he and his wife Val departing after a very successful tour. Flight Lieutenant Mike Barringer also arrived at about the same time.

Low flying over the sea was as essential as that over land, the only tactic available to delay acquisition by ship-borne radars. The Hunters in Bahrain had plenty of training in maritime operations (ship searches, surveillance and recce/attack operations) in the politically sensitive Straits of Hormuz, the coastal waters of Iran around Bandar Abbas and in the Indian Ocean. Exercise Midlink West was held in the

Midlink Mission. Ted Edwards photographed by John Houghton during Exercise Midlink West, *en route* to attack a mixed force of RN, USN and Iranian warships in the Gulf of Oman. *John Houghton*

Indian Ocean at the end of 1968, John Houghton recalling that the Royal Fleet Auxiliary *Plumbleaf* presented a particularly juicy target; being very visible and lightly armed, it came in for a great deal of attention.

Another regular commitment, FAC training, was organised and run by a dedicated cell at JHQ and the squadron GLOs, particularly Major Ian Mennell, Royal Regiment of Wales, who helped develop this training with 'live' weapons on the uninhabited island of Yas off the Trucial (UAE) Coast. As well as playing their very active part in these FAC exercises, the pilots delivered mail

Midlink Target. HMS Chichester, a Type 61 Salisbury Class Air Direction Frigate targeted in Exercise Midlink. *John Houghton*

and other creature comforts, together with small essential items, securely packaged, from the airbrakes of their Hunters to the grateful campers manning this temporary range on the island. Derek Whitman remembers dropping a replacement rotor arm for one of the GLO's Landrovers which 'decelerated so quickly that one of the lads was able to catch the package

HMS Fearless. Tim Thorn finds Fearless in the Persian Gulf. *Tim Thorn*

No Escape. This Royal Navy frigate could not hide from the prying eyes of this FR10 pilot. *Tim Thorn*

before it landed'. Such was the innovation of the time.

Further FAC training took place very close to RAF Masirah, using HE ammunition only, with mentors and students discussing tactics and procedures as together they watched some impressive firepower demonstrations. Army officers gazed in awe as pair after pair of Hunters pitched up from behind a mountain ridge on time, from very low level, to deliver rockets with devastating effect onto their targets. On being told that there was no place for a gunner to accompany the pilot, one cavalry officer observed: 'My God, the ability of these pilots!' Yes indeed. Airmen were impressed too, Tim Thorn recalling: 'The most magnificent demonstration of Hunter firepower I have ever seen' when Fred Trowern 'pulverised' authentic military targets (redundant vehicles) with a salvo of SNEB rockets (which replaced the 3-inch 'drains' in mid 1968).

Despite the valiant efforts of the squadron's engineering officer, Flying Officer Peter Hobbs, and his groundcrew, B Flight continued to fall below their monthly hours targets throughout the remainder of 1968, but in January and February 1969, 120 and 129 hours were generated respectively before serviceability fell again and thereafter fluctuated widely. Jock McVie explained why: 'A combination of lack of personnel and spares, together with competing priorities, meant that the normal time for a Hunter's Minor Inspection could be doubled or even trebled, but Gulf HQ still required us to meet our monthly SD98 flying hours. This meant that all the serviceable aircraft available had to be flown to their maximum, with the result that we ended up with two aircraft sitting on the tarmac out of hours. At this point, Peter Hobbs and I decided to limit the flying of those aircraft within 100 hours of a Minor to two sorties, or even one sortie a day to prevent an increasing number of aircraft bunching up on the second line'. It was also non-productive for FR10s detached to Sharjah for an exercise to be held on standby for long periods between short interceptor missions against 'hostile' FGA9s.

Despite these difficult troughs, there were peaks of serviceability to be proud of, John Houghton remembering that the unusual event of all FR10s being serviceable was celebrated with a close box of four flying a few turns and wingovers over Muharraq. The squadron as a whole had some very good spells, on one occasion flying nine aircraft in arrowhead while on another Jock McVie led a mixed eight-ship formation (with an FR10 taking photographs). The squadron commander was surely right in his belief that these simple displays had an uplifting effect on the morale of all, especially Peter Hobbs and his hard-pressed groundcrew, out of all proportion to their short duration.

Eight's Eight. Squadron Leader Jock McVie leads 8 Squadron's 'canard'. *Jock McVie*

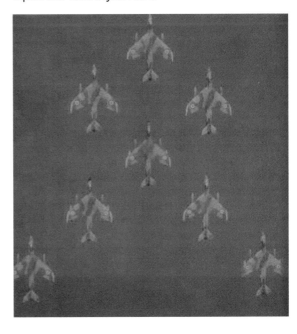

Zulu Survives. Despite trying all the tricks, Tim Thorn was unable to get the nose wheel of Zulu to lower – but the aircraft suffered very little damage. *Tim Thorn*

I'm Right Behind You. 8 Squadron's B Flight Commander John Houghton puts Mike Barringer through his paces on a difficult, two sortie 'op ride', high and low level through mountains and over flat deserts, covering many assorted targets – and declared him 'combat ready'. *John Houghton*

Minor incidents did not help aircraft availability, Tim Thorn having more than his fair share. On one sortie Jock McVie, flying as wingman, was able to confirm that the nosewheel of Tim's aircraft (XE599) had failed to emerge after he had selected gear down. Recycling whilst bunting the aircraft failed to dislodge the recalcitrant wheel and the FR10 was eventually landed gently, with very little damage, on the two main wheels. Sadly, one of the Bahraini crash crew had two ribs broken when the de-clutched canopy slid forward and crushed him as he was helping the pilot vacate the cockpit. In a second incident, Tim experienced a fire on take-off in XF436, caused by the spontaneous ignition of fuel between the jet pipe and outer fuselage. Unable to extinguish the flames, he dropped his tanks and completed a very rapid flame-out landing in time for the fire crews to save the aircraft. In a third incident, some 95 nm from Muharraq at 41,000 ft and with minimum fuel, Tim had an engine 'explode' and grind to a halt. Gliding home silently, with plenty of time to think, he carried out another faultless flame-out landing. The engineers who met him held their noses as they discovered that the engine intakes were filled with the remnants of what looked like a vulture, and that the compressor was badly damaged.

Mike Barringer was now operational, having gone through the usual rigorous checks at the hands of John Houghton, but the shortage of serviceable aircraft in the spring of 1969 hampered the operational work-ups for Chris Marshall, Frank Hoare and Malcolm Lovett, who arrived in time to join the squadron for an APC in July. By this time another renowned 'hours hog', George Lee, had left the squadron and Tim Thorn would depart soon after, giving some hope that the newcomers would get their fair share of the flying. By the end of the APC the squadron had achieved an air-to-ground gunnery average of 43 per cent but in the subsequent detachment to the Sharjah Range in December this increased to 52.5 per cent (academic) and 30 per cent (operational). Jock McVie agreed with others that elevator control was significantly lighter in the FR10 when, for instance, pulling out from a strafing dive, thus increasing the risk of overstressing the aircraft. Indeed, he remembers invalidating several scores when the maximum permitted 'G' was

Worm's Eye View. A range officer's view of the strafe target (obscured here). *Mike Barringer*

Royal Pleasure. 8 Squadron found Royal favour with this fine shot of the Sheik's Palace. *John Houghton*

Downtown Isa. Despite every facility and amenity, this venture into the twentieth century, encouraged by the Sheik, may have been slow to attract those more used to traditional Arab lifestyles. *John Houghton*

Muharraq Island. The airfield, with the capital Manama above and beyond that the causeway to the main island. *John Houghton*

exceeded. Other pilots seemed oblivious to such problems.

Jock wonders whether this increase in scores could have had anything to do with the appearance on the ground of the then Miss World and Bob Hope, when their C-141 stopped at Sharjah to refuel en route to Vietnam for one of their visits to the American troops. They and their entourage were entertained in the Officers' Mess where a huge 'Welcome Bing' sign had been posted above the bar. Despite this, Bob Hope was in good form and said to be 'a most genial,

unpretentious gentleman who chatted to one and all', but Miss World was the main attraction for 8 Squadron. To show they cared, the Hunter men 'kidnapped' her and returned her safely to the C-141 themselves, where Jock introduced three airmen who were waiting beneath its wing to bid her farewell. The first two shook hands and said 'how d'you do' rather blandly but the third, suddenly realising who the lady was, just stood there with his hand outstretched and his mouth open – unable to speak. That was not the end of the matter. A few weeks later, a photograph in the Daily Express showed Miss World at Heathrow holding a red 'bonedome'. In reply to a question from a gentleman of the press, she said she 'got it from a fighter pilot at Sharjah'. (By this time Squadron Leader Frank Spencer, the Senior Equipment Officer at Muharraq, had organised a replacement for John Bolton).

Occasionally the Hunter squadrons, including the FR10s, had the opportunity to fly the low level routes over the south of Iran, staging through Sharjah to refuel. The maps available were again very basic and once away from the coastal strip the terrain was another 'moon country', with very few discernable contours and even fewer targets. However, these trips (which may have been the last to be flown there by British combat aircraft at low level) made a change from the routine of flying over the main training areas around the Gulf.

Staff Flying. John Houghton took this photograph of his wingman, Hunter staff officer at Gulf HQ 'Tinkle' Bell, in the sensitive Jabal Akhdar. *John Houghton*

A few lucky pilots flew 'Ranger' flights to Pakistan and Kenya, and on one memorable occasion four B Flight pilots took two FR10s and two FGA9s to Nairobi via Addis Ababa (Ethiopia) and back through Jedda (Saudi Arabia). All went well until one FR10 trundled

Going Home. An FR10's 'nose-facer' catches the Muharraq based Hunters returning from an APC at Sharjah. *Fred Trowern & Tim Thorn*

off the end of the runway on to a heavily pitted overrun at Jedda, the cause unknown to the author, and an FGA9 ended up in a monsoon ditch after landing with one wheel semi-retracted due to a sequence valve failure. The pilot is reputed to have broken the world sprint record fleeing from this aircraft and escaped injury. Tinkle Bell conducted one of the Boards of Inquiry at Jedda, remaining in touch with Bahrain via a support Argosy's HF SSB radio but he was beset by the problems of Ramadhan, because his witnesses had to answer repeated calls to prayers. While their aircraft stayed behind with Cat 4 damage, the two B Flight pilots flew back to Muharraq to be greeted with a banner displayed by their colleagues on A Flight which read: 'Welcome Home Wrecky Flight'. More in hope than expectation, given that the days of the Hunters in Bahrain were now numbered, Peter Hobbs requested replacements – but to no avail.

Authorities and agencies in the area had been quick to recognise and capitalise on the value of B Flight's capabilities in airborne photography. Under the guise of an 'intelligence requirement', one FR pilot was tasked to take a photograph on one frame of the new bridge linking Abu Dhabi island with the mainland, the excellent result probably used to impress the Royal family. Similar photographs were taken of Sheik Isa's Royal Palace in Bahrain, a newly commissioned Government building on the then western edge of the capital Manama and the new town of Isa on the road south from Manama. The FR Flight was in much demand for many diverse purposes.

Colour photography with the F95 camera was largely unknown, but John Houghton and staff officer Tinkle Bell had acquired three rolls of Kodachrome film and in mid-1970 flew a special assignment together into the Jebel Akhdar in Oman, normally a 'no-go' area for the Hunters because of political and military sensitivities. Whatever the purpose or authority, such opportunities to fly over unfamiliar terrain against new targets were welcomed. The reasons for and results of this 'classified' mission remain unknown and there is no record of any further use of colour film in the FR10 force. Tinkle's close involvement with the Hunter squadrons at Muharraq was valued highly, and Jock McVie was generous in his gratitude for the help he gave them, saying: 'Understanding our problems

Stoker's men. Perhaps the last formal photograph of 8 Squadron before their departure from Muharraq to Sharjah in early 1971. Squadron Leader Bill Stoker, front and centre, incommand. *John Houghton*

at the sharp end and endowed with a huge amount of common sense, he was a good ally who helped us immensely on many occasions'. That was how it should be.

The ORB records that early August 1970 was one of those times when very hazy conditions locally made photography, indeed recce in any form, very difficult, so it was with some relief that the whole squadron left Muharraq for another APC at Sharjah. On the final day of the detachment the squadron enjoyed rehearsing napalm tactics with redundant drop tanks delivered on the range; although filled only with water, the tanks destroyed two 5-ton trucks. As a result of a splendid effort by the ground crew throughout (endorsing the value of having them as dedicated squadron members), the squadron raised twelve aircraft for a 'balbo' formation departure.

After two months on the squadron, Flight Lieutenant Al Cleaver took over command of B Flight from John Houghton in September 1970, a routine month in which 90 hours of FR flying were generated before the totals dropped to 63 hours and 26 hours respectively in the next two months because of poor aircraft serviceability. Nevertheless, B Flight took part in exercise Bugle Call in the Sohar area and shipping strikes against HMS *Tartar*, a Tribal Class frigate.

On 16 October, Squadron Leader Bill Stoker, another very able and experienced Hunter fighter pilot and 'bon vivant', took command of 8 Squadron from Jock McVie. Then in November the newly married Ron Elder arrived on B Flight and quickly proved the value of his FR training on II Squadron in Germany by becoming

operational during the following month. Exercise Breakfast promised to be an interesting experience for a B Flight pilot who accompanied FGA9s of 208 Squadron to Sharjah on 14 December for a 'cleaning up' operation against suspected dissidents in the Khasah area, north east of the airfield. The SAS and Royal Irish Rangers were involved but it all came to nothing and the Hunters returned to Bahrain in time for Christmas.

FGA9s and an FR10 were back at Sharjah again in January 1971 to take part in the very comprehensive training offered by Exercise Arabian Nights, in which the Abu Dhabi Defence Force (ADDF) provided 'no mean opposition' as the Hunters practised FAC work, in-flight tasking by and for the FR pilots, fighter interceptions, air combat and operational FR, all in simulated war conditions. Flying was plentiful throughout this first month of 1971 but tapered off to 103 and 53 hours respectively in February and March, as the number of pilots on B Flight fell to four, Peter Boulter having departed to leave only Al Cleaver, Grant Taylor, Pat Kiggell and Ron Elder. Things perked up again in April with 132 hours and in May with 93 hours flown by the FR10s, during which time the flight participated in exercises Hot Rod and Hard Climb, the latter with the Trucial Oman Scouts (TOS) acting as the enemy in the mountainous area of Ras Al Khaimah.

Bill Stoker had been a member of the famous Blue Diamonds Hunter aerobatic team and proved to be a very smooth formation leader at the head of a nine-ship squadron flypast (followed by a four-ship display) at the opening of the new International Airport at Dubai. This so impressed the Sheik of Dubai that he presented all the pilots with expensive wristwatches, and Bill himself with a far more ostentatious model, diamond chips marking the hour points, which he took care to wear whenever in the company of notable Arabs. The officers were also invited to a party at the Sheik's Palace, this being a unique experience for most of them because it was 'dry' and because it provided a rare chance to taste truly Arab food.

The TOS acted as the enemy again in Exercise Raabita, which took place between Abu Dhabi and Burami in June, 8 Squadron rehearsing its full repertoire in support of 'friendly' forces with the FR pilots again proving their versatility in the FGA role.

A programme of comprehensive, fully integrated training continued throughout July and August, until cracks appeared in some of the Hunter pitot tubes, resulting in temporary 'G' restrictions and more moderate activity.

With only three full time FR pilots now left on B Flight, Al Cleaver, Pat Kiggell and Ron Elder were joined by Flight Lieutenants Pete Griffiths and later Dave Ainge from A Flight who underwent short but intensive programmes of FR orientation. There was a further dearth of FR10 flying with only 39 hours flown in September, but the B Flight pilots were able to negotiate additional flying on the FGA9.

Then came the bombshell (although perhaps foreseen by those in the know) that Sheikh Isa, the Ruler of Bahrain, no longer required the presence of offensive aircraft on the island. As a result, the four FR10s returned to the UK on 24 September and a reduced 8 Squadron moved eight FGA9s and twelve pilots to Sharjah on 29 September.

With Al Cleaver, Ron Elder, Pete Griffiths and Dave Ainge remaining on strength, visual recce expertise proved its worth again in October's Exercise High Point, the Staffords taking full advantage of timely in-flight reports on 'enemy' movements in the Wadi Shimal. This was believed to have been the RAF Hunters' last significant FR contribution to military exercises in the Gulf.

In November 1971, No. 8 Squadron left the Middle East for good after 51 years and 2 months of unrivalled, sometimes spectacular service in the theatre. The squadron had always depended on (and had often provided) aerial reconnaissance, perhaps more than any other squadron in the region, making a significant contribution to exercises and operations before, during and after WW2. For their part the Hunter FR10s excelled during the Radfan conflict and subsequent operations in the Federation of South Arabia, before spending their last more peaceful but still very active years in the Gulf.

Al Cleaver led the last four Hunters back to RAF Kemble via Tehran, Akrotiri, Luqa and Istres, arriving on 10 December 1971 at night in low cloud and driving rain. True to form, Bill Stoker was there with other squadron members, wives and children, armed of course with champagne. So ends the story of the RAF's Hunter FR10s in the Middle East; it is of significance in that it includes the aircraft's only commitment to active service in a hostile environment – and in this, as in all things, it did well.

No. 8 Squadron then went into a very short period of suspended animation, before being resurrected as a Shackleton Airborne Early Warning squadron at Kinloss in January 1972.

Chapter 11
Film Stars

Throughout the preceding chapters, the author has been at pains to persuade readers that tactical reconnaissance in the Hunter era was not solely about photographs, because visual sightings passed promptly (ideally by in-flight reports) could also make major contributions to fast-moving events. No more need be said of that, except that this reminder of a reality should have in no way diminished the great value which could be derived from the FR10's F95 photographs. Accordingly, this chapter offers a separate tribute, albeit reiterating some of what has been written before, to all those who were involved before, during and after a mission, with the cameras and photography, film processing and photo interpretation.

To maximise their potential the cameras had, firstly, to be maintained in peak condition and set up correctly so that they operated efficiently in the air; this was the role of the camera technicians. It was then up to the aircrew to bring back film properly exposed and with the target fully covered, for the MFPUs in Germany and the photographic sections in Aden, the Gulf and Chivenor to process and print as required, expeditiously and to the best of their ability. Finally at the station level, the GLOs and the PIs were responsible for extracting and recording the information required from the film and passing it upstream without delay to the battle managers most likely to need it. These were indeed the 'film stars'.

Sufficient has been written on the excellence and simplicity of the F95 camera in its operation and of its capabilities in the demanding high speed/ultra low level regime – ease of camera maintenance and film management adding to its attractions. The camera technicians working out of sight in the workshops were all too easily forgotten, with the first sightings of camera men at work coming at squadron level as they off-loaded magazines from the FR10s after flight. This could be accomplished very rapidly, with the nose section of the aircraft detached as the aircraft's engine wound down and the pilot signalled which cameras he had used. Many action photographs of this scene pervade squadron albums, with fast feet, bicycles, motor cycles and other vehicles all used to speed the precious film from flight line to processing facility. An error at this stage could cost dearly.

The fully mobile MFPUs came to life in 1943 to support the tac recce units (Mustangs, Spitfires, Mosquitos etc) committed to the invasion of continental Europe in WW2. They were soon proficient, one unit producing 30,000 prints in the 24 hour period within the first week of arrival on the Continent, and their performance with new technology improved progressively thereafter. In the beginning, each unit was commanded by a flight lieutenant and manned by some eighteen NCOs and airmen, mounted in eight assorted vehicles. Based on their success during this campaign the MFPUs were enlarged and modernised after the war, with Blue Train trailers accommodating Williamson film processors and multi-printers with autograders, Hunter-Penrose copying cameras and offices. Blue Trains were drawn by Thornycroft prime movers, with support being provided initially by 15-cwt and 3-ton lorries, water bowsers and diesel generators. The Blue Train vehicles were replaced during the 1950s by Von Lienen trailers which continued to serve at the time of the Hunter.

Although the MFPUs in Germany operated as separate entities, every effort was made to ensure that they were inseparable from their associated flying squadrons. They were, of course, collocated and always included in any celebrations, social or sporting events; such allegiance fundamental to the essentially collective and harmonious effort. That said, these otherwise self-contained units were known for their ingenuity and determination to be 'one up' on the flying squadrons and David Jenkins, one of their number in the 1950s, claimed that they often did. He remembers a detachment to the Belgian base at Bierzet at which they set up camp in a prime position in an orchard, complete with electricity from their organic generators and a much-needed shower. No. II Squadron, camped nearby, envied such luxuries. Another MFPU

It Goes In Here and Comes Out There. A IV Squadron photographer demonstrates the F95 camera. *IV Sqn*

Speed Can Matter. Photographers at squadron level could have the first rolls of F95 film on the light tables in five minutes from 'engine-off'. *II Sqn & IV Sqn*

man, Stan Peachey, had equally good memories of their life 'al fresco' but one initiative might have gone badly wrong when they lit a campfire on what transpired to be a WW2 explosives store near Kleve, a residue of live ammunition soon becoming apparent below the embers. Likewise the GLOs, albeit with their separate sections manned by soldiers, were also considered integral parts of their parent squadrons.

With apologies to those who dealt with the film in Aden, the Gulf and Chivenor, an outline of how it was handled after off-loading from the aircraft is based here on experience with the MFPUs in Germany. At best, the first roll of F95 negatives could have been on the light table for viewing some 5 minutes after engine off, a MFPU NCO in attendance throughout to advise on technical quality and printability, to take instructions and expedite selected negatives to the adjacent printer trailer. First prints from these negatives could be expected 10 minutes after engine off.

Meanwhile, the GLOs and PIs who had been at the pre-flight briefing and already knew a great deal about the targets from their study of large scale maps, earlier photographs and any in-flight reports from their pilots, would be preparing their MISREPS. They would also seek further amplification from the pilot as the latter completed his VISREP on the ground. In rehearsing for war, competitions called for these reports to be completed within 30 minutes of engine off. Should further details be revealed

after deeper study of the negatives or prints a Hot Report would follow the MISREP.

Unlike the Swift FR5 squadrons before them, the FR10 equipped II and IV Squadrons were each established with a resident PI (on the Swift squadrons PIs were co-opted for exercises only). This increased the amount and quality of the intelligence gleaned at this stage from the photographs and the speed of output, invaluable factors in the many academic competitions as they would have been in war. Flight Lieutenant David Oxley, II Squadron's highly respected PI, commended this decision; he recognised the value of having PIs on strength to gain an intimate knowledge of the unit's role, local procedures, equipment and individual pilots, not only to enhance their own worth but to act as mentors to the reinforcement PIs. He saw the need for these dedicated PIs to get to know the particular operating problems of achieving well-positioned, correctly scaled, good quality photographs while extracting visual information from a target, by flying as frequently as possible

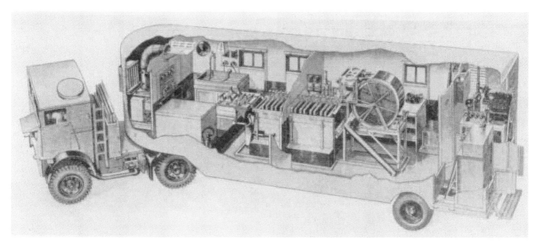

At Your Service. A Mobile Field Processing Unit (MFPU) Processing Semi-Trailer. *Joint School of Photography (JSP) Museum*

with different pilots in the T7, and this he did whenever possible. He believed that a tour on an operational tac recce squadron was invaluable to a PI's personal effectiveness and the squadrons were equally adamant that a resident PI was essential to theirs.

These assigned PIs were assisted in competitions (as they would have been in war) by very willing reinforcements from JARIC, RAF Voluntary Reserve (RAFVR) and photo staffs from RAF Germany. At the outset these were all greeted with some apprehension on the front

Exercise Conditions. The number of units deployed on exercise would be determined by the requirements and the circumstances. *JSP Museum*

line, primarily because most had very little training or continuity in working with the fast-jet force.

When flying for the RAFVR ceased in 1954, some of the incumbents were offered further service in photographic interpretation, within No. 7010 Reserve Flight. Whatever their background in the service or civilian life (which included civil servants, engineers, university lecturers and school teachers) they were all required training to master new equipment and the quickened pace of generating intelligence from fast-jet recce. This training started in a very basic way at RAF Culham, then moved to Nuneham Park, Oxford, where it developed with ever-increasing intensity, crammed into the minimum requirement of 15 days and 2

The Waiting Game. II Squadron's PI, Flight Lieutenant Eric Lockwood, ready and waiting for film to view at his PI's van. *II Sqn*

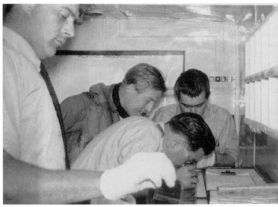

It's All There! Eric Lockwood studies negatives on the light table while the mission's pilot, Hugh Cracroft, looks on anxiously. *II Sqn*

little if anything about 7010 Flight. They were well aware that the PIs were crucial to their chances of doing well in these prestigious competitions, and did not relish the prospect of having to work with what they saw to be a bunch of amateurs. The worst of their fears proved ill-founded, the II Squadron history reporting: 'The impact of part-timers upon a dedicated and professional squadron was not without some problems and tensions, yet on the whole there were very few and they were quickly ironed out'. One prominent member of

The End Product. Selected prints could be to hand within 10 minutes of engines off, ready for the PIs to annotate target details. *II Sqn*

weekends active service each year. It is to the great credit of these enthusiastic officers, to the Joint School of Photographic Interpretation (JSPI) and JARIC that the flight survived several attempts to have it disbanded, although it did have to accept a reduction in size from 150 to 57 members. At this time the part-timers were seen merely as war reserves to supplement regular staff at the Photographic Intelligence Unit (PIU), but a decision was made by wise men at the JSPI, JARIC and the Central Reconnaissance Establishment to disperse them periodically to the operational squadrons for 'on the job' training and to assist the regular PIs in times of need. Their main commitment in this context would be the Royal Flush competitions.

It was understandable that, at the outset, all this worried those on the front line squadrons, who were not involved in the decision and knew

the then 7010 Flight, Flight Lieutenant Fred Piper, sensed the competition atmosphere on 'his' squadron (II Squadron) well: 'It is not easy to describe the overall air of tension which infected the squadron at the time of the exercise, it extended from tarmac to kitchen and, inevitably, wives and families were caught up in the fervour of the competition. Easier to understand were the many parties which followed the end of these exercises – happy and liberated!' Very soon, the squadrons welcomed this addition to their ranks as a valuable contribution to the collective effort. David Oxley spoke well of the reinforcement PIs, but believed they could not have been expected to have the same 'feel for the business' nor enjoy the degree of confidence that the resident PI hoped to have from the pilots. For all that, selected augmentees with the necessary skills and enthusiasm, given the proper orientation, training and continuity, became indispensable when workloads and tensions were high, as in competitions, and many became very welcome and loyal members of the squadrons which adopted them. The dedication and enthusiasm of these officers, whose expertise grew in leaps and bounds, won against the odds professionally and led to social relationships between them and the Hunter pilots they served which continue to this day.

Some of the 'film stars' involved in the chain of events described have been named hitherto for their efforts in connection with specific events as they unfolded in this story of the FR10, but the majority went unsung and had to be satisfied with the plaudits accorded to the collective efforts of their units. For example, the exemplary performance of 4 MFPU in IV Squadron's victorious Royal Flush of 1966 was recognised formally and officially, NATO-wide and locally, as was that of the PIs and 2 MFPU in winning trophies with II Squadron in the 1970 Big Click. There were no competitions in Aden or Bahrain but there was real conflict, giving the hierarchy plenty of visual evidence that the 'back-room boys' there were providing the necessarily continuous, crucial service to the FR10's truly operational effectiveness in the Federation of South Arabia.

Returning to the totality of tactical reconnaissance, there should have been no conflict between the relative contributions made by the human eye and the camera; they were complementary, albeit with one or the other option sometimes more appropriate to specific demands or circumstances at the time. What cannot be disputed from experience is that film from a fully serviceable and properly operated F95 camera, exposed in the right light conditions and processed efficiently, could reveal more than the human eye and brain was able to absorb in the type of low level operations imperative in the Cold War era.

The camera did not lie.

The Victors. No 2 MFPU – winners of the 'Best Photo Lab' trophy at AFNORTH's 1970 Big Click tactical reconnaissance competition. *II Sqn*

Chapter 12
'Plumbers', 'Fairies', 'Sooties', 'Bashers' et al

It has already been acknowledged that the undisputed reputation of the FR10 force was not due solely to the aircraft and pilots in the cockpits, but also to the collective efforts of the many unsung heroes within the ever-ready and very willing supporting elements at all levels, on the flight lines and throughout the stations. Chapter Eleven paid tribute to those who were involved with the all-important cameras and film, and this chapter attempts to do likewise for those who kept the aircraft flying: the 'plumbers', 'fairies', 'sooties', 'bashers' et al (depending on their specialisations). It provides a brief insight into the roles and lives of some of these men, as they worked tirelessly on sometimes difficult jobs in unpleasant conditions and with finite resources. They too were the 'best of breed'.

Engineering support for the four FR10s assigned to B Flight, 8 Squadron, depended on whether the squadron was operating autonomously or beholden to the centralised servicing system in Aden. On 1417 Flight, a number of airmen were held on the strength for first line duties but otherwise the aircraft were supported by the centralised resources of

Tactical/Strike Wing. It was different again on 229 OCU at Chivenor where, in the early 1960s, the FR cell was part of No. 234 (R) Squadron, and its staff had to vie with the air defence, ground attack and instrument training interests for the aircraft it needed from an associated engineering squadron. This was no longer the case from 1967, when a dedicated FR flight with two FR10s and two FGA9 Hunters was set up within a resurrected 79 Squadron, but the squadron itself remained subject to centralised servicing.

Nos II and IV FR10 squadrons in RAFG were autonomous units, established with eight FR10s plus an 'in use reserve', and later a T7, in an organisation which followed the traditional pattern. Completion of assigned tasks, first line aircraft servicing, safety procedures, organic facilities and the well-being of the groundcrew were the ultimate responsibility of the squadron commander, then a squadron leader, who delegated authority to his engineering officer, a flight lieutenant or flying officer. This assignment may have been 'bread and butter' to experienced officers but it was certainly a tall order for those on their first or second tours who had little practical experience to back up their

Trade Training. IV Squadron recruits the young during its 50th Anniversary Open Day in November 1963, Corporal Ayers describing the finer points of the Aden cannon while SAC Mule explains 'black box' technology. *IV Sqn*

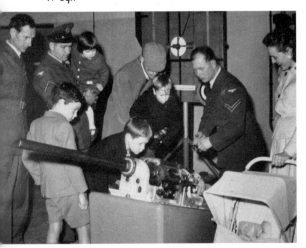

Flight Lieutenant 'Ging' Shaw, IV Squadron's Engineering Officer 1962–63. *Mike Plimmer*

S50B. Time to Go, Engineer Flight Lieutenant Peter Scott and his wife Maisie on their way after a fine tour with IV Squadron. *IV Sqn*

training at Digby, Cranwell or Henlow. However, they could rely invariably on their experienced Hunter warrant officers, NCOs and specialist tradesmen to provide the necessary

Tradesman McGarvey. Flight Lieutenant John McGarvey, II Squadron's Engineering Officer 1965-1967, posing as an 'instrument basher' to do the job his way. The excellent serviceability throughout his tenure earned him an MBE. *II Sqn*

skills and leadership and these teams served their squadrons well. Indeed, the FR squadrons seemed to be blessed with 'can-do' men on the ground at all levels. In the early days they were led by the likes of Flight Lieutenant Pat O'Connor of II Squadron, Flying Officer 'Ging' Shaw of IV Squadron and Flying Officer Owen Truelove on 8 Squadron; Flight Lieutenants Peter Scott and John McGarvey followed on IV and II Squadrons respectively and others have been mentioned in Chapters Four, Five, Nine and Ten.

Best known to the author was John McGarvey of II Squadron, a man of great resource, energy and industry, always in the limelight at work and play. He was equally at home beneath a Hunter getting his hands dirty (thus endearing himself to both aircrew and fellow engineers) and in the Cellar Bar at Gutersloh – doing what Irishmen do so well when the sun goes down. In the hangars and on the flight line, NCOs presided over the airframe, engine, instrument, electrical, radio, photographic and armament specialisations. The squadron undertook first and second line servicing, engine changes, primary and minor servicings, with some deeper servicing or rectification carried out by or with the help of Engineering Wing. The FR10s went to 431 MU at Bruggen for 'majors'.

Mike Plimmer was posted to IV Squadron as a 22 year old corporal technician instrument fitter (a 'basher') in 1962, and was employed primarily in the hangar rather than on the flight line. He remembers that the squadron's old *Luftwaffe* hangar at Gutersloh, with its huge but efficient steel doors still bearing the scars of WW2, was a comfortable workplace; the groundcrew occupied small offices and workshops on the ground floor, the officers those on the floor above. Crewrooms above and below were filled with mementos of past times, places visited around Europe and a variety of artefacts of particular interest at the time. Having spent his previous three years solely on helicopters, with only cursory experience on the early marks of Hunter from his training at Halton, Mike admits that this was 'a bit of a culture shock'. He was responsible, in particular, for the gunsights, oxygen systems and the notoriously unreliable fuel contents gauging, the latter considered by many instrument men to be their most demanding and unpopular challenge.

The Hunter's fuel system was complicated, particularly with the number of fuel tanks involved. In addition to the four external drop tanks, two 230 gall inboard (with their own sensors) and two 100 gall outboard (without any electronic gauging), there were twelve separate internal tanks, each with its own fuel contents sensor. An abundance of high-level float switches, low-level switches, fuel pressure switches, 'bingo' light switches, 'dolls eye' indicators and innumerable relays, made trouble-shooting very daunting. Accessibility was also a major problem: every tank was hidden deep in the fuselage or behind the wing leading edges (involving the removal of scores of fasteners) while access to the fuel gauge amplifiers in the roof of the radio equipment bay required the removal of the bay's cooling-air 'Christmas tree' of pipes. The fuel gauges themselves were nicely to hand on the starboard shelf of the cockpit, but all too vulnerable to damage by carelessly shed buckles from the ejection seat harness (a protective perspex cover eventually solved this problem). Despite the gauge readings, if maximum range was required and there was any uncertainty over the contents of the 230 gall drop tanks, a screw would be loosened on the top of each until fuel seeped out,

after which the tanks were replenished. All in all the fuel system was unreliable and often a nightmare for those who had to put it right so often, but it had to be right for mission success and flight safety, because FR sorties often went to extreme ranges at low level, when fuel was at a premium. It was to the credit of the instrument bashers that no FR10 was known to have been lost due to fuel problems.

Given that the FR10s operated primarily at low level, Mike Plimmer was surprised that so much oxygen was consumed by the pilots; perhaps this was due to the conviction that a session on 100 per cent oxygen helped remove any residual hangovers? It was very important that the system was never fully exhausted and that it was recharged as soon as possible when less than full; otherwise, it had to be purged using a hygrometer and this involved a lengthy and complicated charge/discharge procedure to remove any moisture. The oxygen demand system, based on an American design but British built, had many fail-safe features and gave few problems; so it was with a regulator which had a replacement life of two years or 400 flying hours. It was fortunate that the regulator rarely needed unscheduled replacement because access was again very difficult, and for this reason routine changes were normally programmed when ejector seats were removed for other reasons. Oxygen charging was heavy work; without mechanical handling aids each 2 cwt oxygen transport cylinder had to be manhandled on to and off the four-cylinder trolleys at the gas cylinder compound, the trolleys then towed to the aircraft. Bob Hillman, one of II Squadron's flight commanders, remembers watching with horror as a fully loaded trolley became separated from its Landrover tug and trundled with increasing rapidity down the sloping apron towards the hangar until it buried itself neatly in the back of the station commander's staff car. The station commander, Group Captain David Evans, was flying with the squadron at the time and Bob spent the next hour rehearsing how he would report this to his grand master. He need not have worried; perhaps because he had had a good trip or realised that, by his own orders, the car should not have been parked on the apron, the station commander was at his most human, with words to the effect that accidents will happen – and left Bob to do what he thought was necessary. This entailed a ticking off for the corporal involved, the replacement of all tractor towing eyes and pins and a promise of many beers for the Mechanical Transport Officer and his men who repaired the car. The oxygen trolley was undamaged.

Of course, oxygen was a ready candidate for blame when any pilot felt unwell after landing and, with all the oxygen coming from one source in the command, this could start an almost unstoppable chain of events. This so nearly happened when one Hunter pilot reported to the Senior Medical Officer, feeling hot and sweaty and complaining of nausea, upon which the engineering officer prudently forewarned possible oxygen contamination. The grounding of all RAF Germany's operational aircraft was narrowly avoided when it was revealed that the pilot in question had just returned from his honeymoon, had missed breakfast and endured a very bumpy ride at low level. There was nothing wrong with his oxygen system.

Compass swings on the far side of Gutersloh airfield were a mixed blessing for the instrument men, they were all very well on a nice sunny day but far from fun in the cold, windy mid-winter, particularly when an increasingly bored or perhaps very hot pilot in the closed cockpit did not do exactly as he was told and then taxied back to the hangar without calling for transport for the man outside.

SAC Ian Sharples, another instrument basher, found the same conditions and working routine

on IV Squadron some two years later. He recalls that they started work at 0800 hours by towing all serviceable aircraft to the flight line some 100 yards in front of the hangar. There was just enough room on the hangar floor to park ten Hunters providing they were manhandled with great care along the demarcation lines provided for the purpose. Even then, with all the other ground equipment and spare drop tanks also stored therein, movement was severely restricted and, after the German cleaner injured an eye when coming into contact with a Hunter's aileron, every wing-tip sprouted black and yellow warning discs. Having worked on a farm, Ian became one of those invaluable volunteers who drove the towing tractors, a highly skilled job with no small risk attached when it came to reversing all the aircraft into the confined space of the old hangars at the end of each flying day, when everyone was tired and wanted to go home. Be that as it may, these worthy volunteers could expect no quarter if they got it wrong, even if only slightly grazing an aircraft in the process. However, the author recalls one such minor incident in which an otherwise most reliable and

Risky Work. Ex-farm worker Ian Sharples volunteered for towing duties on II Squadron – knowing the risks involved in manoeuvring up to ten Hunters in the confined space of Hangar 2. *Ian Sharples*

Routine Servicing. Instrument mechanic SAC Ian Sharples replenishing the oxygen system in his adopted FR10 'Tango' on the line at Gutersloh in February 1964. *Ian Sharples*

conscientious airman was clearly at fault. In this case, his fellow tradesmen got together to carry out immaculate repairs to the two aircraft involved throughout the night; they then had the results fully (but covertly) approved by the necessary authority in order to have both aircraft on the first wave the next day. In another very human incident, Senior Aircraftsman George Eccleston (an electrician 'fairy') working on II Squadron, had been helping to rectify a fault in the reversing contactors which controlled the flying tail and tailplane trim at the base of the fin. As was his habit, he placed his handkerchief under the contactors to catch any of the many small screws which had to be removed to gain access, and thereby avoid the risk of FOD. It was only when the job was done and the panels replaced that he remembered the handkerchief. Fortunately, he admitted this oversight at once to his warrant officer, before undertaking the laborious process of retrieving the errant item, 'his pump screwdriver working as if motorised', and his honesty paid off; no harm was done and no retribution followed. Had these incidents been dealt with officially 'by the book' severe punitive action might have resulted, whereas this demonstration of squadron spirit, honesty and camaraderie at all levels enhanced morale; no flying was lost and reputations were saved. So many of these experiences and tales remain in the memories of the long-suffering groundcrew, some having added to their tribulations at the time while others were merely a source of amusement, particularly when they were at the expense of the pilots.

At Gutersloh, a hut or caravan on the flight line accommodated the line chief and a small cadre of first line tradesmen responsible for replenishing fuel, oxygen, film and ammunition before flight, on turn-round and after flight; armourers ('plumbers') had the job of replacing the brake parachutes, a difficult task requiring muscle to squeeze the pack into the container and secure the door. There were times when the line crews, their jobs repetitive, tended to envy those working in the relative comfort of the hangar, particularly in the poor weather which prevailed at Gutersloh for much of the time. On a good day, there might be six aircraft on the line at the start, leaving one or two only in the hangar, but inevitably the latter would be joined by others as the day wore on and evening work for some was far from unusual. Careful man management was needed to share the workload.

Instrument fitter Ben Bennett arrived in Aden after 18 days on Her Majesty's Troopship *Dilwara* in May 1960, and worked on 8 Squadron's FGA9s until the FR10s arrived in the following April. Whilst sharing Mike Plimmer's and Ian Sharples' experiences, he specifically remembers the difficulties they had removing the armour plating on the walls either side of the cockpit before any of the instruments in these areas could be changed: 'a very hot and sweaty job in the heat of Aden'. Ben had accompanied the squadron to Kuwait when General Kassim precipitated the crisis there in 1961 and recalls: 'I thought Aden was hot but there we managed to fry an egg on the wing of a Hunter'. Ben

Hard Times. II Squadron groundcrew de-frosting an FR10. *II Sqn*

Signing In. No time wasted, Kit Netherton signs the F-700 for IV Squadron ground crew on the flight line. *IV Sqn*

Line Marshal. Ben Bennett brings an 8 Squadron Hunter safely back to the flight line at Khormaksar in 1960. *Ben Bennett*

'Moonies'. Ben Bennett draws attention to white-kneed 'moonies' just arrived in Aden from the UK in 1961. *Ben Bennett*

returned to the cool of the UK in 1962, to serve on the ground attack Hunters of No. 1 Squadron at West Raynham, but became re-acquainted with the FR10 on 79 Squadron at RAF Chivenor in 1967. He remained there until 1973 and earned great credit by developing a rapid gun harmonisation system; he also received an AOC's Commendation and was promoted to sergeant. Experience and hard work paid off.

Airframe rigger ('tin basher') Peter Marshall arrived in Aden in January 1962, emerging from the door of a British United Britannia aircraft at 0730 hours into 'hot, moist air that hit me like invisible soup, and as we walked towards the Aden Airways terminal the sweat was already rolling down my back. The humidity was incredible and was always a feature of life on the line in Aden'. Peter had a relatively easy first two weeks with what remained of 8 Squadron at Khormaksar while the rest were on detachment elsewhere, shadowed by one of the old hands until deemed fit to carry out 'before flight' (B/F), 'after flight' (A/F) and turn-round inspections on the Hunters on his own. Delighted to be on an autonomous squadron, Peter was relieved to find that centralised servicing had yet to be introduced on the base. He also found that, on the whole, the Hunter FGA9s, FR10s and T7s of 8 Squadron (1417 Flight had yet to form) were kind to the airframe riggers, although keeping

the sand-blasted canopies clean was a 'bind' and brake changes in the frequent sandstorms 'tested one's sense of adventure'.

Whether it was pressure to meet a deadline, simply human error or over-enthusiasm in the highly competitive climate of aircraft generation exercises and the many FR10 competitions, there was always the temptation to cut corners, and a

Old Hand. Ben Bennett, who put his Hunter experience to good use on 79 Squadron's FR10 Flight at Chivenor, is seen here on a detachment to Gibraltar in 1969 – his contribution rewarded that year with promotion to sergeant and a C-in-C's Fighter Command Commendation. *Ben Bennett*

potentially disastrous incident occurred on II Squadron in 1968 when the four Aden cannons of an FR10 were fired inadvertently in Hangar 6. The aircraft had become unserviceable during an exercise and been moved into the hangar fully armed, where checks were to be carried out to ensure that the air scoop below the fuselage extended to purge the system when the guns were fired. For reasons unknown to the author, all the safety procedures were overridden and the guns triggered. Fortunately, each gun was loaded with five rounds of inert ball ammunition ahead of 130 HE rounds and only the first 20 rounds of ball were fired. The effects were dramatic enough, blowing a hole some 5 ft in diameter in the hangar wall to fill both lower and upper rooms on that side of the building with choking dust, smoke and fumes, but had the HE rounds been fired the results could have been disastrous. It is also remarkable that, with all the pilots in the hangar doing odd jobs, relaxing or preparing for ground training on that Friday afternoon, there were no injuries. Not long after the dust had settled, Pete Atkins and other pilots in the crewroom heard the definitive version of the incident on an East German radio station in detail and with the squadron engineering officer named. It had long been thought that East German or Russian spies were operating in and around Gutersloh, and this seemed to be graphic confirmation. Perhaps it was a little unfair that a German cleaner, who was on the spot throughout, was regarded with no little suspicion thereafter. The outcome of the exhaustive investigation which followed cannot be verified.

Necessary for flexibility, especially when mass launches were required, all squadron tradesmen were qualified to send off and receive FR10s on the line. First they would help strap the pilot into his parachute and seat harness, making sure that he connected his ejector seat leg restraining straps, oxygen and 'G' suit tubes, and finally that the seat pins had been removed. After ensuring that wheel chocks were in place and a fire extinguisher readily available, they would clear the pilot for start-up, watching carefully for anything untoward. They were often rewarded with well-published accolades for spotting such potentially dangerous signs as smoke, fire, leaking fuel or hydraulic seepage and thus played a vital role in flight line operations. These responsibilities were not without risk and there was plenty of room for error.

Peter Marshall's normal routine was to launch a pair of aircraft three times during the morning and then cease work at lunchtime, but extra flying was sometimes scheduled for the afternoon. On one of these days, he returned from an early lunch to be greeted with much hooting and shouts of derision accompanying the news that an aircraft he had seen off earlier had shed its 'Sabrinas' (containers fitted below the fuselage to catch the cartridge links from the Aden guns), one having somehow ended up in an engine intake. It could have been worse had not the pilot, Flight Lieutenant Ken Hayr, managed to bring the aircraft back safely but the sortie, a rehearsal for a solo aerobatic display on the forthcoming Open Day at Khormaksar, had to be aborted. Peter's punishment was 14 days 'jankers' and a rather one-sided interview. He was in no way connected with another mishap on the line at that time, when a Hunter's jet pipe blank blew out with a mighty bellow after the engine had been started with it still in place. That evening, it was laughter and drinks all round in the Camel Club on the engine fitter ('sootie') responsible.

Starting could be hazardous, with an explosion and fire always possible. Mike Plimmer likened AVPIN (Isolpropylnitrate) to nitroglycerine in that, when ignited, it generated huge amounts of the gaseous combustion needed to turn the starter, and hence the aircraft's engine. Once the engine reached the required rpm within the starting cycle, it was necessary for the groundcrew to brave the carcinogenic cloud of burnt AVPIN and 'scuttle under the aircraft to peer into the dark recesses of the starter bay to ensure that all was well before shutting the bay door'. To this end, he had a torch (hardly necessary since the red hot starter glowed throughout the bay) and an asbestos glove to smother any residual flames issuing from the starter exhaust. On several counts this was an unenviable task, as the inexperienced would testify. In the first place, while the asbestos glove did not burn it offered little protection against the intense heat. Then there were the small drops of AVPIN from the starter drain which could burn holes in protective clothing and the adjacent 'sharks fin' aerial which was always there to cut the unwary. Perhaps the Hunter groundcrew bore these trademarks with some pride.

There was a bigger risk. Occasionally, the electrical starter control box would not shut down but initiate a second starting cycle and thereby feed another quart of AVPIN into the already glowing starter motor, where it would ignite. At this point, and as the overheated starter began to scream in anguish, the required reaction was for the groundcrew to leap outside the danger zone and gesture the pilot to shut down and vacate the cockpit with similar dispatch before any explosion. Ian Sharples would bear witness to one such incident on the line while he was seeing off a II Squadron Hunter, an airframe rigger apparently bursting into flames as he went to close the aircraft's starter hatch during a faulty start. The nearest fire extinguisher did not work, but the fire and crash services were on the spot very quickly to find that the rigger had already beaten out the flames himself. Unperturbed, everyone went about their business after what was seen to be little more than a routine event.

George Eccleston was serving on IV Squadron when he was directly involved with his squadron commander in a starter fire. He failed to put out the flames with the asbestos glove and his beret, as did the CO with a 'throttle slam', before it ignited some residual fuel. As his boss leapt from the cockpit and hared across the airfield George continued to fight the flames with a CO2 extinguisher, poking its 'pole' into every possible crevice to eventually master the flames. He was awarded a 'Good Show' for his courageous determination. AVPIN starters may

have behaved well normally but Mike Plimmer was quite unequivocal: 'give me compressed air or cartridge starter systems every time'.

With the potential for mishap and error, it is perhaps surprising that very little seemed to go wrong when the FR10 squadrons in Germany were sorely stretched during the many 'no-notice' alert exercises that kept everyone on their toes. Indeed, this was when the groundcrews gave of their best, often from a standing start in the middle of the night and in bad weather. With their single accommodation so close to the hangar, the airmen of IV Squadron were often at their place of work before those from other units. Then came the frustration of waiting for the duty NCO to draw the hangar keys from the guardroom to open up, at least until someone found that a well placed kick could release a lock in the main doors. Groundcrews rarely had to wait for their pilots, most of whom (in common with their peers on other squadrons) kept their flying suits in their room or car, to drag on as they raced to whichever aircraft had an F-700 strapped to its drop tank to signify that it was serviceable. In the words of Mike Plimmer; 'this displayed some exotic tastes in their choice of pyjamas'. Pilots were often already strapped into their seats, signed up and ready to go before they could be towed to the flight line. All this caused many a raised eyebrow among exercise umpires, especially those from other NATO bases who may not have been accustomed to such ways, but

Sportsmen All. No. II Squadron (left) did well in the Gutersloh inter-squadron football tournament 1965, and even 1417 Flight, despite being only 20 men strong, also managed to field a highly competitive all-ranks football team. *Hugh Cracroft & Dick Johns*

Getting Away From It All.

Close to Home. Ian Sharples(far left) and members of Gutersloh's Mountain Expedition Team spend a weekend training in the hills around the 'Dambusters' Eder See. *Ian Sharples*

Far Afield. Ian Sharples (foreground) with the team climbing the 8000 ft Altspitz. *Ian Sharples*

Amsterdam Culture. Instrument mechanic Ian Sharples (left) and electrician George Eccleston take advantage of the weekend 'cultural' trips organised by Gutersloh's WVS. *Ian Sharples*

they generally turned a blind eye to these laudable initiatives. Back in the hangar every available hand played some part in attending to any 'hangar queens' which may have been sitting there gathering dust for some time. It was amazing how, with determination and 'cannibalisation', some were recovered in double quick time to take to the air again during these exercises.

Of course, when the raucous siren summoned everyone to work there was no knowing whether it was for the real thing or just one more exercise. Such uncertainty was rampant when, as one IV Squadron corporal remembers, an alert was sounded at the time of the crisis in Cuba, and on another occasion just after President Kennedy's assassination. In any event pride in unit performance alone energised everyone and the adrenalin ran high.

For the same reason, groundcrew pulled out all the stops during the many academic competitions, with IV Squadron noted for training long and hard, and very much as a team, for these events. In the words of one: 'It was a joy to see a well-drilled team of three men removing the nose cone, disconnecting the electrical supplies and off-loading the camera magazines as the engine wound down and the pilot leapt from the cockpit'. Pride was a great motivator. Some of the NATO competitions took place away from home and there were many other detachments, whether for the annual exchange visits, operational or administrative reasons, all calling for various levels of ground support. Ian Sharples remembers an exchange with a USAFE Voodoo squadron which took him to Laon AB in France, not via the usual uncomfortable road journey but by courtesy of an RAF Beverley transport. This unique aircraft caused wonder and amusement among the Americans until they saw it back up to within inches of the visitor's hangar, and with only inches either side on a very narrow taxiway. The hosts were also surprised by the RAF groundcrew's capacity for German beer, which they had kindly supplied on the assumption that because their guests came from Northern Germany, they must be German. Ian remembers the comment: 'Gee, you guys speak good English!' The strong beer certainly had a greater effect on the hosts, some of whom were soon fighting amongst themselves, generally causing mayhem and ending up as guests of the USAF's Air Police. This was quite unlike the all-ranks parties and sports events within the FR10 fraternity, which brought the squadrons together and added to the corporate spirit which paid such dividends at work.

There were many less exciting times for the groundcrew with their secondary duties and extraneous commitments seemingly ever on the increase. In addition to the traditional station duties the squadron tradesmen took their turn manning the duty crew at a very busy Gutersloh, the airfield being open at all times for local troop movements, civilian charter flights, visiting NATO aircraft on cross-servicing exercises and 'booze runs'(the RF-84F could carry copious quantities of whisky in its camera compartment). Much of this was dull routine but sometimes there were interesting visitors and servicing opportunities which taxed the mind. Again, pride invariably ensured good service.

There were also plenty of diversions for those off duty, particularly perhaps in Germany. At one time, II Squadron dominated the station's mountain expedition club, comprising some twenty men, half of whom could be expected to attend the weekend forays into the nearby Sauerland and Harz mountains, and there were plenty of volunteers for more ambitious ventures throughout Europe.

For those looking for something less physical, there were trips organised by the various welfare organisations at Gutersloh, Ian Sharples and several of his friends having good cause to remember one of the regular 'cultural' visits to Amsterdam sponsored by the WVS. On their final evening they decided not to waste their last guilders on accommodation, it being so late and with their coach returning to Gutersloh very early in the morning, but rather to spend what remained of the night on benches in the Amsterdam railway station. At midnight, however, the station closed and a porter ushered them out to a waiting policeman; he listened to their predicament and made an incomprehensible call on his radio, with the result that a Dutch army officer arrived shortly thereafter in a military van. In perfect English, he offered them a bed for the night, if only in a military prison. There they were given a cell apiece (with the doors left unlocked) and provided with coffee in the morning before being put on a tram to rendezvous with their coach. The NATO spirit was alive and well that night.

It was not all work and no play for the men who helped keep the FR10s in the air – and they excelled in both.

Fire! It was all hands to the pump in this fire practice at Khormaksar – two FR10s and an FGA9 being pushed hurriedly to safety as firemen pour foam on a fuel spill and a Sycamore rescue helicopter hovers overhead. *Ray Deacon*

Epilogue

All good things must come to an end but the Hunter FR10 would survive for decades after its retirement from the RAF in 1971, albeit in several different forms elsewhere in the world. The RAF no longer occupies the stations on which it served but many of the men who manned the cockpits and kept them flying have survived to tell the tale.

The success of the aircraft had not gone unnoticed in other countries, with previous and new Hunter customers anxious to capitalise on the good deals which came on offer when the RAF released the aircraft back to Hawker. With plenty of life left in them, the redundant Hunters were refurbished and modified to customers' requirements, and reconnaissance variants were high on the shopping list.

In the late 1960s and early 1970s, for instance, Chile received six Hunter FR71s, one of which has been traced. Originally Hunter F4, XF317, this aircraft served on 67 Squadron in Germany, carrying the name of its pilot: now *Scale Aircraft Modelling* editorial consultant Mike McEvoy. When that squadron disbanded, XF317 became an instructional airframe at RAF Halton, before being purchased back by Hawker in December 1971 to be converted to an FR71A, No J734, and delivered to Chile in January 1974. Determined to find his old mount, Mike contrived to include a stopover in Santiago while travelling to New Zealand in 2002 and made straight for the airfield museum which he had heard might have acquired the Hunter. His persistence through language and security barriers paid off when he was allowed access to a part of the airfield where museum aircraft were stored. There he found his quest, indeed bearing the number 734 with the white star of Chile on its fin, apparently in good condition having been retired only three years before. The camera fit was clearly visible and it would seem that the aircraft had also been modified to carry the large external fuel tanks. With the current interest in recovering Hunters to flyable condition, could this be another suitable candidate? Mike McEvoy has hinted that he might not let the possibility rest there.

Several Middle Eastern countries were also in the market, Iraq acquiring four FR59Bs and Abu

Hunter FR in Jordan. This ex-FR10 is awaiting delivery to Jordan. *David Lockspeiser*

Dhabi three FR76s, one of which went eventually to Somalia, while Jordan operated a single F6 (Ex-RAF XF426) which was later transferred to Oman as Serial 853, an FR73. However, by far the largest overseas order came from the Republic of Singapore Air Force (RSAF), where four F6s were brought up to FR10 standard in 1971 and designated FR74s. This preceded an order for twenty-two FR74Bs, for delivery to the RSAF in 1972.

In 1977, Lockheed Aircraft Services Singapore offered ex-Hawker test pilot David Lockspeiser the job of carrying out the test flying on an extensive weapons upgrade programme they had undertaken for the Singapore MOD, the design work having been carried out by ex-Hawker chief stressman Bill Weetman and the work completed in Singapore. An enhanced reconnaissance capability was included in this programme, consisting of custom-built modifications to gun packs to enable them to carry KA56 low and KA93 high altitude panoramic cameras. A third pack was fitted with a 116 camera and Infra Red Linescan for strip recces. These installations were flight tested to evaluate the environmental system designed to prevent misting of the camera lens and window, to check operation of the protective doors and eyelids and to prove that gun firing, if applicable, had no injurious effect or adverse aerodynamic behavioural problems.

By this time, Tim Barrett had been seconded to the RSAF as a lieutenant colonel to command the strike wing at Tengah, once more coming under the command of his one-time OC Flying at Gutersloh, David Rhodes, now General Rhodes, head of the RSAF. Both were then flying ex-FR10s from their Germany days, including Tim's old mount as CO of II Squadron, 'Sierra' (XF432), resplendent in its new livery and flying as an FR74B, No 526.

Two 'hybrid' FR10s exist, one has been languishing for years on the edge of the airfield at Long Marston, Worcestershire, and the other is on show at the City of Norwich Museum, on the north side of the old RAF Horsham St Faith, now Norwich International Airport. With a fuselage from an F6 (XG172), wings from elsewhere and an authentic FR10 nose, this is a laudable attempt to replicate the ex-II Squadron FR10, XG 168, 'N', despite carrying the insignia of 79 Squadron (229 OCU at Chivenor).

The only legitimate FR10 known to be in the United Kingdom at this time, with every prospect of being maintained in its present display condition, is XF426 at the Royal Air Force Museum. A nomad typical of many FR10s, this aircraft began life as part of a batch of 100 F6s built by Armstrong Whitworth Aircraft at Baginton. It was delivered to 5 MU at Kemble in February 1957, where it underwent modifications before being stored at 19 MU, RAF St Athan, until March 1958, when it was allotted to 208 Squadron at RAF Nicosia. This squadron disbanded a year later but XF426 was held in Cyprus until its return to St Athan pending conversion to an FR10 by Hawker, this being completed in April 1961. After further storage and a two year loan to the Ministry of Aviation, the aircraft made it back to the front line with II Squadron at Gutersloh in June 1967. For reasons which are not clear, its operational life in Germany lasted only six months, after which it was re-assigned to 79 (R) Squadron, 229 OCU at Chivenor, where it served until March 1972. XF426 was then presented to the Hashemite Kingdom of Jordan, where, with the number 853, it joined another FR10 within a fleet of Hunters of various original marks. In May 1975, this entire force was passed to the Sultan of Oman's Air Force (SOAF), where 853 saw action against rebel forces with the added capability of unguided 80mm Hispano SURA rockets, often in the hands of RAF pilots seconded or on contract to the SOAF. The aircraft continued to serve there for eighteen years, testament to the aircraft's resilience and longevity (although, for reasons unknown, it had a port wing replaced in 1987) until final retirement in October 1993, by which time it had 4,131 flying hours to its name. SOAF retained 853 in a generally serviceable condition for use in a ground instructional role at the Oman Trade Training Institute at Seeb, until graciously presented to the RAF Museum by the Sultan of Oman. Painted in its operational grey with low visibility SOAF markings, it was transported to RAF Brize Norton (less engine) in an RAF C-17 on 6 September 2003 and completed its trip to Hendon by road. Initially, this sole monument to a highly successful Cold War FR aircraft was very visible in the corner of the primary car park between the Main Hall and the new Milestones of Flying Hall, but it was then moved to between the Milestones Hall and the old Station Workshops.

For its significant contribution to the FR10 force as a two-seat basic flying, weapons and instrument trainer, also used extensively for supervisory checks, the Hunter T7 should not be forgotten in this success story. Fortunately, at the time of writing, a most appropriate survivor of

Hendon Hunter. XF426, Ex-Hunter F6 converted to an FR10 and posted to II Squadron for less than a year before beginning a nomadic life which took it to 79 Squadron at Chivenor, then to Jordan and Oman. In October 2003, it was presented to the RAF Museum at Hendon. *Author*

'Romeo'. This ex-II Squadron T-7, beautifully restored with the original II Squadron markings, is owned by Barry Prescott, based at Kemble and at the time of writing fully airworthy. *Roger Lindsey & Glen Moreman*

Fifty Years On. Geoff Hall, Margreet Walpole, Peter Riley, the author and Hugh Cracroft meet among others again in 2005, at the home of the late Air Chief Marshal Sir John Thomson – one of the best of breed. *Lady Thomson*

Nostalgia Trip. A few of those who flew the Hunter FR10 among the many who gathered at the memorable Hunter Reunion in Barnstaple in 2000, seen here at Exeter Airport where variants of the Hunter were still flying – and doing what they still do so well after the sun goes down. *Author's Collection*

this excellent variant, WV372, 'Romeo', still flies in II Squadron's colours. Romeo was originally an F4, assigned to 222 Squadron at RAF Leuchars in 1956 until it suffered a serious accident when the jet pipe became detached from the engine and caught fire. Rebuilt as a T7 by Hawker in 1958, it joined II Squadron in 1960 and served on various units in Germany before being committed to advanced flying training at RAF Valley from 1971 to 1979. The aircraft then supported the Buccaneer force at RAF Laarbruch and later RAF Honington until 1984, when it was transferred to the Royal Navy to serve on the Fleet Requirement and Air Direction Unit. In 1997, its military service over, Romeo was bought by Barry Prescott and now flies in splendid condition at Kemble.

First to go of the RAF bases from which the FR10s operated was Khormaksar in 1967, and this was soon followed by Muharraq, Salalah and Masirah. Chivenor went next, very soon after a massive and costly redevelopment optimised for Hawk fast jet lead-in training, Royal Marine Commandos now enjoying its excellent facilities. Then came the end of the Cold War and drawdown in Germany which saw the demise of Gutersloh as a fast-jet airfield; the station then passed to the Royal Logistics Corps and was renamed the Princess Royal Barracks.

What of the men who flew the thoroughbred FR10? Many went on to make a name for themselves in one way or another in the RAF. Of the station commanders, Keith Williamson became Chief of the Air Staff (CAS) and a Marshal of the Royal Air Force, while David Evans commanded Strike Command as an Air Chief Marshal. Dick Johns, from 1417 Flight, became an Air Chief Marshal and was appointed CAS, at the time of writing continuing to serve the Crown as Constable and Governor of Windsor Castle. No. II Squadron's Sandy Wilson and John Thomson also became Air Chief Marshals in charge of major commands. Many others from the FR10 fraternity achieved air rank or distinguished themselves in other ways in the service. Dave Bagshaw, for instance, who had flown the FR10 with 1417 Flight, 8 Squadron and II Squadron, went on to become a most revered recce and ground attack pilot in the Jaguar force, and is believed to have been the oldest fast jet pilot to fly in combat in the first Coalition war with Iraq. Many ex-FR10 pilots continued flying in one way or another in civilian aviation and at least three, Colin Richardson, Bill Norton and Al Mathie built their own aircraft and have been flying them happily around East Anglia.

There have been a number of reunions embracing the whole Hunter family (inevitably very large events) the last of which was organised by Hunter pilot and one time station commander at RAF Brawdy, Tim Webb. No. II and IV Squadrons have their own reunions, embracing all their aircraft types, and the FR community (Meteor, Swift and Hunter) held reunions in the 1960s and 1970s, but there has been no specific Hunter FR10 gathering to date. Perhaps this is timely, for who is to say that they and the thoroughbred FR10 did not all belong to 'the best of breed'?

Bibliography

Armitage, *The Royal Air Force – An Illustrated History*, Arms and Armour Press

Bowman, Martin, *The Hawker Hunter in British Military Service*, Sutton Publishing

Boyd, Alexander, *The Soviet Air Force Since 1918*, Purnell

Deacon, Ray, *Hawker Hunter – Fifty Golden Years*, Vogelsang Publications

Handling Squadron, RAF, *Pilots Notes - Hunter FR10 and FGA 9*, Air Ministry

Jackson, Robert, Hawker Hunter – *The Operational Record*, Airlife

Kipp and Lindsey, RAF *Hunters in Germany*, Kipp and Lindsey

Mason, Francis, *Hawker Hunter – Biography of a Thoroughbred*, Patrick Stephens

Onderwater, Hans, *Second to None*, Airlife

Operations Record Books, *Nos II, IV & 8 Squadrons, 1417 Flight*, Public Record Office

Richardson, Colin, *Masirah*, Pentland Press

Index

All numbers shown in *italics* refer to a photograph.